Behind Frenemy Lines

Advance Praise

"Dr. Tichenor makes the crucial point that when women see each other as allies, opportunities increase for all of us to succeed. This book is a 'must read' for women looking to break the frenemy cycle and for leaders looking to attract and retain the best female talent."

> —**Anne Devereux-Mills**, Founder of Parlay House, and author of
> *The Parlay Effect: How Female Connection Can Change the World*

"*Behind Frenemy Lines* presents the bold and compelling case that as women our power doesn't come from tearing each other down, but from building each other up. Dr. Tichenor combines impressive research with introspective exercises as she puts our competitive behavior under a microscope in order to help us be better and do better in the future. It's a must-read for any woman struggling to enhance her own self-esteem (which let's be honest is all of us)."

> —**Katherine Wintsch**, Founder & CEO of The Mom Complex
> and author of *Slay Like a Mother*

"Amber's work is transformative. Not only because it gives voice to the suffering of so many women but because it provides a framework that every woman can use to make a better choice when confronting learned rivalrous behaviors. With women dropping out of the workforce in record numbers, leaders need to know how to identify, confront, and eradicate female rivalry from their organizations so that women feel safe returning to the workforce."

> —**Sara James Shelton**, Managing Director,
> Human Capital Practice Area Lead, Fahrenheit Advisors

"This book gave me much needed closure about an old rivalry that I never understood. Female rivalry is not an easy topic to discuss but Dr. Tichenor takes care of her reader with relatable stories and tools to recognize and resolve these issues. If you're a woman, read this book!"

—**Eva DeVirgillis**, Actor, Speaker, Communication Consultant,
www.evadevirgillis.com

"Can't we all just be nice to one another? The well-researched and numerous personal stories in *Behind Frenemy Lines* shows that this is easier said than done. Dr. Tichenor brilliantly broadens your understanding and experience of conflicts with other women. And then gently guides you with a practical approach to respond and move into being a truly, supportive friend and human being."

—**Mary Foley**, Founder of REV UP Society for Women Entrepreneurs
and author of *Bodacious! Woman: Outrageously in Charge
of Your Life and Loving It!*

"If you've ever experienced rivalry, you know firsthand the damage it does to relationships, self-confidence and entire organizations and ecosystems. Dr. Tichenor illuminates the stories and experiences from women who are seeking a better way to bond with and empower other women and heal from past rivalry. The practical, reflective exercises throughout the book will help you make peace with rivalry you've experienced, reconnect to how you want to forge relationships with the women in your life, and dismantle rivalrous situations so they can be a thing of the past."

—**Michelle Mercurio**, Brand Writer, Catalyst, Authenticist

"*Behind Frenemy Lines* is a fantastic resource for anyone looking for a deeper understanding of female rivalry. Amber addresses this often unspoken topic head on by interweaving stories of women who have experienced it firsthand, with fascinating research on why women are so competitive in the first place."

—**Wendy Urquhart**, Business Development Executive +
Relationship Manager, Mother of Teenage Girls

"If you are a womxn in corporate America struggling to find support and sisterhood from your workplace, the wealth of personal stories in this book will help you feel seen and heard. The book includes helpful tips and resources to foster more self-awareness and support networks. Reading this book really made me appreciate the importance of strong, supportive sisterhood of womxn helping one another navigate life and work."

—**Seo Kelleher**, founder of Alpha Female Sisterhood
and author of *Don't Be a B*tch Be An Alpha*

"*Behind Frenemy Lines* should be required reading for every female. No matter who you are, or where you come from, if you're a woman, this book will hit home. From the 'friend' who always makes you feel like you're walking on eggshells, to the co-worker who's determined to make your life an absolute hell, Dr. Amber Tichenor gives us a raw and real breakdown of the many layers and ways that female rivalry can manifest and have an immense negative impact over the course of a woman's lifetime. The real-life stories of girl-on-girl crime will give you all the feels, but the real-life tools and strategies she shares for overcoming (and stopping) female rivalries will leave you feeling empowered to reignite your spark within. From cover to cover, Dr.Tichenor reminds us just how much brighter we are able to shine when we share our light with our fellow sisters, instead of trying to put each other's out."

—**Lauren Steward**, M.S. | CEO, Stewart Media

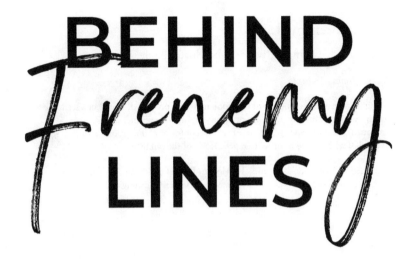

BEHIND *Frenemy* LINES

Rising Above Female Rivalry *to be* Unstoppable Together

Dr. Amber Tichenor, PhD

NEW YORK

LONDON • NASHVILLE • MELBOURNE • VANCOUVER

Behind Frenemy Lines

Rising Above Female Rivalry to be Unstoppable Together

Published in New York, New York, by Morgan James Publishing. Morgan James is a trademark of Morgan James, LLC. www.MorganJamesPublishing.com

Morgan James BOGO™

A **FREE** ebook edition is available for you
or a friend with the purchase of this print book.

CLEARLY SIGN YOUR NAME ABOVE

Instructions to claim your free ebook edition:
1. Visit MorganJamesBOGO.com
2. Sign your name CLEARLY in the space above
3. Complete the form and submit a photo
   of this entire page
4. You or your friend can download the ebook
   to your preferred device

ISBN 9781631955419 paperback
ISBN 9781631955426 ebook
Library of Congress Control Number: 2021932757

Cover & Interior Design by:
Christopher Kirk
www.GFSstudio.com

Morgan James is a proud partner of Habitat for Humanity Peninsula and Greater Williamsburg. Partners in building since 2006.

Get involved today! Visit
MorganJamesPublishing.com/giving-back

To all the women who have trusted me with their story...
The women who were exposed to a deep, ruthless pain
and chose to relive it again to share their experience.
I am humbled to be your voice, thank you.

For all the women who've kept silent.
The women who felt alone and have lost their voice...
May you find a sisterhood of support
and join in the revolution of collaboration over competition.
For what we can do together is far greater than what we can do alone.

Table of Contents

Acknowledgments

The undertaking of this book was a journey leading to a destination of the path I was meant to be on.

Every time I've had a vision of what I thought it should be, life came along and let me know I was not always the one in charge. With each adventure along this path toward reaching my destination, I hopefully learned to be a bit more patient and to appreciate the moments and time that was given to me. It was in those moments, over a span of several years, that this book grew to what it was meant to be.

Special gratitude is extended to Kim Eley, of KWE Publishing, who has guided me on this journey with endless insight, expertise, and humor. It's crazy to think that less than a year ago I first met you at an NSA Virginia meeting. Our paths crossing was meant to be.

To David L. Hancock and Morgan James Publishing (MJP), thank you for believing in my book. I look forward to our continued partnership (and more books), in the years to come!

To the women who trusted me with their stories. Although each of you is an individual, it is your combined experiences that create a full narrative to make this book complete.

It is from support of family and friends that I was able to accomplish this leg of my journey. I am so blessed to have women in my life that uplift, support, and motivate me to be a better person. I only hope that I, in turn, can inspire someone to be the same.

And finally, this book is dedicated to my family with great love.

To my mom, the first "doctor" in our family, thank you for inspiring me to follow in your footsteps. For pushing me to pursue education, even at such a young age when it was not as appreciated as it is now. For setting an example of what a strong woman can do, how she can pursue her dreams while at the same time be an excellent mother. For setting an example of how this journey can be completed and the destination is well worth the ride.

To my husband, Andrew, you may not always have known or understood what I was writing about but your on-going support on this journey has been a constant. Thank you for your love and encouragement. I love you.

To my children who fill my world with more joy than you'll ever know. Life is at your doorstep…

Harrison, may you always approach it with the same outlook as you do now, with open curiosity and fierce determination.

Audrey, I've thought about you so much as I wrote this book. May your path in life be filled with genuine sister-like-bonds of friendship. To have such women by your side is truly one of life's greatest blessings.

First Word

"It takes a thousand voices to tell a single story."
—Native American Proverb (Native Partnership, 2020).

Female Rivalry. It's More Than Competition.

The backhanded compliment. The fake smile. The passive-aggressive comment. The takedown that occurs behind closed doors. It's happening everywhere. In your workspace, your community groups... even on the soccer field with another mom.

Most of the time, it's the elephant in the room.

I say that it's time to be different.

It's time to talk about female rivalry to know how to dismantle it, one action at a time. It's time to be more intentional with our words and our leadership. It's time to build up our self-images and to love ourselves more.

Because true power doesn't come from rivalry, it comes from uplifting, empowering, and supporting our sisters, our friends, our daughters, and womankind. The cards are already stacked against us. Why would we want to be the ones to stack them against ourselves?

It is my intent, with the publication of this book, to expand understanding of the experience of rivalry between women. These stories portray women in their everyday lives, at work, at home, at the Parent Teacher Association (PTA), on the tennis team, at a mom's group, with a neighbor, or at a book club. You name the place and you can be sure that it exists. This type of rivalry does not discriminate, because with rivalry between women, nothing is out of bounds.

Rivalry Defined

I'm positive that you are familiar with the term "rivalry." But do you know what it means as it pertains to this topic? I specifically pose this question to you because I've received a lot of questions about it. Many people are not familiar with the term as it's used in this context of female rivalry. It's not until I provide descriptions and well-known phrases that they'll say, "Oh yes… that. I definitely know what you mean now."

My personal definition of this behavior is, "Female rivalry is one woman minimizing another woman so they both feel small—smaller than they really are. Female rivalry hurts individuals, teams, and organizations." Formally, rivalry is defined as,

ri·val·ry. /ˈrīvəlrē/. *noun.*
"competition for the same objective or for superiority in the same field."
(Merriam Webster, 2020).

Rivalry is the act of competing for the same thing against another person. Rivalry comes from the noun rival, the person you compete against. Often a rivalry starts when people want the same reward—and their talents are just about equal (Vocabulary.com, 2020).

Other common terms for female rivalry include: aggressive, b*tchy, bully, catty, competitive, contentious, hostile, opposing, prickly, resentful, spiteful, and vicious.

If you still are not overly clear, I can assure you that by the end of this book you will know without a doubt what rivalry means as it pertains to female behaviors.

Why I Wrote This Book

This book is about women, because of women and ultimately, for women.

The fundamental essence of this manuscript is rooted in the testimonies, conversations, and interviews I've collected over the years. It includes women sharing their experiences of rivalry between another woman, either from within their working environment or in their everyday life.

To corroborate my initial research findings, personal narratives are interwoven throughout the following pages. These candid stories portray the raw realness of this behavior, and they give life to the findings. The women who gave voice to my research gave me permission to use their stories. Every single story is true. Specific names, organizations, places, and other identifying details have been modified to protect identities.

I initially began collecting these stories about 15 years ago, circa 2007, as research interviews for my Ph.D. dissertation. My qualitative thesis, *A Phenomenological Study of the Experience of Rivalry Among Women in the Workplace,* highlighted stories from nine women, whose ages ranged from 36 to 45. They all were college graduates, the majority of whom had higher professional degrees, and between them they had 15 to 44 years of professional work experience.

The purpose of my research study was to give voice to these women who'd experienced rivalry within a working environment. I am very passionate about women's issues, especially those pertaining to the workplace. Up until that point, while I'd certainly been exposed to certain types of "passive-aggressive, non-tangible, mean-girl, or Queen Bee behaviors," I'd not yet experienced a "full-on-b*tchy-rivalrous-want-to-have-control-type-of-situation" targeted directly toward me, in or out of the workspace.

Don't get me wrong. Although I hadn't been on the receiving end of it, I saw firsthand the outcomes of the behavior. I saw what it did to the women on the receiving end. How cruel the behavior was, how passive-aggressive and disruptive... not only to the targeted individual involved but to the organizational culture. I became curious as to why this sort of behavior seemed to occur predominantly between women. While it's been shown that some men do act inappropriately in the workplace towards women, typically they do not show *these* types of behaviors to other men or even women, for that matter.

Utterly astonishing to me was the fact that the negative behavior continually seemed to just be "swept under the rug" because it wasn't talked about. There it was, this big pink fat looming elephant, just sitting there... but people tip-toed around it. Organizations were doing absolutely nothing to deal with it and the women experiencing it had zero support. By ignoring it, the organizations were endorsing the negative behaviors... and so it continued. It was this endless cycle of negativity that motivated me to research and write about it.

Minimal popular research was available on this topic but there was no scholarly literature at hand that seemed to elaborate about these particular types of behaviors. The lack of academic research on this topic completely baffled me.

Because I was so curious about the "why" of the behavior, I began to talk to women about their personal rivalrous experiences in the working environment. Initially, I was hesitant to ask them to share such personal stories, but that feeling didn't last long. I was blown away by the responses. Not only did these women want to share... they told their friends, who told their friends, and so on. They were so happy that someone wanted to listen to them, to understand them, and to have empathy about what they'd gone through. They wanted to feel understood. My documentation of their stories helps to fill a void for them personally, and ultimately for broader research awareness.

After interviewing the women who willingly participated in my study, I became motivated to tell their stories. On behalf of the women telling their stories, I desired to be their voice. My other objective was to provide a voice of awareness. My goal and hope of this initial research was to yield a voice to the women who had or currently were experiencing rivalry within the workplace. I wanted to better understand why these types of behaviors occurred. Furthermore, I also wanted to understand what could be done from an HR or senior leadership perspective to help alleviate these types of situations from materializing. I wondered if companies were equipped to handle this type of rivalry (or not)—and if that was the reason why it appeared these types of behaviors were often left unacknowledged.

In 2011, I completed my schoolwork. Even though I'd obtained my Ph.D., I was still drawn to collecting female rivalry testimonies. I wanted at some point to help other women by sharing these unembellished stories, to give them a voice, and to let them be heard.

After graduating, I continued to collect descriptions of rivalries from women in situations that occurred in the workplace as well as in other parts of their lives. I've captured so many representations from brave women who have opened up, bared their souls, and shared their most personal and often excruciatingly negative experiences with me. These stories ooze vulnerability, shame, and sadness. Some of the stories will make you cry. Some of the stories will make you angry. Some of the stories will completely blow your mind.

There is a tragedy to so many of these narratives because often at the time of the incident occurring, their voice was not heard. And because of that, they suffered silently, in great pain.

Behind Frenemy Lines: Rising Above Female Rivalry To Be Unstoppable Together is about awareness of this phenomenon. My goal is to promote a full understanding of what rivalry between women means and how harmful the behaviors can be. Not in the frequently, jokingly called, "catfight" or "that's just women being dramatic" type of manner, but in the true psychological, mental, emotional, and physical way. The way that perhaps until reading this, you can only really know and comprehend if you've been a recipient of the contemptuous conduct. It isn't pretty. It can be raw, ugly, confusing, and very painful. And if you've experienced it, you really know. You know it so well that you may be afraid to trust other women, work for other women, or have close female friends... ever again.

As a female, I am sure there are men in your life who support, love, and greatly understand you. Additionally, I am sure, these men have also witnessed this behavior in some form or another within their family or loved ones, from friends, or at work with colleagues. Really, who hasn't seen it at some point? But in all honesty…. they will never understand and fully comprehend the deep dark depths of female competition, rivalry, and bullying because they are men. And men traditionally do not act this way toward each other.

Until this type of behavior is brought out in the open, addressed, and dealt with, it *will* continue. Female rivalry is boundless. As a result, there is a hunger for this topic. We long to better understand it, to curb the behavior, and to dive into the misconceptions and reality that it's not just a catfight. It's much more than that.

Behind Frenemy Lines is a practical guide to help women find their peace, explore how they trust, establish true connections, and know they are not alone when they are experiencing these types of behaviors. By sharing personal and relatable stories, this book addresses the raw ugliness of female rivalry head-on. It offers tips with a structure to educate and to help women connect with one another about the seriousness of the phenomenon so that they can forge relationships that help them be unstoppable, together.

How to Use This Book

You will find "*Your Turn*" sections interwoven throughout the text. I've added these sections to not only be interactive but to treat the content like a conversation, like what you may discuss with a girlfriend. You can read the book all the way through in its entirety and return to the "*Your Turn*" sections later or address each one as it pops up. I frequently like to read all the way through a section, not only because I'm eager to see what comes next... but also to let what I've just read, marinate, and digest a bit. However you do it, my aim is for this approach to be helpful to you.

Whatever the size of your circle, squad, or tribe, I am sure you have one or two women with whom you are good friends. At least, I hope you do. If you don't, you should. And by the end of this book, if you don't, I hope you are on a path to where you do.

My hope is that the stories I share with you will help you to understand the truth about what rivalry between women truly means. You should know, especially if you have ever or are currently experiencing it... That you can say, "*It's not just me,*" and know you are not alone.

—Amber

PART I:

The Opposition

op·po·si·tion. /äpəˈziSH(ə)n/ *noun.*
"resistance or dissent in action or argument.
A group of advisories or competitors" (Merriam Webster, 2020).

"When they judge you, yawn.
When they misunderstand you, smile.
When they underestimate you, laugh.
When they condemn you, ignore.
When they envy you, rejoice.
When they oppose you, prevail."
— Matshona Dhliwayo (Quotesphilia, 2020).

Chapter 1:

When the Claws Come Out

"The connections between and among women are the most feared, the most problematic and the most potentially transforming force on the planet."
—Adrienne Rich (Goodreads, Inc. 2020).

Natalie's Story

"She was a really good friend of mine... We'd been friends for a few years, to the point where we'd spent holidays together with each other's families. Not something I'd done lightly.

I'd been at my job for a while. She was looking for something new and said, 'Wow, that place sounds amazing. I would love to work there.' So, I referred her. She got the job and ended up on my team. I was one of the people on my team that trained her, along with another person.

Within three to four months of working together, she stopped talking to me. I assumed it was for a completely different reason, a social thing which I thought was ridiculous, so I didn't acknowledge it. I was just like, 'Ok, well if you're mad, that's weird, but whatever.' But it finally got to a point where it was uncomfortable. She was rude to me in team meetings and other types of interactions. It completely affected the work we were doing.

I went to our manager and said, 'Hey, something's going on here. I've never seen her like this but it's affecting our work. If it's a social thing, I can separate that away from my day, but we need to be able to get the work done.' And my manager said, 'Well, she's had a problem with you for a while now and has been telling me about it for a few months.' I was shocked and said, 'And you didn't tell me?'

As it turned out, she'd told my manager crazy things about me that I hadn't done. She was very accusatory... It was like she was bullying me. It was the strangest thing. It got to the point where she wouldn't even let me ask her a work-related question. If I asked a question, she'd immediately start screaming at me. Everyone on our team noticed it. It was hard not to.

Our female manager, though, didn't believe me. She said, 'You know, I think you just thought that you two were friends but really you weren't.' Our manager ended up becoming friends with her and socializing with her outside of work. And then our manager would tell me, 'You know it really bothers me when I bring her name up and you get all prickly. It makes me really uncomfortable.'

For whatever reason in the office, my 'previous friend' singled me out as the enemy. No matter what she was irritated about, she would just dump it on me. I never understood how we went from friends to enemies in just a few short months. It was baffling."

Do You Compete or Empower?

Frequently when I speak to a group of women, I'll ask the audience to participate in an exercise before diving into the presentation. I'll say... "As a woman, young lady, or girl, think back to your childhood, your teen years, your college years, and your entry into the workforce. Now, please raise your hand if you've experienced being left out of a clique or group of girls, with one girl as the ring-leader." "Please raise your hand if you've experienced a 'destructive or deadly' type of friendship, friends one day, backstabbing the next." "Please raise a hand if you've experienced rivalry or competition about your looks, clothes, or the way you dress." "Please raise a hand if you experienced rivalry or competition from a family member, mom, sister, cousin, aunt."

I'll continue to ask questions about various types of rivalrous experiences they may have encountered throughout their lives in sports, in school, in social situations, at work, etc. If one hand is raised, I'll ask them to raise a second hand. If both hands are raised, I ask them to stand.

Often by the end of my questioning, every female in the room, whether a group of 15 or 100, is standing. I've had women who've participated in this exercise stand with their eyes shining because they were on the brink of tears. I've had moms with looks of complete disbelief on their faces, as their daughters raised their hands, and ultimately stood, as they answered all my questions. I've had women approach me afterward to say, "Thank you. I thought I was the only one."

Every single time I do this exercise, I get chills because it highlights the magnitude of the occurrence of this phenomenon. It's a widespread problem and no age, demographic, or status is off-limits.

1.1: Your Turn. Dear reader, before diving into all the outlandish aspects of what denotes the behavior of rivalry between women... please share your initial thoughts of what you think it means now, before gaining a better understanding of the juicy details. Take a moment now to write below, based on your own beliefs, your own experiences, society's viewpoint, etc., of what you think female rivalry means.

_____

_____

_____

_____

The Power Struggle Between Women

The power struggle between women is immense. The divide of women opposing women is something that often occurs. It is clearly illustrated in the classical French musical and historical novel storyline of *Les Misérables*. Written in 1862 by Victor Hugo, there is a haunting point in the composition where, had the women supported one another, the outcome of the story would have been significantly altered. Granted it was a very different point in time. During this era, women followed a patriarchal rule and were not allowed to speak forthrightly, especially as it pertained to feminist views.

In the musical, although her love child was kept a secret from others, the female character, Fantine, would do anything to support her illegitimate daughter, Cosette. The women in the factory in which Fantine worked found out that she was an unwed mother. Because of their dislike of her secrecy, overall situation, and beauty, they grouped together, ganged up on her, and ended up telling their supervisor the truth. Tragically, Fantine was fired. As a result of being let go from her job, Fantine worked from home, making barely enough money to support her daughter. She resorted to selling her possessions, her hair, and her teeth. Ultimately, she resorted to prostitution, was thrown in jail, became sick, and died, all without ever seeing her daughter again. Although this analogy is extreme and not necessarily applicable to the present, it is telling regarding the power struggle between women. It is significant to how far back in history this power struggle has existed.

Fast forward to modern-day, to a similar story-line about women opposing women showcased in a high-school setting that is very much a universal theme for tweens and teens. Debuting in 2004, American actress, comedian, writer, producer, and playwright, Tina Fey wrote the script for the movie, *Mean Girls,* based on certain elements from her own high school experience as well as from aspects of Rosalind Wiseman's 2002 non-fiction book, *Queen Bees and Wannabes.* The film, a pop-culture phenomenon, is technically a comedy. However, its depiction of "girl-on-girl" cattiness, spotlights an all too real truth about female high-school social cliques, mean girls, and Queen Bees. The storyline reveals the damaging effects that female rivalry can have on girls, regarding their self-esteem, self-image, and the behaviors they may exude, simply to fit in with the "in" crowd.

In an interview about the film, Fey noted, "Adults find it funny. They are the ones who are laughing. Young girls, however, are watching it like it's a reality show. It's much too close to their real experiences, so they are not exactly guffawing" (Fey, 2004).

When the Claws Come Out

In groups of women, you routinely see the moment when the claws come out. The stance becomes a bit straighter, there's a bit of perceived, light-hearted laughter, and then BAM! The passive-aggressive remark is made to let the other female know. It's the one-up to not-so-lightly say "I'm doing more than you. I'm better than you...because I'm on this path, and you're not." It's her dig for awareness, for power, and to make herself feel better. Then more laughter too, of course, making it all appear carefree and cheerful. To demonstrate to everyone else that we are friends having a nice, pleasant conversation and everything is just fabulous.

But really, it's not. And really, we aren't friends.

This type of rivalry occurs daily, in so many situations about so many topics. To dive into each one is exhausting because there are too many to count. So instead, it's covered up. We act as if we didn't hear her. But I did, you did, we all did because she is always there in some form or another. However, it's rarely confronted, and so the behavior continues.

1.2: Your Turn. Dear reader, have you ever been in a situation where you've seen the claws come out? Was it directed at you or someone else? How did it make you feel? Did anyone else notice it? Take a moment now to write your thoughts below and why.

_____

_____

_____

_____

The On-Going Rivalry

Women around the world continually deal with pressures that are exclusive to females. Pressure by a certain age to get married, to have babies, to work or not, to juggle motherhood and work, to be the perfect mom, or to deal with the glass ceiling (an unofficially acknowledged barrier to advancement in a profession where it's challenging to be considered equal to their male counterparts). Pressure to make as much money as their male counterparts, to have the perfect body, to have the perfect family, to have no wrinkles, no grey hair, to be physically fit, to be smart, to be successful... with that in mind, this list could go on and on.

Historically, we as women are taught to not bring attention to ourselves. We're taught to, "sit still, look pretty, be quiet, be nice, don't rock the boat, don't be loud, don't stand out, don't be bossy, don't be aggressive, don't be difficult, don't be awkward," etc. To summarize the words of Chimamanda Ngozi Adichie, in her book, *We Should All Be Feminists,*

> *"We teach girls to shrink themselves, to make themselves smaller. We say to girls, you can have ambition, but not too much. You should aim to be successful, but not too successful. Otherwise, you would threaten the man. We raise girls to see each other as competitors not for jobs or accomplishments, which I think can be a good thing, but for the attention of men"* (2014).

Additionally, a lot of these external pressures stem from "envy." We live in an image-heavy society, which is infatuated with the idea of the "perfect body" as it's portrayed in movies, TV, online, magazines, etc. If someone doesn't fit the societal mold, they are considered "less than," "not beautiful," or "not worthy." And many women in general, whether they overtly show it, already struggle with self-confidence. If we are not feeling good about ourselves, while someone else is flourishing, looking good and is perceived as "having it all"... it's easy to want to see her fail.

In her book, *Tripping The Prom Queen* (2006), Susan Shapiro Barash summarizes envy and female rivalry as having three sources. 1) There is our own sense of despair at the ways in which modern society, apparently so open to female success, still makes it so difficult for women to get ahead. 2) Even healthy competition for women is still largely taboo. It's very difficult for most of us to admit that we want to win, snag the promotion, or rise to the top. And, 3) the third reason for our fascination with other women's failure is rooted in female identity. For virtually every woman in this society, our definition of ourselves is bound up in the perception of other women. We see ourselves through comparisons with our mother, our sisters, our friends, and our colleagues. For a whole host of reasons, we have a hard time seeing ourselves as separate individuals with destinies of our own. Instead, we view our identities as a kind of zero-sum game: we succeed *where our mothers fail*, we gain *what other women lose*. We can't envision succeeding or failing on our own terms; we can only measure ourselves against other females. So first we envy the powerful women and then we symbolically triumph over them as they crash and burn (pp. 17–19).

The age of the internet and social media further contributes to the negative aspect of female rivalry. It's all too easy to shame someone when hiding behind a screen, to make her feel inadequate. Keyboard Courage is, "a false bravery possessed by an individual who does not possess the true quality in person. It's typically portrayed in a confrontational attitude exhibited by someone (via an anonymous entry) to an internet web-page or posting" (Urban Dictionary, 2020). Keyboard Courage plays a key role in making cruel and disparaging comments online. It's very cowardly and easy to hide behind the screen to make other women feel bad about themselves. It's especially prevalent in social media groups and settings that make it *easy* to blatantly target and hide behind words.

With these unrelenting societal and self-inhibiting restraints, why do we then continue, as women, to add to that pressure by judging and not being supportive of one another? Why do women enjoy seeing other women fail, especially when and where we need it most—in the form of support, to and from each other? As a result of these feelings of envy and wanting to see "her" fail, we as women, pay a dreadful price for these unimaginative defeats.

Every time we cheer the downfall of a powerful woman, we're giving ourselves the message that power is bad and we shouldn't desire it. Every time we revel in a beautiful woman's aging or weight gain, we reinforce the idea that we, too, are less valuable if we are old or overweight. Every time we gloat over a woman's loss of a husband to a younger, prettier rival, we are reminding ourselves that our own relationship is unstable, that someday our man, too, will move on to greener pastures. Moreover, in savoring women's defeats and seeing other females as our rivals, we lose out on the chance to make women our allies. Who better than other women to understand what we are going through—on the job, with men, in friendships, with our family? Who else should we look to for support, empathy, and assistance? With whom should we join to improve conditions for us all? But we cannot expect other women to join us in true solidarity if we are continually reminding ourselves that these very women are our enemies (Shapiro Barash, 20016, pp. 19–20).

Selena shared her thoughts about society and powerful women,

> *"So, I think that as women, we are taught to mistrust other women who are strong. Let's say you are in a board meeting and there are other women in leadership positions, who are speaking up to a group of men, or are challenging things. I think we've been told (consciously or not) to avoid them or to not support them. You know what I mean? Number one, I think we were raised to mistrust other women trying to be powerful. When women try to be powerful we are taught, 'She's trouble, don't trust her.' Growing up I think I already had some of that type of mistrust built up and it was really hard for me to align myself with the right leadership.*

So, then I'd align myself with leaders who were total push-over women. Women leaders who were not really leading. They'd jump at everything that was said. I was working way too long and too hard and was getting frustrated. I look back now and had all of these women just worked together, they could have been so much more powerful. But they were all isolated, fighting for themselves, to stand out."

1.3: Your Turn. Dear reader, do you believe there is an ongoing rivalry between women? Do you agree with the concept that women often shrink themselves to be smaller? To not rock the boat? Do you think that society endorses the message that a powerful female is bad? Do you have your own story about this? Take a moment now to write your thoughts below and why.

What Rivalry Looks Like

Dear reader, as you dive into this book, I want to keep you interested and not get "too scholarly." However, I think it's so important to also illustrate the significance of this phenomenon, by providing awareness about the type of research that is currently available and what has previously been conducted. Rivalry between women is not just a "light-hearted label," it's a real behavioral issue with long-lasting impacts. These insights set the foundation for the rest of what I'll share with you.

Rivalry and competition are common traits of indirect aggression and passive-aggressive behaviors portrayed by women. Rather than using a direct technique of aggression, females often express hostility indirectly in a roundabout approach (Duncan & Owen-Smith, 2006, pp. 493–494). Also, there is an indication that women primarily target their aggression towards each other rather than focusing on the opposite sex (Bjorkaqvist, 1994, p.

179). Dr. Chesler (2001), Emerita Professor of Psychology and Women's Studies stated the following,

> *"Girls and women are as competitive as men, but mainly toward each other. However, unlike men, middle-class white women and all those who aspire to that position have learned that open competition among women...is taboo" (p. 335).*

Historically, it's the overall perception of open competition between females being off-limits that has ultimately resulted in indirect aggressive behaviors of rivalry and competition between women. Vast research has been conducted on women in the corporate arena in terms of breaking through the glass ceiling. "Female leaders in all countries have gradually had to find their place in organizations, in which the senior and top ranks were male-dominated" (Rojahn, Fischer & Willemsen, 1997, p. 183). However, limited research exists addressing the topic of how women are experiencing or handling aggression and rivalry.

The first real acknowledgment that rivalry among women occurred in the workplace was in a compilation of essays printed in 1987. Published by editors Miner & Longino, *Competition, A Feminist Taboo?* openly addressed women and competition. It's a collection of essays that focuses on competition and provides various points of view from a variety of authors. Each essay addresses the following points,

> *"How does competition motivate us, do we feel more competitive with women than with men, what are the intersections between competition and cooperation, what are the differences between our internal and external experiences of competition, and how can we distinguish between striving for excellence, striving for success, and striving for control?"(pp. 6-7).*

Shapiro-Barash (2006) conducted a study with 500 women on the topic of female rivalry. Her findings resulted in two conclusions. One conclusion suggested a continuing and troubling pattern of rivalry she described as "cut-throat." She said, "Women will do anything rather than face up to female envy and jealousy—especially our own" (p. 7). The second conclusion suggested that women are not supported when confronting the problem of rivalry. "In these post-feminist times, women were often rewarded for romanticizing female friendship and punished for telling the truth about female rivalry" (p. 7).

Phoebe shared a story with me about another woman turning away from the female rivalry she experienced,

> *"It was so very subtle the way it began but occurred over a three-year period of time. I worked with all blonde women who were five to ten years younger than me. I am a minority, so there were also cultural differences besides just the female factor. I was outnumbered by white, blonde women. The women would have lunches and not invite me. There was a lot of exclusion as well as cutting remarks and passive-aggressive digs about me in general and my work too.*

> *I didn't say anything about it until it escalated to hateful behavior. We had to hire a new director for our department and there were two main candidates, an African American woman with braids and a tall, bubbly, nice blonde woman. I am not putting her down at all. She was just pretty boring. But these women were mean to the African American candidate. The ringleader said, 'I want someone who can teach me something!' She also said, 'My grandfather would not want to see braids in this office!'*

> *To seek help, I went to the woman in HR and said, 'I've noticed these things and I can't stand this. And furthermore, I don't feel like I personally fit in either.' I knew it was discrimination. As well as the mean girl thing too.*

> *And after that... nobody talked to me. They somehow knew I'd gone to HR, which was supposed to be confidential. Word travels fast though,*

and I could tell they weren't happy with what I'd said. For a whole year nobody talked to me at all. I was the persona non grata."

Recall Natalie's story at the beginning of this chapter? Natalie's manager did not believe her. Natalie, because of telling the truth, was punished in the sense that nothing was done to modify the negative behavior.

"I went to our manager a couple more times and said, 'This hasn't been solved. It's still a problem. Other people on the team notice it and we need to fix it.' She said, 'I think it's just because your feelings are hurt because you think that you two were friends when you really weren't.' And I said, 'You just don't understand.'"

There are many external factors that cause women to resort to indirect aggressive habits. Many women use indirect, aggressive behaviors to feel more powerful especially in situations where they were lacking in power (Duncan, et al., 2006). Corporate consultant Judith Briles (1989) conducted a survey among women business executives. The result of the survey showed that to move up the corporate ladder, women were more likely to behave unscrupulously toward other women than toward their male counterparts. This behavior manifested due to the feelings of jealousy, envy, and even fear that another woman was competing for her job.

The following three studies are also important to the research on women and rivalry as they pertain to indirect aggressive behaviors and its effects on females.

Study #1: Dr. Chesler (2001) investigated relationships between women, how they view and treat each other, focusing specifically on how indirect aggressive behaviors between women unfold. Her work summarized that women truly need each other to bond and foster relationships of emotional intimacy. She also said that on the flip side, women form cliques, exhibit behaviors of avoidance, and envy other women.

Betina. *"I've wondered if these behaviors are inherently just human? Is it the way we're socialized? I do think there are certain things, like the way our society is set up, that it definitely ends up pitting women against women. I think all women want to be perceived as beautiful, I don't know if that's a strength or weakness in us. But you know, no matter what our age we always want to feel validated in that way. And I think that is an underlying factor to the behaviors of women against women. Whether it's socially or at work, women are vying for that attention. And if someone thinks you are very pretty, it feels like you are a threat. And frequently too, other women will treat you differently based on how you look."*

Study #2: Duncan & Owen-Smith conducted a study on female friendships (2006) that highlighted the feeling of powerlessness, which resulted in indirect aggressive behavior. They found in peer relationships when anxiety was high, indirect aggressive behaviors were more present. Because indirect aggression is not as blatant as direct aggression, individuals can express their feelings without bringing a lot of attention to themselves.

Thea. *"I thought there must be some deficiency in me that brings out this quality in people (to me) and then in turn I feel self-doubt. I've wondered if I needed to learn how to better manage the politics in the office. But when you are a target, it's hard to do that very well. But managing office politics is one thing, and mean girls are another thing. There is that vindictive behavior from a female-targeted to another female. And often it's so calculating and smooth and it makes you doubt yourself because sometimes you even wonder, you'll think that didn't just happen, I perceived it incorrectly."*

Study #3: Loya, et al (2006), explored the notion that women's hostility towards other women is not necessarily a common attitude. Hostility toward other women can be influenced by circumstances in which women generate negative feelings about themselves as women. To summarize, they defined this type of hostility as a component of competition. It's when women have a general tendency to stereotype other women negatively, which can include feelings of hostility toward them.

> **Helen.** *"My experience has been that women will assess you and decide whether you are pretty or not, and then from that, they will categorize you. And based on that, let's say they think you are attractive, they will assume that you are dumb. If you are nice, they will assume you are also not smart. And they start making some generalizations. And so, when they find out that you are attractive; and you are smart, and have some other great qualities too... Well, that just ratchets it up a notch to a whole other level. Some of them threaten you and can get really nasty. And what's been interesting to me is how utterly nasty it can get."*

1.4: Your Turn. Dear reader, do you agree that men and women exhibit different traits of aggression? Do you agree that females are more indirectly aggressive than men? Have you experienced this personally? Have you ever experienced a situation where other women turned against the rivalry you were experiencing or did not support you? Do you have your own story about this? Take a moment now to write your thoughts below and why.

_____

_____

_____

_____

Two Key Definitions are Rivalry and Competition

Now that you have a general understanding of the *"why,"* let me share with you the specific significance of the *"what."* This will help you have a better understanding of the terms you will see interlaced throughout this book.

Rivalry is a component of aggressive behavior. For the sake of this topic, I often use the word "rivalry" as the broader banner for various types of "mean girl" behaviors that can occur, such as bullying, judging, acting passive/aggressive, having intangible behaviors, etc. When I conducted previous research for school, the closest defined word to "rivalry" in the scholarly literature was the term "competition." And while it has similar aspects, it is a kinder, less abrasive meaning than rivalry.

The word *rival* most commonly refers to a person or group that tries to defeat or be more successful than another person or group, which means that rivals tend to come in pairs. Thompson (2020) defines rivalry as,

> *"The state of two people or groups engaging in a lasting competitive relationship. Rivalry is the 'against each other' spirit between two competing sides. The relationship itself may also be called 'a rivalry,' and each participant or side a rival to the other."*

Competition is defined as, "the desire to excel over others, and better them" (Lugones & Spelman, 1987, p. 237). Competition is a component of aggressive behavior.

Additionally, Matsumoto (1987) claimed competitiveness was a state of mind,

> *"Although potentially constructive, competitiveness also includes those less ethical but very human characteristics such as spite, envy, egoism, and duplicity"* (page 81).

Rivalry as a Banner for Broader Behaviors

As gleaned from the research descriptions, rivalry is often a "banner" for other broader behaviors that women experience, or a result of other extensive circumstances.

A key construct of this book is the idea that rivalry and negative competition create obstacles to building strong female relationships or sisterhoods. While I wholeheartedly believe in positive competition and think it's definitely a motivator when used in the proper situation, it also has to have parameters to ensure it doesn't turn divisive. In an isolating manner, it's not a sustainable long-term strategy for an effective team-based culture, social relationships, sisterhoods, etc. It's simply negative behavior.

Women typically tend to display indirect aggressive behaviors versus a more direct method. Females use indirect aggressive behaviors as a way to be and feel more powerful, especially in situations where they are lacking power. Indirect aggression is not as obvious as direct aggression. Because the actions are often not tangible to others, they can slide under the radar. It's a sneaky, slippery type of projected behavior that may be discernible only to the individual it's projected toward. In all of the stories that were relayed to me, when the experiences began, they were barely noticeable. The subtleness of the targeted behavior made the women question if indeed it was occurring. As the indirect acts escalated, they traditionally became more frequent but often, were not discernable to others.

> **Beatrix.** *"She had sat herself where she would be out of the line of sight of the Vice President while we were having the discussion, but she was in my line of sight. And anything I said, I don't care if she agreed with it or didn't agree with it, she would just glare at me. The anxiety would just bubble up in my stomach into my chest. I felt like I was just going to throw up on the spot."*

In other words, feelings can still be expressed without bringing a lot of attention to oneself. The person being aggressive can simultaneously still "fit in" with their peer group, especially in situations where others in the group may be more powerful. Females use indirect aggressive behaviors as a way to feel more powerful, especially in situations where they are lacking power (Duncan, et al., 2006).

1.5: Your Turn. Dear reader, have you ever heard female aggression defined in the way that I have shared it, in terms of competition and rivalry? Do you agree with the concept that negative rivalrous behaviors are a banner for other underlying issues? Take a moment now to write your thoughts below and why.

_____

_____

_____

_____

My Story

In the introduction, I mentioned why this topic piqued my interest. I'm very passionate, as you can probably already tell, about women's issues. When I began my initial research, I was especially devoted to better understanding why women in the work environment so often lack support for one another. It completely baffled me because I'd never looked at other females through this type of lens. I tend to see the good, the positive. As time passed and I became more familiar with the traits of the occurrences, I also saw how extreme this type of behavior was for women, integrated as a part of everyday life.

To a degree, I'd also been on the receiving end of certain rivalrous behaviors throughout my life, in social groups, at school, in sports, at work, etc. As a result of those interactions, I knew just enough to slightly understand it personally. I had the belief "that was just how certain groups or types of females were going to behave." I was extremely compassionate about my research. I had nothing but positive intent to share the ins and outs of this negative behavior. The combination of what I'd witnessed and experienced, as well as the powerful stories women shared with me, gave me a strong belief that I genuinely knew what the phenomena entailed. And because I was *so* aware, this also led me to the belief that I truly knew what an in-depth female rivalrous experience felt like.

Really though, I didn't. Because then I experienced it first-hand and I didn't even know it was occurring for several months. It was the best negative thing that could have ever happened to me.

In mid-2017, I was working at a job that was no longer fulfilling nor healthy. I didn't sleep well at night, and when Sunday morning rolled around, my weekend was pretty much over as I was already dreading going back to work on Monday. Daily, as I was driving into the office, I'd have a pit in my stomach. I lost my ambition and was unmotivated. I felt a lack of joy. I was short-tempered with my husband, children, family, and friends. I didn't feel like I was doing my best job as a wife, mother, daughter, friend, etc., simply because the ambivalence toward work was seeping into everything else in my life. I was unhappy but I also was not fully consciously knowledgeable or aware of the reason "why." I didn't have the correct words to verbalize it appropriately because in all honesty, it was not something I could consciously pinpoint.

It wasn't always that way. I used to enjoy going to work. In fact, I'd been there for almost six years and used to really like my job. The source of my anxiety was an unpredictable female named Whitney, who led the team I was on. Nice or mean, each day, each hour actually, I never exactly knew what temperament I'd be dealing with and the sound of her voice began to grate on my nerves. Her laugh sounded evil. Her mood swings were like a pendulum.

There was constant conflict and rivalry among our team members, and, if you didn't kiss Whitney's ass, you definitely were not "in" with her or the rest of the group. She had a small posse comprised of a few females who hung onto every word she said as if she were speaking the gospel. They emulated her every action as if she could pave the way for them. And as a result, they followed her blindly, always doing what they were told.

I noticed frequently that conversations with Whitney, either in a meeting or in general, changed. And then over the course of several months, I realized that certain information was relayed entirely differently to individuals in other meetings or discussions that I was no longer a part of.

I've always been a note-taker. But at that point in time, and because I am a fast typist, I began typing meeting discussions verbatim. On several occasions Whitney would comment, "Amber, you have such great note-taking skills." And I did, but unbeknownst to her, I was documenting our exchange to have proof of what we'd talked about. I wanted proof that certain events had occurred, to cover my backside. That documentation came in handy too many times to count as it gave me proof of the dialogue we'd had, "Well, actually Whitney, on this day, you actually said this, and gave me this work to do… not that," etc.

On more than one occasion, I approached Whitney about our apparent disconnect. Each time, I was intentionally objective and consciously chose to not point fingers at her inconsistent behavior. I even went so far as to put the blame back on myself asking, "I feel things from a project perspective are not progressing as efficiently as they could be. Is there something I can do on my end to help the project, and ultimately make our communication more efficient?" In hindsight, I wondered if my approach in talking to her last minute via an unscheduled meeting had caught her off guard. She did not like conflict and was very calm, almost fake-happy, as she responded, "No Amber, everything is just fine."

Not even a few short days later, she pulled me aside, furious, alone in a conference room only to shout at me, "I just need you to lead! You are not leading the team or this project!" I was completely caught off guard by her erratic behavior. I was mystified as to why this hadn't come up in our conversation a few days earlier. I also was furious. Did I show that to her? No, I calmly listened, then got up and left. It took all I had to not tell her off, to not walk out that door and never come back.

I'd been trying very hard to lead this project team. It was something I'd done previously on many occasions for this client and additionally, it was something I was very good at. But until this point, with this particular individual, every suggested framework, solution, and idea had been shot down. Mind you, the solutions she was rejecting were based on industry respected tools. I'd implemented similar proposals on previous projects and had been quite successful.

Whitney was the roadblock and she obstructed me from effectively doing my job.

Before coming to our team, Whitney had a vastly different business background and came from an entirely different sector within the same organization. She'd managed the inner workings of the business in her area to make things run as efficiently as possible. She was used to clear, definite processes, a black and white approach, per se, to getting things done. With my psychology background, I focused on utilizing organizational tools to help individuals and teams adapt to change. To a degree, I was also very used to clear, definite processes as the proactive foundational piece of the work I was doing. However, there was also a lot of grey in my approach as it pertained to the reaction(al), dealing with people components (i.e. the things you can't always plan for). In retrospect, I think initially, this is where we began to clash. We had unique differences in our approaches, and I had expertise in an area she did not. I now realize she was put in a position to lead a team in which she had absolutely no understanding at all about the methodology, concept, or foundation of the type of work she was tasked to do. It was the type of work I was very knowledgeable in.

I began to be "uninvited" to regular long-standing meetings, as well as some of the separate, less formal conversations. This made it hard for me to do my work efficiently because I needed interaction and input from individuals on those broader teams to successfully implement the work I was doing.

Work that had been given to me to take on or lead was also often given to other associates from her posse to also lead. This often resulted in a duplication of efforts and wasted time. When I'd voice my comments about redundant work, I was told very clearly that "I was not being a team player and that type of attitude would not go far as it went against the overall company culture."

To help me learn to "lead" better, Whitney had a female associate from her girl-posse schedule weekly meetings to "coach" me on how to interact appropriately with senior leadership. It was humiliating and demoralizing. I'd been a consultant for years at a Big 5 Firm, led major projects, as well as led and facilitated numerous meetings with generals and colonels at the Pentagon. I had no problem at all interacting with senior leaders. However, Whitney had a problem with me. She was not verbally articulate about it but definitely wielded her power of control by her actions. It was subtle and all on the premise of "helping me do better and improve."

Though I was unhappy, on edge, and seemed to have misplaced all power of articulation to speak up for myself, I'd also lost all passion for work. Any effort to make a change seemed utterly overwhelming. As a result, I did nothing.

Until one day, while driving to work, I was talking to my mom about the situation. She'd been aware of the circumstances for quite some time but on this particular day, she said something that ignited me. "I really hate to see how, because of this woman, you are doubting yourself so much and the work you do. Especially, because you are so good at it."

And that's when I had a "lightbulb moment!" I physically felt like the wind had been knocked out of me, that I'd been punched in the stomach... I suddenly realized I was knee-deep in a rivalrous situation that I'd completely not seen. To say I was blown away was an understatement. My next immediate thought was, "If I knew about this topic as much as I did...researched it, studied it, wrote about it, and yet, when it was happening to me, I failed to realize what was going on. If that was the case, what was it doing to other women who weren't as familiar or knowledgeable about it? How was it making them feel? How were they coping?"

This realization inspired me to make an immediate change. I promptly gave my two-week notice and quit. The ironic thing was, wait for it... I was a consultant! Technically, I was not even an employee of the organization I'd served for almost six years. All that I'd been experiencing and feeling was sheer misery. I truly began to wonder, what in the h*ll was wrong with me?! I must note that the consulting firm I was working for during all of this was extraordinarily supportive. They'd been aware of the situation and knew at some point I'd want to make an exit. Until my "light bulb moment" I'd told them it was okay, and I was handling it. I didn't know how wrong I was about that choice until I'd removed myself from the situation and ultimately felt like the weight of the world had been lifted off my shoulders.

Beyond the fact that, as a consultant, I could have left ages ago, I was aware that I had been putting up with a situation that I should have recognized and avoided from the onset. This was an extremely frustrating realization for me to wrap my brain around and because of it, I was very hard on myself.

In my post-graduate work, I studied rivalry between women in the workplace extensively. It's what I do—my thing. To find myself in a situation where I was experiencing what I'd researched and had absolutely no idea that I was knee-deep in it was perplexing. It was definitely a slow progression. I didn't fully get it until my mom mentioned something to me, and by then, I'd felt trapped with no way out.

I'll dive into more detail about this in the following chapters, but in a nutshell, because I lived it, I now better understand the challenges and behaviors. Like so many women who shared their stories with me, I too lost my voice. I lost my sparkle and my shine... I didn't like myself. I didn't feel like a good wife, mother, or friend. I was just getting by, day by day. Because I truly knew what it felt like, I understood the aftermath of coping and the recovery steps. That it takes time...sometimes a long time. Several women have also shared with me that after their experience was over, it felt like they had Post Traumatic Stress Disorder (PTSD). As I've never had that, I can't say for sure. But I do know the thought of seeing Whitney's face, hearing her voice, hearing her "put-me-on-the-edge" laughter, or going back to that same working environment again, gives me huge thoughts of anxiety and feelings of physical discomfort. It is doubtful because of this experience that I will ever work for that organization again—all because of her.

I knew I didn't like working with this particular female. At the time it was occurring, I was so entrenched in the problem that I simply could not see what was right in front of me. I was too close. I'd blocked out everything except literally focusing on how to cope, to just get through each day, one day at a time. I had lost my voice and didn't know how to speak out about it.

Taking the leap to do what I knew in my heart was the right decision gave me strength and peace. I felt a sense of exhilaration! It was like an enormous weight had been lifted off my shoulders.

1.6: Your Turn. Dear reader, based upon the sharing of my story—did anything resonate with you? Do you have your own story to share? Take a moment now to write below, if any of the points or actions that I shared, resonate with you and why.

_____

_____

_____

_____

"An old Cherokee told his grandson:
'My son, there's a battle between two wolves inside us all.
One is Evil. It's anger, jealousy, greed,
resentment, inferiority, lies and ego.
The other is Good. It's joy, peace, love,
hope, humility, kindness & truth.'
The boy thought about it, and asked:
Grandfather, which wolf wins?'
The old man quietly replied: 'The one you feed.'"
—Cherokee Proverb (Native Partnership, 2020).

Setting the Context

As mentioned in the introduction, when I first began my research on this topic for my Ph.D., I focused solely on this phenomenon as it pertained to women in the work environment. I interviewed at great length nine women of diverse working levels in a variety of organizations. These women are key, fundamental players in my initial research and helped kick-start my passion for this issue. My own experience pushed me to expand it. Throughout this book, you will meet many brave women who've experienced this sensation at work, home, school, or in their neighborhood. The context or space of the occurrence doesn't really matter. *These women are just like me and you.* And this can happen anywhere, anytime, anyplace.

You will see many names appear in the following chapters. The names of the initial nine women, however, are a constant throughout. I'd like to introduce them to you.

Amy has a Bachelor of Science degree in education and worked in the educational field as an elementary school teacher for 39 years. She is a petite woman, with a dry sense of humor and personality. Amy relayed her experience in a matter-of-fact type of demeanor. As she began talking, she did not get emotional as she spoke about her experience. In fact, right from the beginning, she was quick to praise the other woman's skill and competence as a teacher.

> *"The first one being, my observation of this co-worker of mine, I will call her Karen, is that she is and continues to be an excellent teacher. I mean there's absolutely no doubt about that."*

Beatrix has a Bachelor of Science degree in chemical engineering. She specializes in supply chain management and worked in the chemical industry for 15 years when her experience occurred. Beatrix was direct, to the point, and spoke matter-of-factly about her experience with a female supervisor. A down-to-earth individual with a quick wit, Beatrix was not overly comfortable in singing her own praises. As a result, even though it was important to note, she was hesitant to say that she was a high-performing individual within her company.

> *"This is hard for me to say, but I'll say it. I'm what our company calls a high potential employee. Some of my moves are very scripted and this was one of them. I needed supply chain experience and this was a global role."*

Clio has a Bachelor of Musical Arts degree and 20 years of work experience in a variety of industries, which include construction management, medical, program management, and retail development. Clio was very dry and direct, warmly smiling at times throughout the interview, letting you know she had a sense of humor. She spoke candidly about her first professional working experience out of college with a female boss.

> *"I mean she was just so mean to me. It was to the point where I was afraid to talk to her unless it was absolutely necessary because she just was so angry, she would take it out on me."*

Dana has a Bachelor of Arts degree and worked in the insurance industry for 40 years. Dana is a licensed chartered property casualty underwriter (CPCU), a professional designation in property-casualty insurance and risk management. Dana spoke directly about her experiences with two different female supervisors. In one experience, she acknowledged how the men and women were treated in the work environment. Dana described the controlling behaviors of one of her supervisors.

> *"The women were in the office all of the time. She did not treat the men as poorly as she treated the women. One woman that worked there could do no wrong. But everybody else in the department she terrorized by threatening them, or putting them on probation, just different things like that."*

Eleni has a Master's in Business Administration (MBA). Specializing in media marketing, she has 19 years of professional working experience within her industry. Eleni was very candid as she spoke about her experience of rivalry with another woman in the work environment, an experience that lasted over 16 months.

> *"I think from the beginning she felt threatened by me because I think. She perceived me as being more competent, more intelligent than she was. She didn't like the fact that I was getting more face time with the execs and having conversations about priorities with them, than she was. So yes, I think it was a form of control—it came down to her managing other people's perceptions of her. And for me to meet with other people without her, she thought, made her not look good."*

Faith has a Doctor of Philosophy (Ph.D.) degree in social work and worked in the health behavior change and social work industry for 44 years. Faith was direct and to-the-point in her delivery. As the situation escalated, Faith kept trying to do a good job at work.

> *"Being in a leadership position, I did a lot of community work. I tried to keep the reputation of the agency and the services high."*

Grace has a Master's in Business Administration (MBA) and 15 years of professional work experience as a consultant for the United States Intelligence

Community (IC). Although soft-spoken in her demeanor, Grace's manner was very forthright as she spoke about her experience of rivalry with another woman. Unemotional, she described the indirect aggressive behaviors of the other woman, a consultant from a different company who worked on the same team of which Grace was in charge,

> *"The other woman had some very direct aggressive behavioral traits that she exhibited. What I experienced with her was very insidious. She would always smile and grin to my face, but then I would find out after the fact that she was doing things to undercut the team and undercut the team camaraderie."*

Hannah has a Bachelor of Arts (BA) degree and worked in the business development and sales industry for 15 years. Down to earth and approachable, Hannah displayed a character of strength and ambition. Possessing an awareness of self, she spoke candidly about several experiences of rivalry with peers and an employee who worked for her, in various work environments.

> *"I am very goal-oriented. Just because other people weren't like that, I think that's in part why I stood out. I felt bad that because other people didn't have the same drive as me, that they were being measured against me in that aspect."*

Although the companies in which she worked for varied, Hannah self-reflected as to why she was the common denominator for the behaviors she was subject to.

> *"I'm somebody who wants to have a list and check it off, every day. I get a big sense of accomplishment from that. When I was in college, and we would get our syllabus at the beginning of the semester, I would get my papers done in the first week of school, and people were like, 'What is wrong with you?' I don't have the ability to procrastinate, and just because that has helped me, I can't apologize for*

that. That is who I am. But to other people... to other people it's like, 'What?' They don't get it."

Ilene possessed a master's degree and had 26 years of professional working experience in the United States government Intelligence Community (IC). Although very direct in her approach, there was also an undertone of an energetic personality that came through when she spoke about her experience of rivalry with a woman senior to her that covered a 10-year span.

> *"Well, let me start by saying, it wasn't necessarily a direct rivalry. I would consider it a direct rivalry one, where she and I were at the same level, we were competing for the same job, and we were kind of working on all those same issues. It is a little different because she was a senior in my chain of—well, not even in my chain of command, but within the office that hired me, so she had the same specialty and held what would become the jobs that I would grow into."*

Closing

The aggressive behaviors named in this chapter that occur from one female to another—can be females of any age who are failing to help each other. The subtleness of indirect aggressive behaviors makes it difficult to pinpoint because it's so often hard to see. This makes the situation even more burdensome. If the receiver of the behavior wants to confront the other woman, how can she directly do so, without proof or specific evidence that the behavior exists?

I'm sure in some form or another you've witnessed these types of behaviors. Perhaps, you have experienced it. If not personally, I am sure you know someone who has. Indirect aggressive behavior is devious in nature, and its approach is artful. The sad thing is, the women emanating these types of behaviors are often fully aware of what they are doing.

If you or someone you know has experienced it, but are at a loss of what to do, keep turning the pages! The following chapters will give you an insight into what the behaviors look like, how to know if you are dealing with it, and how to move beyond it.

Chapter 2:

Myth: It's Only a Catfight

"At some point just about every woman realizes that she is seen not only as not-good-enough but also as a threat, that some person wishes to eliminate her from competition while another seeks to engage her in it. Both situations indicate pernicious rivalry. Unwelcome competition satisfies neither the inventor of the competition nor its object, neither of whom probably feels strong. If ever cooperation should be substituted for competition, it should be in such a situation. Sadly, lack of self-confidence, which engenders senseless competition, also render collaboration difficult."
—N.E. Painter (Miner & Longino, 1987).

Melissa's Story

"A friend of mine asked me to be a guest speaker at a class at my local university. After my presentation, she said, 'I'm going to introduce you

to someone in the health services department that is trying to build a resource for students on campus.' Soon after, I met that contact and she said, 'I love what you are doing! I'd like to bring you on campus to do more of this work.' She then started the paperwork for me to be a contractor and continue my work there.

Later, when I was back on campus, I saw flyers for a yoga class that my friend Amy was teaching. For years, Amy and I ran around in the same circles, as we'd come from similar lines of work. I'd even mentioned to the contract lady that I knew Amy. She thought it was great that we were friends.

I later talked to Amy, congratulated her, and told her it was cool to see that she was spreading her wings. I told her I was also going to be on campus and maybe we could collaborate at some point. She said, 'Oh, really? What are they going to have you do?' I told her what it was and said, 'I recommended using one of the curriculums I've used for other clients. And the contract woman agreed, and really liked it.' Amy said, 'Are you sure? Who did you talk to? Are you really sure?' I told her who it was, which was one of the same people she'd also talked to.

I thought it was odd... she was questioning me so much. It felt like she thought I was making it up. She said, 'I thought I was going to be doing some of that work.' I said, 'Well, I don't want to step on your toes. Why don't you circle back with your contact and see what she says?' And literally, I was not planning on stepping on her toes. Especially if she'd already been there. The woman in charge of contracts liked what I was doing and said there was room for both of us. But I encouraged Amy to talk to her, to get clarity, and see how it'd be best for us to both move forward and see what that best fit was.

I also kept saying if she was already there, I didn't want to take her work. Amy kept on insisting that 'No, there is so much work to do on campus. There is more than enough space for both of us.' I got no negative vibes at all from her about it. All in all, I thought it was a great conversation.

The following week I reached out to the contract lady at the University. She began the conversation with a really concerned tone, asking, 'Did you tell Amy I was bringing you on as a contractor?' I said, 'Yes, I told you we knew each other. She was excited about it.' The lady let out a big sigh and said, 'Amy called my supervisor and told her it was not a good fit to have you come on board and that it'd be a conflict of interest to have you on campus. That she feels disrespected and if you were to come on board to work, it would have to be under her, Amy, as your manager.'

Mind you, Amy was a contractor too. She had a lot of guts to say that to the vendor who was in charge of her paycheck. Amy also referenced my experience to the contract's director, and said, 'They should see if I had experience working on a campus.' Which I did. A lot of it. She was trying to stir the pot. What she said to my face was totally different than what she said behind my back.

Someone I thought was a friend totally insulted me, cancelled me out, questioned my experience, created doubt as to what I would deliver, and doubt as to the quality of my business. It was shocking. My stomach dropped when my contact told me what Amy had said about me. I was so very hurt. I just couldn't believe she would do that to me. It hurt so bad too because I was at the point in my life where I was trying to see if I could support myself with my company. It was so hurtful for someone to go behind my back and say things that were not true to jeopardize my business.

I didn't then and still don't understand now, why she acted that way. We may not have been best friends, but I at least thought we were social friends. I'd known Amy for years. I realize now that I'd been trying to cultivate a friendship that 'could be.' As I looked back, I realized that sometimes she was a bit standoffish but I always chalked it up to her 'just being busy.' But now I see it may have been something other than that.

And even after all of that happened, Amy kept trying to contact me. I ignored her because I was still trying to process the conversation I had. I was at a loss as to what to do with her. I don't even know if she knew that I knew what she had said."

Catfight Defined

Although the term "catfight" was introduced in 1824, it was first recorded in 1854 as a characterization of what a fight *between women* looked like and was described as, "a woman who was regarded as spiteful, backbiting, and malicious" (Herbst, 2001). It's a term that is frequently used to describe women insulting each other verbally or engaged in an intense competition for men, power, or occupational success (James 2016).

Historical Evolution of the "Catfight"

While the use of the term is often considered derogatory or belittling, it's been a staple of American news media and pop culture since the 1940s (Douglas, 1994, Sweeny 2007, Heim, Murphy & Golant, 2003, Dowd, 2005, Douglas & Michaels, 2004).

Over time the physical emergence of "catfights" evolved to showcase women wrestling in short film clips in the 1950s, to B-movies in the 1960s (e.g. *Faster, Pussycat! Kill! Kill!* by Russ Meyer). "In the 1970s the American news media began to use the term catfight to describe women's disagreements about issues related to women's rights, such as the Equal Rights Amendment" (Douglas, p. 221, 1994). The 1970s and 80s introduced "catfights" to television drama series (e.g. *Dallas* and *Dynasty* nighttime soap operas) with Linda Evans and Joan Collins. "Catfights" then, more consistently began to appear in popular movies, *2 Days in the Valley* (1996) with Teri Hatcher and Charlize

Theron, and *Catwoman* (2004) with Halle Berry and Sharon Stone, to name a few (Douglas, 1994, Sweeny 2007, Heim, Murphy & Golant, 2003, Dowd, 2005, Douglas & Michaels, 2004).

Advance to present-day television with the existence of reality TV, daytime soaps, and talk shows that include such titles as, *The Bachelor*, *The Real Housewives Series* and *Jerry Springer* (Pozner, 2010). In 2009, ABC-TV promoted the evening reality show, *The Bachelor*, with the voiceover narration, "Let the catfights begin." Additionally, reality television shows have frequently overlaid sound effects of hissing cats onto scenes featuring women arguing or competing with each other (Pozner, 2010).

Silent Epidemic (Societal Views)

There is a general awareness of rivalry between women, commonly, often jokingly, referred to as a "catfight," as referenced by its evolution in U.S. popular media. It's a phenomenon that many people recognize but grossly underestimate. It's routinely voiced as, "It's just women, being dramatic or difficult." OR "Typical female behavior!" OR "It's nothing serious—they just need to get over it!"

Societal views tend to make light of this behavior. In its regular portrayal on reality TV shows, movies, and social media there often is an aspect of comedy or entertainment to the negative conduct. And certainly, while some of what you see on reality TV is staged for viewer ratings, the "behind the scenes" behavior, the real-life behavior that's not portrayed in pop culture, is often a result of the "pop influence" and not taken seriously.

However, the term "catfight" discredits the seriousness of the situation and trivializes an important topic. It is a silent epidemic. Silent in the aspect that women who are recipients of this type of behavior often do not speak about their experience until it is behind them, or near to being over. Silent in the fact that there is often awareness by others about the behavior as it is occurring, but traditionally it is not overtly dealt with until after the fact, if ever.

Habitually, there is more to this type of conduct than what meets the eye. After the initial rivalry begins, there is a unique pattern to how it unfolds. If it is apparent to anyone else at all, it may look and start out as appearing "dramatic." To the "receiver" however, an indirect, aggressive pattern of behavior tends to follow. Often, especially in the beginning, the subdued manner of indirect aggressive behavior is difficult to identify and is not overtly visible.

I've witnessed this behavior first-hand as well as from stories women have shared with me. It isn't pretty. It can be raw, ugly, confusing, and to say the least, very painful. Indirect aggressive behavior is calculated and is not as blatant as direct aggression. This type of negative behavior is infectious. If left unaddressed it will influence the morale of others.

2.1: Your Turn. Dear reader, what are your thoughts about the term "catfight?" Do you think society highlights and endorses these types of behaviors for entertainment or media purposes? Why or why not? What do you think when you hear people say, "It's just women being dramatic or difficult?" Do you agree or disagree? If so, why? Has anyone ever told you that you were being dramatic or difficult as it pertained to this type of behavior? If so, how did it make you feel? Take a moment now to write your thoughts below and why.

_____

_____

_____

_____

Theories of Aggression

Rivalry is a component of aggressive behavior. Indirect aggressive behavior is a component of an aggressive act. Indirect aggressive behaviors fall into the category of women failing to help each other.

To better understand the underlying nature of these actions, bear with me for a moment as I dive into a bit of psychological history, to highlight what experts say about "Theories of Aggression."

"Aggression as a behavior has many appearances and manifestations and is portrayed by action or words, as well as being triggered by violence, anger, hostility, or an emotional response" (Brehm, et al., 2005).

While most people are familiar with the basic term, "aggression," it has a variety of underlying meanings depending upon the context in which it is used. For its use in psychology, and specifically for how it's addressed in this book, the broader term aggression is defined as, "behavior whose intent is to harm another" (Duncan, et al., 2004).

The topic of aggression is not a new discussion. Its various theories have been debated for decades by some of the world's leading psychologists such as Sigmund Freud (Campbell, 1993), John Dollard (Dollard, Doob, Miller, Mowrer, & Sears, 1939), and Albert Bandura (Bandura, 1980). What is newer to the discussion is the evolution of aggression. For several (recent) decades psychologists debated about three various theories of aggression, including:

1. Aggression as an instinctual behavior,
2. Aggression as a predictable or functional reaction, and
3. Aggression as a learned behavior

Sigmund Freud, an acclaimed psychologist, viewed the behavior of aggression as a learned instinct (Campbell, 1993). John Dollard, social psychologist, and Yale graduate viewed aggression as a functional reaction to the defined stimuli of, the feeling of frustration (Dollard, et al., 1939). Lastly, Albert Bandura, social psychologist, viewed the behavior of aggression as a learned behavior within a social context (Bandura, 1980).

Bandura's (1977) social learning theory emphasized, "behavior is learned through the observation of others as well as through the direct experience of rewards and punishments" (Brehm, et al., 2005, p. 410).

A study Bandura and colleagues conducted in 1961, called the *Bobo Doll Experiment*, observed children who had previously watched adults modeling various activities. Children that witnessed adults exhibiting overt aggressive types of behavior modeled a similarly aggressive type of behavior in their own play. Similarly, children who witnessed adults exhibiting a quiet non-aggressive type of behavior modeled a similar manner of behavior in their own play (Brehm, et al., 2005, p. 410). Bandura believed, as a result of this study, that children learned by observation. They observed an action and then emulated the behavior they saw. He also believed that if acts of aggression remained unpunished, they would continue and increase.

Gender and Aggression

Studies that focus on understanding aggressive acts of behavior in children are relatively recent. However, what is known offers insight as to how aggressive behavior first appears in boys and girls, the gender differences as to why, the reasons why it continues to grow and develop, and how it can later impact adult behavior.

Gender research offers two major explanations for why this is. As infants and toddlers, males and females display similar traits of overt aggression (Bjorkqvist, 1994; Chesler, 2001; Duncan, et al., 2006). When children are young, exhibiting direct aggressive behavior is traditionally not encouraged in little girls. "Proponents of classic social learning explanations have argued that girls are more frequently and consistently punished for being directly aggressive than are boys, and so tend to express their aggression indirectly" (Duncan, et al., 2006, p. 494). When you think back to how you were raised, does what I am describing sound familiar?

> ***Phoebe.*** *"My candy analogy about this topic as it pertains to men and women is… When men fight or have disagreements it is like bubble-gum. They've chewed their gum, blown the bubbles, and then when they are done with it, they spit it out. For women, it's very different. Female fighting or this indirect angst and disagreement is like putting pop rocks in your mouth. They make your mouth hurt and it hurts so bad. It burns. It burns even after you spit them out. So, it's bubblegum versus pop rocks. And that's a big difference."*

Wendy. *"There is a different overtness about male behaviors. They just sort of size each other up and get the aggression out that they need to and then they move on. There's not this pent-up hostility, this subversive behavior. I think that is what becomes the insidious thing this is, is that this just kind of gets under the surface... And it really can destroy a whole working relationship or a friendship relationship. I just feel like there is so much sizing up and it is based on the external versus the internal."*

Did you know that almost 60 years ago, researchers believed only men exhibited aggressive behaviors? This is very telling regarding societal views and gender research. It shocked me when I first read this, as 60 years is not that long ago at all! Researcher Arnold H. Buss (1961) claimed the phenomenon of aggression was typically a *male characteristic*. He believed that women *did not* display aggressive types of behaviors and therefore it was not a phenomenon to be studied in women. It's only been in recent decades that the discussion of aggressive behaviors has been highlighted based upon gender differences between men and women.

It's a known fact that men and women, for the most part, communicate differently. Think of the book series, *Men are From Mars, Women are From Venus*. Traditionally speaking, men are more violent than women in almost every culture (Brehm, et al., 2005, p. 402). Women feel anger the same as men do but often portray it in a different manner. Women tend to use different strategies of aggression versus the aggression strategies demonstrated by men. Males are more physically aggressive, exhibiting overt, direct behaviors, while females traditionally resort to more indirect forms of behavior, less physical in nature (Chesler, 2001; Brehm, et al., 2005; Duncan, et al., 2006). As defined by Dr. Bjorkqvist (1994), indirect aggression is "when social skills develop, even more sophisticated strategies of aggression are made possible, with the aggressor being able to harm a target person without even being identified" (p. 179). What's even more fascinating is, some women may not even be aware of or know why they exhibit indirect aggressive behaviors. Ultimately, many women may even *refuse to believe* that they exhibit indirect and passive-aggressive types of behavior toward other women.

And while it's so very common to hear about female-to-female rivalry and competition, competition between men and women to the same extreme is very rare. This can occur but may not be as disruptive or as passive-aggressive as female to female rivalry can be.

2.2: Your Turn. Dear reader, do you agree or disagree that there are different types of aggressive behavior? What are your thoughts that theorists, as little as only 60 years ago, believed that women did not display aggressive types of behavior? Do you think that men and women display different types of aggression? Why or why not? Take a moment now to write your thoughts below and why.

_____

_____

_____

_____

Social Intelligence

Along with gender, Social Intelligence (SI) plays a big role in the behaviors of aggression. It's been proven that at a young age all children exhibit *similar direct* aggressive traits. Indirect aggressive traits, however, begin to appear in little girls around the ages of six to eight. It's typical that little girls develop Social Intelligence before little boys do. As a result, they can begin to exhibit indirect aggressive behaviors earlier than their male counterparts. Boys routinely use direct forms of verbal *and* physical aggression more so than girls, while indirect verbal aggression is more common in little girls than little boys. (Bjorkqvist, 1994; Chesler, 2001; Duncan, et al., 2006).

First mentioned in 1920 by Edward Thorndike, Social Intelligence is defined as, "the ability to understand and manage men and women and boys and girls, to act wisely in human relations." Psychologist Nicholas Humphrey of Cambridge, MA (1986) believes that it is social intelligence that defines who we are as humans.

"Social Intelligence is the capacity to know oneself and to know others. It develops from experience with people and learning from success and failures in social settings. It is more commonly referred to as 'tact,' 'common sense' or 'street smarts'" (Riggio, 2014).

A theory developed by Bjorkqvist, Lagerspetz, Kaukiainen, & Osterman (1992) linked different aggressive styles to interpersonal aggression and Social Intelligence. According to this theory, aggressive behavior tends to appear in the following order:

1. Direct physical
2. Direct verbal
3. Indirect aggression

The meaning of "indirect aggression" is defined as,

"social manipulation: the target is attacked, not directly, but circuitously, and the aggressor can thereby remain unidentified and avoid counterattack. The use of indirect aggression requires a certain amount of social intelligence; indirect aggression correlates with measures of social intelligence" (Bjorkqvist, 1994, pp. 183–185).

In summary, how aggression is defined and what contributes to it is not just "black and white." Aggression is a multi-defined, multi-faceted behavior. Young children often exhibit similar types of aggressive behavior regardless of gender. As a result of the development of Social Intelligence and classical learning explanations (to name a few), aggression traits usually evolve and show up differently in adults versus children.

Rivalry and Women

It is not uncommon that people may embrace the concept of "stranger danger."

"The idea or warning that all strangers can potentially be dangerous. It is an example of a moral panic that people experience regarding anyone that they are unfamiliar with in society" (Wikipedia, 2020).

Did you know however, that aggressive acts of behavior are traditionally targeted toward an acquaintance rather than a stranger? As quoted by the U.S. Bureau of the Census (Richardson, 1993), "most aggression occurs in the context of everyday conflict and involves interactions between people who are familiar with one another. Even assaults are less likely to be directed toward strangers than toward familiar targets" (as cited in Richardson, 2006, p. 2492).

Prior to the feminist movement, women and competition was a subject traditionally not discussed because it was not overtly seen or acknowledged. If competition occurred among women, there was a societal belief it pertained only to beauty pageants, cooking contests, and dating. Just think about what the outcome of what these contests entailed... The outcomes or the "winners" of these competitions were directed toward men. In today's world, when women compete in the workforce, they are competing against themselves. It's an entirely different kind of competition.

2.3: Your Turn. Dear reader, what are your thoughts about Social Intelligence and the role it plays in aggression in males and females? Do you think aggressive traits evolve as children grow to be adults? If so, why? Do you think that women are set up to compete with one another? Take a moment now to write your thoughts below and why.

_____

_____

_____

_____

Layers of Rivalry

Susan Shapiro Barash (2006) tackles female competition head-on. She described competitive female behaviors as having three forms: competition, envy, and jealousy.

> **Competition** *is the most benign form of female rivalry. When we compete with one another, we're saying, "I'm willing to fight you for what I want." It's an aspect of rivalry that is perhaps the least harmful. This isn't necessarily a bad thing, particularly when we're competing for limited resources. A woman who withdraws from consideration for a job, for example, simply because she knows other women are up for the position would be almost pathologically unwilling to engage in the normal, healthy competition that is simply a part of life.*

> *This can be positive until it escalates...It's when healthy competition for what we want turns into a problematic desire to have something merely because a rival already has it. "Oh, you're going to Bermuda for vacation, well I'm going to go to Bermuda too!" OR "Hmmm, Sally is hanging out with a new guy. I think I'd like to date him." OR "Oh you're pregnant? We were going to wait but I want a baby now too!" "I'd like to have that job, promotion, board seat, lead starter on the soccer field, etc., and will compete with you for it."*

> **Envy** *is when healthy competition gets an edge. It's the, "I want what you have" type of behavior. There still may be some positive components of this behavior, if it doesn't get out of control. Think of a friend having a baby and you'd like to have one, too. Either you can't for medical purposes or your childbearing years are over. You are still happy for your friend but you are envious of her situation. A little bit of envy is not a bad thing. A bit of envy can help you explore uncomfortable feelings that you may have been avoiding.*

Jealousy is the, *"You've got something I want, and I want you out of the picture so I can have it" type of behavior. This behavior may focus on, "I want what you have or what someone else has and I hate you for it" versus determining what you may want and personally figuring out how to get it (pp. 13–15).*

Internal Drivers

Did you know, we are most likely to shame others in areas where we feel vulnerable? With that being said, the key *internal drivers* of female rivalry are fear and low self-esteem. There are multiple reasons why this behavior evolves. It can be a learned behavior from a key female figure (in your life) who doesn't trust other women, instilled from growing up in an environment of constant physical or emotional rivalry, or a learned behavior by someone leading you to believe you are never good enough. Thoughts of *"I am not good enough therefore I have to compete to be better"* are common.

Who vs. What

The reason this phenomenon impacts women on so many levels is that it's frequently about *"who"* versus "what." Competition between women is about "identity." The *"who"* looks at the *external* side: clothes, hair, make-up, car, boyfriend, etc. These components are the physical, easily-recognizable, visual things that you see. The *"what"* looks at the *internal* side. The internal side is hidden and not easily recognizable until you get to know someone (Shapiro Barash, 2006).

While it's not uncommon for women to "fight" with other females, on the flip side, women also want and expect total union and sympathy from same-sex friends. Additionally, by nature, women's definition of themselves is tied to perceptions of other women. As women, we simply see ourselves through comparisons of other females, mothers, sisters, friends, and colleagues. It is hard for women to view ourselves as individuals with our own path and future (Shapiro Barash, 2006).

In primitive times women shared much more of their daily domestic living with each other than they traditionally do today. Communal lifestyles were common. In this domain, they cooked together, participated in the care of each other's children, hunted for food, and gathered for shelter and fire, all done in tandem with other women.

Today, although women are still customarily the pillars of their family life and communities, shared living is not a commonality. Women are much more isolated from each other. They live in their own homes versus a collective setting, they have their own schedules, and own immediate self and family needs. Occasions to get together are fewer and together-time is lessened. For females, coming together is not as much of a natural everyday support process, as it once was.

External Drivers

There are specific ways in which rivalry manifests itself. These various attributes include the Queen Bee Syndrome and Glass Ceiling which are also external drivers of rivalry between women. In the next chapter, I will explore these in more detail. An organizational setting which is a key driver to this type of behavior, will be discussed further in Chapter 5.

Culturally, have women always been taught to be *"at the bottom,"* and never the top? Therefore, they feel threatened by any woman who breaks the mold. If a woman has succeeded, does she feel other women will undermine her, so she is always on guard? Is it hard for an ambitious woman to admit her desire for power, traditionally reserved for men? Because women's ambition is so often seen in negative terms, it paves a path where it is difficult for her to achieve. If you cannot naturally be ambitious, it will be hard to cope with openly rivalrous behaviors.

Underlying Concept

To the one instigating this type of behavior, once it starts it's hard to stop. Surrendering to this type of behavior—overtly competing with other women over children, men, work, looks, sports, etc.—is dooming oneself to a lifetime of perpetual insecurity. And where does it end? Behaviors of this manner are used as a "false exterior." They are simply a way to try to feel in control and boost self-esteem.

Rivalry is also driven by the inability to manage healthy competition. It's okay to want to win, rise to the top, get the promotion, have athletic children, etc. That doesn't mean that others must go down as a result. Often women in our culture have been forced to hide their ambition. There is a message that *"if you do rise, you have to act like it doesn't matter if you win or lose. Nice girls should only care about being nice."* But everyone, male or female knows, that success entails hard work and a will to win.

2.4: Your Turn. Dear reader, do you agree that there are levels of rivalry? Why or why not? Do you agree with the notion that women fight with each other but on the other hand, also want support and sympathy from each other too? Do you think there are other underlying concepts that drive female rivalry? If so, what are they? Take a moment now to write your thoughts below and why.

_____

_____

_____

_____

Closing

This chapter has taken a deep dive into the scholarly side, to share insight about the history and theories of what this type of behavior stems from as well as examining what the internal drivers are.

Are you ready to discover more? To learn about the nitty-gritty, juicy details of the various attributes and stereotypes that are key components of this negative behavior? Buckle up baby, because I am sure you'll be very surprised at how vast the list is and what it all entails!

Chapter 3:

From Friend to Frenemy

"People will forget what you said, they will forget what you did, but they will never forget how you made them feel."
—Dr. Maya Angelou (Goodreads, Inc., 2020).

Hazel's Story

"I was very young, 20 or so, when I got a job at our local police department in Texas. I worked there for almost 3 years. My husband was in the military, so I was alone in a new city without any friends or family around. Diane was a few years older than me, 28 or so, and was the secretary for the chief of police. She only worked for one person. My job was a lower scale than hers was, as I was the secretary for five detectives and the assistant chief of police. All of those men gave me work to do.

I didn't work for Diane; there wasn't a hierarchical order. She was a peer, just in a higher position. She had her own office by herself, and I worked with the group of men in the common, larger office space area. For whatever reason, the detectives liked me. They used to tease me all the time. It absolutely wasn't anything sexual as they were all married. They were just nice to me. I think that's what started it. She became jealous of the attention I was getting from them, and my teasing and laughing with them.

There was one other woman in the office, the switchboard operator, Mary. Her husband was also in the military. She was quite a bit older than Diane and me. I really liked her and she also was very kind to me.

Diane was the type of woman that was always perfectly dressed. Compared to her, I felt very inadequate. Even though at that time, I probably had a couple of years of college under my belt, I still felt very incompetent around her. She made me feel so inferior about myself and who I was as a person. She'd frequently make comments and snide remarks to me. She didn't say those things in front of the men or even Mary for that matter. I know they'd have shut her down and not put up with it.

This happened a long, long time ago. And because of that, I can't remember all of the words or actions, but I still very clearly remember the feelings. She made my life completely miserable. I felt very bad about myself when I was around her. Because of her, I felt bad about myself in general.

Another reason Diane may have been jealous of me was because of my relationship with Mary. We'd go to her house for dinner and have picnics at the ranch Diane wasn't included because we never knew how she'd respond, and she never showed interest in hanging out with us.

The strange office dynamic of three women and 30+ men...You'd think the three of us could've been close and worked together. Diane set herself apart and just wasn't nice. I don't think Diane was mean to

Mary. Mary was older and wouldn't have put up with it. Also, there were always two people in her office, a lieutenant and Mary, so she really didn't have the opportunity to be mean to her. I honestly too, don't think Mary was a threat to Diane.

You'd think with only three women in the department I could confide in Mary, especially since we were friends. I really liked her, but for whatever reason, I honestly don't know what it was, I didn't feel like I could talk to her about that. Here I am a young kid, pregnant, with no family close by. If I'd had another woman to talk to about it, it would have helped but I didn't. I was all by myself and alone."

By now you can probably tell that I love to provide the meaning of words I frequently use, or that have an impact on the broader message of this book. For this portion of my discussion, I am going to talk about what constitutes a friend, a frenemy, and all, the other components found in between, on the journey of friend to frenemy.

Food for Thought: Chances are if they were your "friend" and now are your "frenemy," they were never really your true friend to begin with.

So, let's be clear about this… the kind of friends who make you doubt yourself, who put you down versus lift up, or who try to change you… they are NOT your friends.

A friend is defined as, "a person whom one knows and with whom one has a bond of mutual affection, typically exclusive of secular or family relations" (Oxford English Dictionary, 2019). A "frenemy" is the opposite of a friend. This term combines the characteristics of "friend" and "enemy" and is someone you do not trust because she has given you very good reason to not trust her. Because it's a foundational premise of this book, "frenemy" will be defined in detail, later in the chapter.

"Indirect aggression" is the main characteristic of this type of behavior. It's what makes an on-going rivalry type of situation hard to identify.

Behavior of Self

As mentioned in the previous chapter, this type of behavior is not just a "cat-fight." It's real. Chances are you may not be doing anything at all to provoke her conduct toward you. But then again, what if you are? It's always good to look inward to see how your behavior could be impacting the situation.

Look at what you are doing. Are you exuding certain types of behaviors or mannerisms that may be triggering the "other woman?" Simply asking yourself the question, "What am I doing?" can help to identify if you have any part in the behavior. Remember, there are always three sides to a story... yours, hers, and the truth. It's very likely in this type of situation that you are not at fault. Understanding the role, you personally play, even if it's nothing, can also help you to better understand your rival's behavior, her intent, and insight to the underlying cause.

The "Other Woman"

The other woman, in these scenarios throughout my book, is the female projecting the negative behaviors. In all the interviews I've conducted about this type of negative behavior, I've only heard a few stories where the victims received confirmation of what the "*other woman*" was feeling, and why. I'll share more on this later in the book in Chapter 10. In various types of situations, the other female typically ended up feeling guilty for how she treated the targeted female. These are examples of directly confronting the behavior and are very rare.

All the women mentioned that the "*other woman*" or "*women*" emanated negative behaviors predominately by indirect, passive-aggressive actions. Some direct aggression was also portrayed by bestowing demeaning behaviors and certain types of public humiliation. Women who shared their experiences with me, often concluded from their own personal involvement in the situation, the other woman was acting out from:

- Jealousy
- Feelings of insecurity
- The need for control

Melissa. "It's too bad. It really was a great space. But it was like it was covered in this gooey-thick-dark energy when she was around. She was building her own barrier by her actions and how she treated other women."

Selena. "This woman's power was obvious. It's like she was so insecure in her own skin, the only way for her to survive was to take down other women. Our corporate office that did nothing at all about her behavior was full of bully-beta-men. Nice men...but don't be a wuss and do nothing. You know what I mean?"

Natalie. "She just made my life miserable. She bad-mouthed me to people in the office. I had people coming up to me and telling me she was saying all of the horrible things. She was accusing me of gossiping, but she was the one running around talking to people behind my back. It was just ridiculous. And the thing is, we were both high achievers and we both could have had a really successful team together."

Maggie. "So. I was part of this team for three years. All the other women were tight friends and I was the new person. My entire first year on the team, every time I went into the office I was misunderstood. I didn't get invited to group outings. I felt very much not included, not invited, not anything... you know, not heard. All those women worked really well together but none of them wanted to work with me. They would actually say, 'That is irrelevant to me, or that is a dumb idea,' From that group of women there was always a lack of wanting to understand what I could bring to the table, even though I saw the opportunities they could bring. It was never reciprocal."

Lola. "I reported her behavior up my chain of command. But she held so much clout with some of the higher-ups that I also think they also felt stuck. She was just a bully. But they supported me, and they tried to validate and protect me. I felt at some point that she was trying to *get me fired. She probably knew I'd gone to HR and my superiors. And that probably pissed her off more than anything. I wanted to confront her but was told not to by one of my sergeants. They said she's not trustworthy. Meaning she spins things. So, if I did confront her, I would have had to have tangible evidence when I did. And I had nothing to show except her verbalizing things. Her verbal tirades. She'd completely gone off on me before. I don't think in front of other people. And she always did it in a very calm, and condescending way. It was very passive-aggressive, and wasn't tangible behavior."*

Behavior of the "Other Woman"

The majority of all the women I've interviewed on this topic can't tell me directly what the *"other woman"* was thinking. They can tell me however, there was something very obvious to them, and that was the *"other woman's"* projected behavior.

The women who've contributed to my research have not always directly named the following terms, "control," "indirect aggression," "direct aggression," "demeaning behaviors," and "public humiliation." These "experience descriptions" are always clear as to the types of behavior she endured. I've highlighted a few examples for you in the following paragraphs.

> ***Amy.*** *"And while I was talking with her, Karen stopped me and started to scream at the top of her lungs, 'Just what is it, do you think that you are doing? You can't come in here and speak to just one student!' And there were parents in that classroom, and it was extremely embarrassing not only for me and the parents but for the students themselves."* (Public Humiliation.)

> ***Faith.*** *"I was the second-in-charge person in our facility, and she was a strong, very attractive young woman about eight years younger than myself. After a couple of years, she not so nicely said, 'I want your job.'"* (Direct aggression.)

Dana. *"And this woman made us do different thing,s so we knew she was always watching us. For example, she used to have us sign in and out, just to go to the bathroom."* *(Control.)*

Hannah. *"As a result, if she had too much work on her plate, and she wanted to go leave early, she would just give me some of her work to do, or she would drop it off at my desk. We were peers. We were peers, but she would just sit there and say, 'Oh, well, Hannah we'll just get it done.'"* *(Indirect aggression.)*

Beatrix. *"And behind closed doors, she would always attack me, as a person, my intellect, my behavior, my professionalism, the way I dressed, you name it. At one point she said, 'You better get your pregnancy weight off because ratings and rankings are coming up and the fat girls never get good ratings.'"* *(Control and direct aggression.)*

3.1: Your Turn. Dear reader, have you ever looked inward to see how your behavior, if applicable, impacted a situation? If so, how did that make you feel? Have you ever been subjected to negative behaviors by the "other woman"? If you've experienced this, how did it make you feel? Did it catch you off guard, make you feel uncomfortable, or embarrassed? Did you feel shame? Take a moment now to write below, if any of these examples have resonated with you and why.

_____

_____

_____

_____

Stereotypes and Personas Defined

Because rivalry between women occurs everywhere in everyday life, the ways in which the behavior manifests also varies. This can be illustrated by various frenemy definitions as well as other types of personas and behavioral roles.

Over the years, I've become familiar with these personas, definitions, and ste-reotypes either by the stories that have been shared with me or by general research and information that's been highlighted in pop culture. I've tried to categorize as many of the rivalrous personas as I can, to spotlight the many ways in which the behavior can appear.

Some of the personas are categorized not as an individual person, but as a familiar term that also impacts rivalry (i.e. Glass Ceiling). Some of the perso-nas are more formally defined (i.e. found in the dictionary) and some are cate-gorized in "*slang*" terms (i.e. found on the internet or in general conversation). The slang terms, although not formalized, are for the most part familiar to most people and/or have been shared with me as a type of female who projects rivalrous types of behavior.

Some of the descriptions and personas are ugly and may be off-put-ting...I'm highlighting this for awareness purposes because ugly and off-put-ting is the premise of this type of behavior.

Stereotype. In social psychology, a stereotype is defined as, "an over-gen-eralized belief about a particular category of people" (Cardwell, 1999). Ste-reotypes are generalized assumptions, an expectation that people might have about every person of a particular group (Simply Psychology, 2011).

Persona. In everyday language, a persona is defined as, "the aspect of someone's character that is presented to or perceived by others" (2019, Oxford Dictionary). For psychological purposes, according to Carl Jung (Jung, 1971) and Jungian Psychologist, "the persona is also the mask or appearance one presents to the world. It may appear in dreams under various guises." As sum-marized by Mark Leary (2011),

> "*People may choose to wear a social mask or 'persona' to make them-selves appear more socially desirable. This is used to impress potential partners or to make new friends. People can have multiple personas that they use in various situations; this can include work; being with friends; at home; etc. Depending on the individual's circumstance, a persona which they consider stronger within their specific social situation can be created because they put a higher emphasis on social interactions*" *(Jung, 1971).*

Personas of Rivalry

The following defined "persona" terms have attributes of or influences on the behaviors of rivalry between women. There may be more. In many instances, I've highlighted the persona with a distinct story to further explain the meaning. In some examples, the meaning is self-explanatory:

- **Abuser.** Abuser is defined as, "a person who uses something to bad effect or for a bad purpose" (Oxford English Dictionary, 2019).
- **Backstabber.** Backstabber is defined as, "a person who backstabs. A traitor or hypocrite, such as a co-worker or friend assumed trustworthy but who figuratively attacks when one's back is turned" (Your Dictionary, 2020). To backstab is to, "harm (a friend, partner, etc.) by treachery" (YourDictionary.Com, 2020). Urban Dictionary defines "backstabber" as "a person who pretends to be a friend but then betrays you" (Urban Dictionary, 2020).
- **Brown-Noser.** To "brown-nose" is defined as, "a person who acts in a grossly obsequious way" (Oxford English Dictionary, 2020). A brown-noser is, "a person who tries to please (especially one's boss) so much that their nose turns brown from kissing their ass" (Urban Dictionary, 2020).
- **Bully.** Bully is defined as, "a person who habitually seeks to harm or intimidate those whom they perceive as vulnerable" (Oxford English Dictionary, 2019). "Especially one who is habitually cruel, insulting, or threatening to others who are weaker, smaller, or in some way vulnerable" (Merriam Webster Dictionary, 2019).
- **Clique**. In the social sciences, a clique is defined as, "a group of individuals who interact with one another and share similar interests" (Salkind, 2008). Chris Labrum also summarizes,

"Interacting with cliques is part of normative social development regardless of gender, ethnicity, or popularity. Although cliques are most commonly studied during adolescence and middle childhood development, they exist in all age groups. They are often bound

together by shared social characteristics such as ethnicity and socio-economic status" (Wikipedia, 2020).

Additionally,

"Typically, people in a clique will not have a completely open friend group and can therefore 'ban' members if they do something considered unacceptable, such as talking to someone disliked. Some cliques tend to isolate themselves as a group and view themselves as superior to others, which can be demonstrated through bullying and other anti-social behaviors" (Wikipedia, 2020).

- **Exclusion.** Exclusion, specifically "social exclusion" refers to, "Keeping an individual or group out of social situations. It typically occurs in the context that the individual or group is believed to possess undesirable characteristics or characteristics deemed unworthy of attention. Acts of social exclusion are observed in humans and other social animals. Researchers agree that social exclusion serves a specific function for those who employ it and that it is unpleasant and painful for those who are denied inclusion" (Williams, et al, 2005).

There are several components to social exclusion but a key premise as it pertains to female rivalry relates to *group identity,* which is defined as, "often resulting in justification for discrimination" (Williams, et al, 2005). Group Identity is explained as,

"The need for belonging is an important basic human need; group identity is often a way of fulfilling this need. Group identity categories are formed on biological factors (e.g., race, sex), socially constructed factors (e.g., social class), or personal beliefs and opinions (e.g., religion, politics). These divisions often lead to an 'Us versus Them' mentality, serving as a way of solidifying group identity, and keeping dissimilar groups on society's fringes" (Williams, et al, 2005).

Lila's Story. *"My husband, fairly new to his company won a Caribbean get-away for achieving top sales in his company and I was invited to go along. I was excited to not only relax, and have a long weekend with my husband, but also was looking forward to meeting some of the spouses of the men he worked with.*

We both work full-time and are in the process of adopting but don't have kids yet. I met the group of stay-at-home women who previously knew each other, by the pool. They totally ousted me. I mean they did not include me in any of the activities or events they'd planned. I even dropped the, 'we are adopting' bomb because that usually is a huge icebreaker...but nope, nothing. I was totally amazed by their behavior. I ended up doing my own thing, took naps on the beach, relaxed, got a massage...If I wasn't confident in making friends on my own and also enjoying some much needed alone time, this incident would have really stung."

- **Frenemy.** The term frenemy is defined as, "An oxymoron and a portmanteau of 'friend' and 'enemy' that refers to 'a person with whom one is friendly, despite a fundamental dislike or rivalry' or 'a person who combines the characteristics of a friend and an enemy.' The term is used to describe personal, geopolitical, and commercial relationships both among individuals and groups or institutions. This term also describes a competitive friendship" (Oxford English Dictionary, 2019).

The frenemy persona is the foundation for a lot of the information I'm sharing with you. I've inserted the initial definition here, to highlight it as one of the key personas for this type of behavior. A separate "frenemy" section later in this chapter dives deeper into the meaning of this persona. This section features the individual frenemy personas and focuses on stories, under the broader frenemy persona banner.

- **Gaslighting.** The term, which has been around for a long time, originated from the 1938 play, *Gas Light*, and has been used in psychological literature, as well as in political commentary, philosophy, and popular culture. It's defined as, "a form of psychological manipulation in which a person or a group covertly sows seeds of doubt in a targeted individual, making them question their own memory, perception, or judgment, often evoking in them cognitive dissonance and other changes such as low self-esteem. Using denial, misdirection, contradiction, and misinformation, gaslighting involves attempts to destabilize the victim and delegitimize the victim's beliefs. Instances may range from the denial by an abuser that previous abusive incidents ever occurred to the staging of bizarre events by the abuser with the intention of disorienting the victim" (Wikipedia, 2020).

When it's directed at you, it can appear in the following types of comments:

- You're overreacting.
- I was just joking.
- You're so sensitive.
- You twist things.
- What are you talking about?
- I never said that.
- Just calm down.
- You're upset over nothing.
- You need help.

- You're remembering things wrong.
- Stop imagining things.
- I never said that.
- It's your fault.
- Why are you so defensive?
- You're so dramatic.
- You must be confused again.
- I didn't do that.
- It's always something with you.

What's worse is, if "gaslighting" is projected frequently toward you, you can, in turn, start to dispense the same type of behavior to yourself, which leads to a questioning of self and a breakdown of confidence.

Werner describes *"self-gaslighting"* as, "the suppression of thought and emotion." For example, let's say that someone says something insensitive or hurtful. You might notice that your feelings were hurt, but then—almost instantly and impulsively—you think: "I am probably just making too big a deal out of it and being too sensitive" (2019). Self-gaslighting can appear in the following types of comments or thoughts to yourself:

- I am too dramatic, emotional, sensitive and crazy
- Maybe it's all just in my head?
- I love them so I should just do this. Why did I do that to them?

- I know they love me and didn't mean it like that at all.
- It's all my fault anyway.
- I am too much/not enough. There's something wrong with me.

Annette's Story. *"After a while, after I'd been subject to the negative behavior from my supervisor for the length of time that I was...I began to believe it myself. I began to believe that I deserved how she was treating me...because I thought it was true. I began to feel it was my fault for not attaining targeted project goals. I began to believe that I was not good enough to be in the position I was in. I didn't feel smart, or worthy and I knew because of that, I could never go after the promotion I wanted.*

It wasn't until after I'd left the toxic environment, got away from her erratic behavior, and engaged in intensive therapy that I found myself again. I realized that all her berating, beating me down, and need for control, although unjustified, was the cause for my low self-esteem and feelings of unworthiness. I'd believed what she'd done and said to me, so much so that in the process of it all, I lost sight of who I really was."

- **Glass Ceiling.** The U.S. Federal Glass Ceiling Commission defines the glass ceiling as, "the unseen, yet unbreachable barrier that keeps minorities and women from rising to the upper rungs of the corporate ladder, regardless of their qualifications or achievements" (Federal Glass Ceiling Commission, 1995).

First, just stop for a moment to reflect, can you even believe that we have a Federal Glass Ceiling Commission? When I first stumbled upon this fact, I was pleasantly surprised that it existed.

The term "glass ceiling" originated by feminists to address the career obstacles high-achieving women face (Wiley, 2012). The perception is, there is not enough room at the leadership table of an organization for everyone, which results in fewer women at the top. "The 'glass ceiling' concept is a metaphor used to represent an invisible barrier that keeps a given demographic (typically applied to minorities) from rising beyond a certain level in a hierarchy" (Federal Glass Ceiling Commission, 1995).

It's a known fact that men hold more leadership positions than women do. Men traditionally make more money for the same type of job or work than women do. This in and of itself causes a huge competitive mindset. Add to that, the fact that women in general, feel competition from other women at work, no matter what the ages of the involved females are.

There are fewer women at the top and this promotes realistic feelings that someone else will take or replace her position "at the top." So as a result, she needs to eliminate the competition. It is hard for a woman "at the top" to feel as if she can win. Especially, if she faces the contradictory demands of being feminine and business-like. "They cannot join as a woman and once they start to behave like a man, they cannot be a 'proper woman'" (Maddock, 1999). If you are a token woman at the top and all your peers are male, it can be difficult to determine how you appropriately fit in.

> *"If as a senior woman you do not lead on the women in management mantle, if you do not conform to a feminine model and you develop commonalities with your peer group, who will be mostly men, then you will be vilified for not representing the interest of women and for becoming more male than men: a no-win situation for women in management" (Mavin, 2006).*

Anne Welsh McNulty shares her Glass Ceiling experience in an article she wrote for the Harvard Business Review,

> *When I graduated college in the 1970s, I believed that women would quickly achieve parity at all levels of professional life now that we had 'arrived'—I viewed the lack of women at the top as more of a 'pipeline' problem, not a cultural one. But the support I expected to find*

*from female colleagues—the feeling of sisterhood in this mission—
rarely survived first contact within the workplace. When I was a first-
year accountant at a Big Eight firm (now the Big Four), I kept asking
the only woman senior to me to go to lunch, until finally, she told me,
'Look, there's only room for one female partner here. You and I are not
going to be friends.' Unfortunately, she was acting rationally (2018).*

- **A "Guys" Girl.** A "guys" girl persona is defined as,

  *"That great girl who can just chill and be 'one of the guys.' She's into
  sports, beer, action flicks, and doesn't 'give a d*mn what others think.'
  The pseudo-definition then goes on to assure, 'However, unlike the
  tomboy, she has her gang of girl mates who she shops with and does
  girly stuff'" (Urban Dictionary, 2020).*

Here is more insight about the term,

*"For some women, the identification of a 'guy's girl' might be, in part,
due to an alleged inability to get along with other women who are
all characteristically vicious, catty, dramatic, and stupid. They feel
unique because of this. For others, I think they might identify with
this persona because they feel alienated by other women. Some might
say they just genuinely find that their interests align more closely with
those of their male counterparts" (Admin, 2011).*

Kendra's Story. *"All during school I was pretty athletic and played a
lot of sports. As a result, I hung out more frequently with guys than I did
girls. I honestly wasn't attracted to them in the 'be my boyfriend' kind
of way. I did have some girlfriends, but we really didn't seem to have as
much in common as I did with the guys. Guys were just easier to hang
out with... less pressure, more real, and direct. I was just completely
myself when I was around them. And with the girls, I always felt like I
was being judged because I was athletic and not more 'girly-like.'*

In grade school and middle school, it wasn't really a big deal but it sure became a one in high school. Girls would say the meanest things to me, thinking I was trying to steal their boyfriend. And some of my best guy friends, due to pressure from their girlfriends, stopped wanting to hang out together. I didn't feel like I fit in as well with the girls, so it was a really frustrating time for me, trying to understand where I fit in and who my true friends were."

- **Mean Girl.** To be mean is to show "unkindness, spitefulness, or unfairness" (Oxford Dictionary, 2019). There are many aspects of meanness, "namely empowerment, bullying, aggression, cruelty, and ruthlessness—which have been incorporated in the late 20th and early 21st century popular cultural concept of the 'mean girl'" (Ringrose & Walkerdine, pp.9–10, 2008).

Valerie Walkerdine, social science professor claims that,

"Meanness is becoming a dominant motif for Western girlhood, as it fits well with the normative, repressive, boundaries of what is appropriate to modern femininity in work and school, and supports the narrative that empowered, successful, females cannot treat empowerment and success positively, but rather always risk slipping into cruelty" (Ringrose & Walkerdine, p. 10, 2008).

Wendy's Story. *"I was asked to work on a diversity group in our organization. It was for women and something I was totally interested in. It was all about elevating women in the workplace. It was right up my alley. I was asked to be an ambassador for our department. My boss's parting shot was to tell the incoming manager that she didn't feel like I had the extra time to devote to that...that it was an honor that I didn't deserve to have. Even though she was leaving...she made sure to tell him that. None of what she did was subtle.*

She was constantly nit-picking and looking for things, of how to exude control over me. Her behavior was such a classic example of being passive-aggressive...She had a partner in crime in the office. Her leadership approach was very 'high school.' It was like, let's go ahead and be mean to that girl, let's go ahead and take her down because she has something that we don't have on our resumes. I feel she was all about competition and volume and for all of the wrong reasons that had nothing at all to do with leadership but to show off and let her be the center of attention."

- **Mommy War(s).** The "Mommy Wars" persona addresses the "battle" between stay-at-home moms (SAHM) and working moms. SAHM's are females with children that work inside the home caring for their children and managing the household. Working moms are females with children that engage in work-life outside of the home. These women traditionally pay for a service or another person to watch their children while they work.

Motherhood has become a venue for resentment, envy, and guilt. There's a lot of judging and feelings of entitlement criticizing how other females undertake parenting, all because someone else is approaching it differently mom-shaming, a key component in the "Mommy Wars," is about two groups of women who misunderstand and envy each other in a fake, passive-aggressive way. Author Leslie Morgan Steiner wrote that "as women struggle to come to terms with their own choices in parenting against society's standards they engage in this warfare that does nothing to promote self-acceptance, acceptance of others, or balance within their individual lives" (2007).

SAHM vs. Working Moms (Real Comments):

"I mean, why in the world should you ask a working mom to bring snacks for a game or school? You should ask the stay at home moms. All they do is sit around in their little tennis skirts, gossip, and drink alcohol." OR "How dare you!!!" Comment from an older woman to a young mother, when she mentioned she worked full time. OR "Oh,

you're just a trophy wife ... IF I stayed at home, fixed myself up and the only thing I did was work out ...well I would like that too!" OR "How do you even stand it, staying home? I can't wait to go back to work!" OR "Seriously, what do you do all day, just hang out? It must be nice." OR "Oh, I've noticed you haven't been to any of Billy's track-meets this season...." (long pause) OR "Did you know she takes both of their kids to day-care, before and after school? I mean why is she even a parent? It's a disgrace!" OR "Yes, I think it's a good decision for you to not go back to work. A woman's place is in the home, with her family." (Comment from a young nanny to a working mom of two).

Melanie's Story. *"An acquaintance of mine at a mom's club event, who I know doesn't have good intentions, was going on about her job and how busy she was and how much she traveled. She asked, 'Do you miss working?' At the time I really didn't, so I said, 'No, actually. Honestly, I don't.' I know she was expecting to put me on the spot and devalue me. I know it because I know her. Then she said, 'Well, it's just so nice to be able to afford a cleaning lady and to be able to buy myself things when I want to.' I wanted to say, 'Well I have a cleaning lady too, and being with my children is more important than buying 'things,' but I bit my tongue and smiled.'"*

Tammy's Story. *"The same moms were at the bus stop every day. I worked outside of the home when we lived there...These women were my neighbors. But when I showed up, they looked at me like I had two heads. They looked my way but never said 'hi'. They were a clique and I wasn't invited in. It just baffled me why they weren't supportive or inclusive. But no, they just stood there and talked poorly about other moms."*

- **Social Media Stories.** Prince Harry's and his wife, Meghan Markle, have been highlighted in the media for stepping out of the British public eye (Jan. 2020). To top it off, Meghan has been the target of "mom-shaming." Critics on social media and beyond called out Meghan for what they saw as "sloppy use of the baby carrier that held her and Prince Harry's 8-month old son, Archie, even though 'experts' saw no problem."

Jenna Bush, President Bush's daughter who has three children of her own, has also been publicly "mom-shamed." A very verbal attack occurred on social media in December 2019 when she left her 4-month old son, Hal, to go to Vietnam with former first lady Michelle Obama to put a spotlight on "Girls Education."

My first thought when reading these "news updates" or any other that are similar, is, "why did experts even have to weigh in on what other women are doing?" These stories simply should not be issues that are highlighted in the news. If children are safe and not being harmed...let her do her and leave well enough alone.

- **Queen Bee Syndrome**. In the early 1970s at the start of the women's movement, a famous study by Staines, Travis, and Jayaratne (1973) coined the term "Queen Bee." This study was important, and one of the first of its kind that promoted awareness about the behaviors of women within a working environment. The study discussed traits that encompassed indirect and passive-aggressive behaviors among women in the workplace, including competition and rivalry.

You've probably heard of the "Queen Bee" expression; she's a b*tch. In this case, "b*tch" meaning a woman who has a dominant or controlling position in a particular group or sphere. This type of woman treats other women in the workplace more critically, disdainfully, meaner than she would a male colleague. It is the tendency for a powerful woman in these types of scenarios to get used to being the only female in the group, and to decide she wants to keep it that way. There may be an internal thought process too, from the Queen Bee of, "I got here on my own. Why should I then have to also help other women advance their career path? If I did it, then they can too."

Often in these situations, men may not even be aware that the "Queen Bee" is targeting other women. They will think she is great to work for and can't understand why their female counterparts are having angst with her. Men will assume "they" are just jealous because she's so cool and such a great leader to work with. These women may try to fit in with their male counterparts by acting like the men in the group. As a result,

> *"If as a senior woman you do not lead on the women in management mantle, you do not conform to a feminine model and you develop commonalities with your peer group, who will be mostly men, then you will be vilified for not representing the interests of women and for becoming more male than the men: a no-win situation for women"* (Mavin, 2006).

The term "Queen Bee" is still being used today as a way to describe women who have "made it" professionally in a world widely dominated by men. Women in these powerful positions typically exclude other women (Staines, et al., 1973; Kanter, 1977; Chesler, 2001; Mavin, 2006a). They are proud of the fact that they have succeeded in a world where most women do not; it's what makes them feel special and unique. The "Queen Bee" Syndrome focuses on the individual woman as one who does not lean toward group strategies or collaboration. They are women who want to *"climb to the top"* and be recognized for their own accomplishments. They do not want to share accomplishments with other women in terms of any type of group recognition.

The "Queen Bee" persona is not limited to the working environment and exists in numerous other types of social situations in everyday living. This persona yields substantial control and power. As she is considered a role model, others often emulate her behavior. She traditionally is the ring-leader of a clique, holds a position of high social status at school or in other social settings, and is frequently stereotyped in pop culture as wealthy, beautiful, charismatic, and manipulative (Tracy, 2003, Wiseman 2011).

Author Sussana Stern established the (social) "Queen Bee" persona as having the following features, *"an overly-heightened self-esteem, which may lead to arrogance; being overly-aggressive, selfish manipulative and confident; behaving like a bully or sociopath; being wealthy and/or spoiled; being pretty, popular, talented, wealthy or privileged; and being envied, hated, admired by peers—mainly female peers" (2001).*

The other side of the "Queen Bee" equation beckons one to look at the aspect of individuality versus group recognition. If one is choosing to be this type of an individual, she often stands out as being b*tchy, or the Queen Bee. Therefore, she is viewed as instigating competition, rivalry, and jealousy from other women.

Ilene's Story. Ilene, who worked 26 years in the intelligence community, shared her experience with a Queen Bee senior. Ilene reflected that 20 years prior, the male-dominated culture influenced the behavior of the other woman. During that time there were only two women holding positions of senior rank. It would have been a perfect opportunity for the other woman to be a mentor and help Ilene grow professionally. That, however, was not the case, as the other woman exhibited characteristics of control and indirect aggressive behavior that Ilene would later find out about.

"It was a zero-sum game. That there was only enough attention for her, or for me, but certainly not for both of us. You would see those things come through in things like assignments. 'Well, you were not viewed as being ready for that assignment because this other woman thought that you did not have enough experience in that particular area or that particular area.' I would think, 'Wow, that is interesting because I have all those things in my resume but all right if that is the way she is putting it.'

My very favorite confrontation was not necessarily directly between the two of us, but it was so, so telling me about her character and outlook. We had a conversation and I said, 'You know I recently served on a selection panel.' She was surprised that we had selected a woman to serve in one of the tough jobs overseas. I said, 'This would be a very good opportunity for her because we have not sent a woman to do that job before' and she just looked at me and said, 'Well there is a reason that we have never sent a woman to that job. These married women, they are not good to us.' Of course, she was single. She said, 'If it were up to me I would make all of you get a hysterectomy before we would even accept you into the career field because all you do is get married and then go off and have babies and then you are absolutely not good to us.'"

- **Women With Children vs. Women Without Children.** This persona is about being judged for a lifestyle because it is different. For a certain population of women, this is a behavior that can be intense, cruel even. The key assumption for a female without children is that she is doing the world a disservice by choosing not to procreate. The key assumption for a female with children is, how can you even bear to have children, they control your life and ruin your body. These assumptions are not always one-sided and go both ways.

While this may not be a direct rivalrous behavior, it most definitely contributes to it. It originates out of judgement that is a form of "societal judgement." It's also a form of a "microaggression." This conduct first coined by psychiatrist Chester M. Pierce in the 1970s, is defined as, "a term used for brief and commonplace daily verbal, behavioral, or environmental indignities, whether intentional or unintentional, that communicate hostile, derogatory, or negative prejudicial slights and insults toward any group, particularly culturally marginalized groups" (Wikipedia, 2019).

Women With Children vs. Women Without Children (Real Comments):

"You are selfish! That is SO selfish of you to ignore the role of women and not fulfill the most incredible thing that women are supposed to do! It is what God intended for you to do!" OR "Who's going to take care of you when you get old?" OR "But how can you stand to

be alone all of the time?" OR "You're not a mom so you just don't understand." OR "Well now that you are married, when will you have kids?" OR "You're just not being sensible. Don't worry dear... you'll come around." OR "Why would you not want to have kids? It's your gift!" OR "You are ignoring the role of the woman!" OR "What's wrong with you?"

Shana's Story. *"One of the funnier things I was once asked, 'Does your husband know that you don't want to have kids?' It's like, how does your husband feel about this as if somehow this is a secret that I am hiding from him. It's like I am this terrible person that has this secretive agenda about something. These types of questions come from women who have children, they usually don't know me that well, but they just don't know how to process the difference between me and them. I don't always think they mean to be rude, but they can't understand it... our differences. I guess it's a way of them saying, 'you are selfish in the way that you are putting yourself first.'"*

Jordan's Story. A married female in her mid-forties who has also purposefully chosen to not have children relayed that during her life she's been subject to lots of discrimination about this personal choice—a choice she and her husband have collectively made together.

"So, my thing is, I'm childfree by choice. We are childfree by choice. I really do not want children. I never wanted children. I'm honestly grateful every day that I don't have children. And I love being friends with women who are moms and I have a lot of friends and family members, who are mothers. But for me, I am so thankful that that is not the life that I have. Even when people don't understand when people are judging or saying these hurtful things without realizing what they are saying."

Kelsey's Story. A female in her late twenties relayed her story.

"For a variety of reasons, it's been a conscious decision to not have children, one I realized when I was very young. I babysat for the entire neighborhood and I liked the idea of being with those kids, taking care of them, and then I liked going home. I'd also heard horror stories of childbirth, my brothers included. And that has always stuck with me. And then, there's the fact that I really want my body to remain the same. That's when I get the well, 'that's just being so selfish.' Like I should have to devote my body to having a child. And it's, I think, that stigma that has been around so long like we're just meant to be an incubator."

- **Women as Single Parents vs. Women in a Partnership.** This persona is also about being judged for a lifestyle because it is different. It may not be a direct rivalry, but it can be a judgement based upon parenting that may be different. You may be familiar with the term "mom-shaming." It's defined as,

"bullying other moms for their parenting choices in subtle (and sometimes not so subtle) aggressions sprinkled into play group conversations. It's a small way for some women to gain stature among a group by tearing down others. And as horrible as it sounds, it's an easy trap to fall into" (Medela, 2020).

Lola's Story. *"What I have, I wouldn't have it any other way, being a single parent. But there's also a price that comes with it. There's judgment. Being judged on not electing to go out to certain events because I have to choose between staying home with my child or the choice of going out, getting a babysitter, and then spending money out...It could be over a hundred dollar evening. And people sometimes don't understand, those are the type of choices I have to make.*

There's a group of friends, three of them that don't have children so they can't relate to any of the kid things that I deal with. They have stopped inviting me to things because I have said no too many times. With the no being, 'You know, I can't afford to get a babysitter and go out that night.' Their response is, 'Yeah. Why can't your parents watch her?' That's just not their business to say that. And my parents already do so much for us. And so that is hard, being left out.

Then there is the judging of my parenting. Most nights my child still sleeps with me. While I know it's my choice, it's also not really what I want. But sometimes it's just easier. When it gets to the point of it being up at 11:00 pm and I can't get her to sleep until 2 in the morning and then I have to get up at 5... I can't tag team with anyone. So, the easiest thing for me to do, to get sleep and save my sanity is to say, it's all right, she's going to sleep with me. I don't have a partner to split the nights with so that's just a battle I don't want to pick right now. It's shocking though what people have to say about it. What they say, is so out of line."

Food for Thought: If you can think of something I've missed as it pertains to unique personas of rivalry, please share! I'd love to hear from you.

3.2: Your Turn. Dear reader, I've shared a lot of personas and stories that hone in and highlight the various, crazy personas of rivalry. As you read the above descriptions did anything resonate with you? Have you ever been on the receiving end of a certain, similar type of behavior? Or maybe, have you ever projected a certain type of behavior toward someone else? Take a moment now to write below, if one or more of the persona examples have resonated with you and why.

_____

_____

_____

_____

Frenemy Persona

Now let's get back to the anchor persona, *frenemy*. To share some more insight, the term frenemy has, shockingly, been around for almost a century! Aristocratic, American-based author and activist, Jessica Mitford (circa 1930) first propagated the word "frenemy" by stating it was,

> *"an incredibly useful word…coined by one of my sisters when she was a small child to describe a rather dull little girl who lived near us. My sister and the frenemy played together constantly… all the time disliking each other heartily" (Mitford, 2010).*

Surprisingly, father of psychology, Sigmund Freud also loosely used the term, "frenemy." He said of himself that "an intimate friend and a hated enemy have always been indispensable to my emotional life… not infrequently… friend and enemy have coincided in the same person" (Jones, E. 1964).

> *"Frenemy" has been used to describe personal and working relationships. Personal relationships are different from professional relationships because they are based upon mutual interests outside of the working environment, whereas a professional relationship is grounded upon a working, professional bond, or interest. In intense surroundings or any situation that demands performance comparing between one or more people, rivalry and competitiveness can develop, stirring up resentment, jealousy, and ultimately damage the relationship. A Businessweek magazine article claimed that "frenemies in the workplace are common, even in business partnerships" (2007, Jap, 2017).*

Sandy Jap summarizes how working relationships have evolved to make the evolution of "frenemy" at work, more common,

> *"Due to increasingly informal environments and the abundance of very close, intertwined relationships that bridge people's professional and personal lives…[while] it certainly wasn't unheard of for people*

to socialize with colleagues in the past, the sheer amount of time that people spend at work now has left a lot of people with less time and inclination to develop friendships outside of the office" (2017).

I've worked in a variety of work environments. Every situation is different but certain types of cultures seem to foster personal relationships more than others do. When I lived in Seattle, I worked at a well-known game company. It was unlike any organizational setting I'd ever worked for; a creative environment with imaginative and innovative people... it was fun! But on the other hand, everyone knew each other because they were friends in and outside of the organizational setting. Many people in fact, were drawn to the company because they were gamers and loved the games the company produced. As a result, there were many levels of personal relationships intertwined with the professional ones... which instilled a bit of a "grey area" in terms of how people socialized together.

It's important to note that the term "frenemy" can pertain to any type of rivalrous female relationship such as, co-workers, mothers, daughters, cousins, aunts, neighbors, sisters, etc. It does not just apply to a "friendship" type of relationship.

While "frenemy" is a stand-alone term, there are several sub-categories used to describe the varying "frenemy" types, based upon specific behaviors. As initially gleaned by a compilation of work by (Clarke, 2017, Edwards, 2017, Haufrect, 2018). I've taken a deeper dive into each one. They are as follows:

- **Ambivalent Frenemy.** This type of frenemy has both positive and negative qualities. Sometimes she can be helpful and polite but sometimes she also acts selfishly or competitively. It's her choice how she acts, based upon what she "gets" out of the situation.

   Maren's Story. "My mom is a first-generation Honduran, female. She is not quite the youngest of nine children. There has always been a type of competition that stems from her Latin culture as well as on-going sibling rivalry. This has impacted our relationship. It's also trickled down to the second-generation family members, and the relationship me and my cousins have. In my mom's eyes, how I make her look from the viewpoint of her siblings is a direct impact on her. My mom and her sisters compete with one another about everything, but it's especially highlighted by what their children do.

For as long as I can remember there was always a pattern of ups and downs between me and my mom. My mom would brag about me, her only child, to her sisters. And while I didn't think this, she would say things like, 'Maren is the prettiest, has the best husband, has the best house, and the most handsome grandchildren, etc.'

When I got divorced, she immediately switched on me, 'You are making me look bad. How could you do that? You are working out and going out and now you just want to go be a whore! You are shaming the family.' It was awful. I have forgotten a lot of what she said or compartmentalized it, and how she acted during that time, or we'd not have a relationship today, at all. It immobilized me, 'I mean hard to get out of bed at all, type of breakdown.' A few years later when I was back on my feet, I was back in her good graces, because now I was making her look good again. 'Oh, look what Maren has done all her own, she is so much more successful, has her own business, remodeled her house, has fantastic children, than what yours are doing.' And so on."

- **Competitive Frenemy.** This type of frenemy is basically a competitor of one. At work, she behaves well, makes compliments, and acts as a well-wisher, especially in front of others. In reality, she never wants anything good to happen to you. She never wants you to be more successful than she is. Socially, she also never wants you to be more successful than she is and will try to "one-up" you any chance she gets, if it gives her the spotlight first, before you.

Melanie's Story. *"My sister-in-law is uber-competitive with me. It was more so in the beginning when I first met her, but still occurs to this day. The first time I met her, when I was dating my (now) husband, she literally would not talk to me at dinner. She answered my questions with 'yes' or 'no' responses but would only really engage conversationally with my boyfriend (her brother-in-law).*

'As soon as we announced our engagement, she immediately announced she was pregnant. Because I'm almost 10 years older, there was general awareness by the entire family that we'd start trying to have kids soon. I thought the timing of her announcement was interesting but didn't say anything. I actually thought, 'I'm being ridiculous for feeling like she is trying to be in the spotlight.' But two other family members, behind closed doors, told my fiancé and I, 'She did that so you wouldn't have kids before her. She doesn't want you to have children first.'

At one time my mother-in-law and I were very close...my sister-in-law didn't like that. She pushed her way into our relationship and made sure we weren't close anymore.

We go to their River House every Fourth of July. This last year we were playing an adult card game and I was winning. She got extremely agitated and just got up and left the table and wouldn't come back to play anymore. So, we've never really been close. Which is too bad. Initially, I was excited to have a relationship with her. To a degree, she is supportive of me, as long as it's not in her lane, against her directly. She likes the acknowledgment that she's first. As we've gotten older, she's backed off a bit, but it's still there, the distance, and her always trying to 'one-up' me."

Lola's Story. *"A good friend of mine whom I've known for years and am actually really close to is also really competitive with me. If I tell* *her I had a good day at work, 'I got a raise today.' She'll say, 'Oh, I got a $10,000 bonus today.' If I say, 'My daughter got a ribbon for her swim team race today,' she'll say, 'My daughter broke all of the swim records today.' I am divorced. She'll jokingly say, 'I'm getting divorced.' It's really...she can never just let me have a moment of my own. It's always been that way, for about 20 years. Ever since I met her in college. I just see this competition between us, from her, and I've never really known why it's there. Our daughters are the same age. My daughter does okay in school but hers had to be held back in grade school. It was painful to watch her feel as if she was a failure. Because of her competitiveness to me, I know that's how she felt."*

- **Controlling Frenemy.** This type of frenemy wants to have all the power. It's "her way or the highway." She makes all of the choices, wants to know where you are at all times, gets upset when you make other plans without her, etc. She is concerned about her needs, not yours. She will exhaust you.

Joanna's Story. "From a very young age, I grew up in a blended family. It was the early 1970s, my dad was a playboy and cheated on my mom. There was a lot of hatred and animosity from my mom after my parent's divorce. After the divorce, he had loads of girlfriends but eventually settled down with Lucy, my 21-year-old stepmom. As a young girl, I loved everything about her—the platform cork shoes, long straight hair, flowy clothes, light blue eye make-up. She looked and acted cool. My mom hated her. Without it being said, I instinctively knew...that I could not bring up any topic at all, about Lucy to my mom.

My brother was not quite two years older than me and lived with my dad. When Lucy and my dad got married, I did not go. I clearly remember my mom telling me I wasn't invited. Often, I looked at their wedding picture and saw my dad, brother, Lucy, and the bridesmaids dressed in all colors of the rainbow. I remember feeling very left out, unloved actually, for not being invited to celebrate their special occasion. Years later, my dad told me, 'Of course you were invited. Your mother would not let you go and there was nothing I could do about it.' My mom had passed away by then but in my heart, I know my dad was right. My mom hated Lucy so much that she lashed out to hurt them by not letting me go to their wedding. Ultimately, I am the one it ended up hurting. I know my mom didn't care...she frequently used what she had in her ability, to control and hurt them."

- **Jealous Frenemy.** This type of frenemy is based upon jealousy. When you share good news, she is not excited—she won't say anything, may put you down, or even try to "one-up" you and turn the conversation to something about her. She may become jealous of you, because of your success, beauty, personality, humor, social status, etc. This frenemy will devise ways to make you feel insecure about yourself.

Melody's Story. "There is a persecutor, victim, rescuer mentality about the relationships my mom has with her female siblings. It's always a rivalry to be on the top, based on who has more. I think that because of our mothers, the relationship I have with my female cousin is not as great as it could be. When things are neutral, or if I am perceived as being 'less than' it's okay. But if I or her friends or anyone close to my cousin has 'more than' she does, she gets angry.

A good friend of my cousin was recently divorced. After her divorce, she came into some money and was able to remodel her house. My cousin was blatantly angry that her friend had the financial means to remodel. We all knew and witnessed her behavior. It was like, 'it's not fair that she has this money, why don't I have it too,' versus the attitude of, 'wow, she's just gone through a rough time, I am happy for her.' There is never that 'I am happy for her' type of outlook."

- **Negative-Difficult Frenemy.** She is "Debbie-Downer" or a "glass half-empty" person. Nothing is ever right and she'll let everyone know it by complaining (loudly) about it. She never wants to hear how you are doing, only to voice what she is feeling. You will feel in despair and without hope if you are around her too much. This type of frenemy is combative, dramatic, and objects to everything. She looks for things to pick at or be upset over. You will feel on-guard, apprehensive, and like you are continuously "walking on eggshells."

Jan's Story. "*I love my friend Tina but after several years I realized I had to distance myself from her. Every time we spoke something was always wrong. I mean every single time! It got to a point when I saw her, I just knew there'd be another negative story she'd share. She'd even asked to borrow money from me. At the time, I felt bad for her, so I let her have it. But then it became a pattern, a continual request, and she never attempted to pay me back. I realized then, I'd never get my money back, so I started saying no. I felt drained, just being around her. It didn't seem from my point of view that she was doing anything to improve her situation... and that became very frustrating. Especially because she constantly complained. Over time, I just started to not be available to take her calls or see her. I felt like I was her constant support system. It didn't feel reciprocal and I just couldn't do it anymore.*"

- **One-Sided Frenemy.** This type of frenemy is unequal. She only reaches out to you when she needs help or a favor. She doesn't care about your life and doesn't have any interest in what is going on with you. When you need a friend, it's hard to find her. It's a one-sided, not mutual relationship. This type of frenemy is continuously in crisis-mode. She's one of those people where everything always goes wrong, and always ready to tell you about her problems, in great detail. She loves the attention and rarely seems to take advice that could help things improve. If you let her, she will suck you dry.

Julia's Story. *"Anytime any issues ever came up between us, she would make me feel like I was over-sensitive and blowing things out of proportion. She never was accountable for anything, always putting the blame on everyone else. If she had a problem, she needed help with, she'd instantly tell you about it, or call and want to discuss it. It was 'me, me, me, me, me, me!' But if I wanted to tell her about something I was experiencing, she never really had the time to listen. I now know, I was never a top priority to her. I'm not sure anyone was."*

- **Over-Involved Frenemy.** This type of frenemy gets involved in your life without your approval. She reaches out to your family, friends, or significant others in inappropriate ways without your permission... all on the pretense of caring or showing concern for your well-being. Her over-involvement bothers and irritates you. It's not real and is based upon using information to make you look or feel bad.

Jessie's Story. *"I've known Donna for such a long time we were almost like family. In fact, she knows my family very well. She got married and had children. I did not. I still am not married and am totally fine with that. At some point, after she had kids our relationship took a turn... not because we didn't care about each other but because we just had different priorities and interests. Of course, I'd still see her, I love her, but it was just different. She didn't take it very well.*

She was on a mission to find me a husband. I however, took up the stance that it'll happen when it happens, if ever. She got very meddlesome... reaching out to my mom, and my sister. Trying to set me up with people, telling them about my dating life, and why I wasn't taking it seriously. It was just too much. I finally had it out with her and told her to stop or we just couldn't be friends anymore. In hindsight, I realize she was doing it on the appearance of my well-being, but in reality, she missed our friendship and thought if my lifestyle changed to be like hers, our friendship would go back to the way it was."

- **Passive-Aggressive Frenemy.** This type of frenemy makes mean remarks and gives backhanded compliments, but never directly to your face. She does something purposeful but then acts like it was a mistake (i.e. deliberately deleting you on social media). She knows what she is doing and will leave you feeling confused and doubting what you have done wrong.

Joanna's Story. "My husband and I were co-parenting our children with our ex-spouses, and each family had equal 50–50 custody. We were 'in it together' to support our children but there was a definite divide between me and my husband's ex-wife, as well as one with my ex-husband's new wife.

It was our week to have my husband's boys and I made homemade blueberry muffins for breakfast. One of my stepson's did not really care for them that much, but I didn't think too much about it. The following week when we picked up the boys from their mother's house, Betsy, their mom leaned in the back window and handed me a package of instant blueberry muffin mix and said, 'These... are the only type of blueberry muffins that my boys will eat.' She was quiet about it as I knew she did not want my husband, her ex, to hear the conversation. I smiled and said, 'thank you.'

Her action and one-liner sentence spoke volumes about her intent. I'm not proud at all of how her behavior toward me made me react toward her in the exact same manner. I probably should have just sat down with her at some point to have it out over dinner and a glass of wine... but I never did. She didn't either. And so throughout the time we raised our kids together, this type of behavior was frequent.

The next morning, I made her package of blueberry muffins. I sat down with my stepson and the package of mix and said, 'I am very happy to make these for you because they are your favorite, but this will be the last time that I do. I know you don't care for my muffins as much, but they are made with real blueberries. This package is made with fake blueberries, and just isn't good for you. I don't make fake food.' But of course, I did. I just wanted to get back at her."

Shelby's Story. *"My husband's best friend and his wife, also a very good friend, used to live next door to us. We used to hang out with them all the time because we were close, and we were all such good friends. Then they got a divorce and he moved out. Initially, she stayed in the house and we continued to hang out with her because she was near. When their divorce was final, he took custody of the house, moved back in, started dating someone new, and ended up marrying her.*

Out of the blue, his ex-wife unfriended me on social media. I texted her and said, 'Hey, what's going on? I noticed you unfriended me on Facebook.' She replied, 'It's nice that you are so 'worried' about me while you're hanging out with them!' She ultimately chose to not be my friend because I was also friends with her ex's new wife."

- **Unfiltered-Undermining Frenemy.** This type of frenemy insults you, makes fun of you, and cracks sarcastic jokes about you so frequently that it gets hard for you to tolerate. She discloses your secrets in public. You will eventually start to hate or dislike this frenemy.

Alyssa's Story. *"A neighbor I used to live by always had some sort of dig or passive-aggressive remark to say to me. They weren't exactly mean but when she said them, they never felt sincere or nice. They were back-handed compliments, given on the pretense of being nice, especially if someone else was listening. 'Wow, you look nice. You're actually wearing color today, not just black and white.' OR 'Well just look at you, you always just look so put together like you're trying to put the rest of us to shame.' OR 'Perfect Alyssa does it again with the best appetizer that everyone loves.'*

She made similar types of remarks to my mom when she was at the bus stop with the kids when we were out of town. I hadn't told my mom about my thoughts about this particular neighbor, but my mom later said, 'Your neighbor does not like you at all. She really likes to say mean remarks about you. I was surprised she said them to me because I'm your mom!'"

Lynette's Story. *"I had a mutual agreement with the woman I reported to that for the remainder of my time on this particular project, I'd work part-time. I worked closely with a colleague named Kelsey who seemed to think I should let her know my whereabouts: when I came in, went home, etc. She treated me like I was her personal assistant and began to micromanage the work I was doing, even though I was not a direct report of hers. I was a consultant and she was an associate, which in her mind, I think, made a difference. She always had a dig or something passive-aggressive to say, usually in front of other co-workers like, 'Oh, you're finally here. I just never know when you'll be working or not,' OR 'Wow, you look like you've been out in the sun. It must be so nice to not have to work as much as the rest of us.'"*

The "frenemy" persona is vast and wide. The types of behavior involved with the various relationships within the persona, the personal descriptions, and the stories are real women encountering real behaviors. That is why it kills me when people say it's women being dramatic or it's just a catfight. With what I've shared, you can see how this is a phenomenon that is prevalent in everyday living. Frenemies have been around for a long time, and if you are involved with one, I am sure that you absolutely agree with me that this type of relationship can have serious repercussions.

3.3: Your Turn. Dear reader, by sharing the different personas and stories that highlight the various characteristics of frenemy behaviors... when you read the above descriptions, did anything resonate with you? Have you ever had or been on the receiving end of a frenemy? Or maybe, have you ever projected a certain type of frenemy behavior toward someone else? Take a moment now to write below, if one or more of the frenemy examples have resonated with you and why.

_____

_____

_____

_____

Chapter Closing

So, wow! Is your mind blown yet?! I know it's a lot to take in, all these different definitions and personas. And the stories... well, I know they've been giving you all the feelings (amazement, anger, disbelief, sadness, etc.). It's these stories that give life to the point I am trying to make in highlighting these types of behaviors. I know my mind has been blown with almost every story that has been shared. And the thing is, they all, are completely real.

Dear reader, this is just the tip of the iceberg.

PART II:

The War

war /wôr/ *noun.*
"A state of competition, conflict, or hostility
between different people or groups" (Merriam Webster 2020).

"It takes strength to resist the dark side.
Only the weak embrace it.
It is more powerful than you know…
And those who oppose it are more powerful than you'll ever be."
—Obi-Wan Kenobi (Star Wars Inc., 2020).

Chapter 4:

Dealing With a Vicious Vixen

"We can say the brotherhood of man, and pretend that we include the sisterhood of women, but we know that we don't. Folklore has it that women only congregate to b*tch an absent member of their group, and continue to do so because they are too aware of the consequences if they stay away. It's meant to be a joke, but like jokes about mothers-in-law it is founded in bitter truth."
—Germaine Greer (Goodreads, Inc., 2020).

My Story

Once upon a time, there was a young girl who was friends with all her classmates. For whatever reason, on that Friday, she was not invited to join the sleepover birthday party with all of the other fifth grade girls in her class. The birthday party that had been the hot topic of conversation, all week long.

Before the school buses pulled up at the end of the day, Lara, the birthday girl, said she'd call her so that she could come too. She went home, excited to finally be included, and told her mom. Her mom listened but didn't say anything.

The young girl sat in the kitchen by the phone... watching it, willing it to ring. Occasionally her mom would look over at her, with a sad expression on her face. One hour, then another went by. Her family had dinner together. Finally, around 8:00 p.m, her mom sat next to her and said, "Come and watch TV with us in the family room." "No, mom. Lara told me she'd call. I don't want to miss it." Her mom said, "Honey, she's not going to call you or she would have done so already." The young girl started crying and said, "But why did she tell me she would? Why did she say anything at all, if she didn't mean it?"

Lara never called. It was circa 1981 and that young girl was me. Was it the end of the world? No. But in my bubble, where everyone liked each other and played nicely in the sandbox, it was the end of innocence as I knew it to be. It was my first encounter of what it felt like to not be included… and that stung.

Was it a direct rivalry? No, but it was my very first interaction with a Queen-Bee-Mean-Girl behavior. One that to this very day, over 30 years later, I can still recall with vivid clarity. My head on the kitchen counter staring at the yellow-corded phone on the wall. My mom, looking at me with sorrowful, subdued eyes. Having overwhelming feelings of unhappiness and loneliness, I felt left out and did not understand why.

Perhaps this resonates with me so deeply because my daughter is around this age. She hasn't (yet) experienced this type of behavior but in all reality, I know it's coming. It's coming because it's inevitable.

Introduction

While you may not always be fully aware of the types of behaviors projected at you, a vicious vixen can make your life a living h*ll. A vicious vixen is the "bad actor" that exudes the many personal qualities of female rivalry that I described in the previous chapter. Any one of the previously described personas could be a vicious vixen, but not every vicious vixen will display all the traits of the personas. In this chapter, I am going to share examples of when rivalry occurs, the varying ages, the milestone stages, what it looks like as it pertains to real life and social settings, and the signs to be aware of. But first, let me define what a vicious vixen is.

vic.ious. *|viSHəs|: adjective.*
"deliberately cruel or violent. immoral. dangerously aggressive malicious, spiteful" (Merriam Webster, 2020).

vix.en. *|viksən|: noun.*
"a spiteful or quarrelsome woman. a shrewish, ill-tempered woman" (Merriam Webster, 2020).

Rivalry comes in many forms and can rear its ugly head at any age. If left unaddressed, it frequently will continue to escalate and at a certain point, can turn into a bullying type of behavior. That's why it's so important to have an awareness of when it's occurring—to hopefully stop it.

4.1: Your Turn. Dear reader, have you ever worked for, or been on the receiving end of a vicious vixen? How did that make you feel? What did you do? When you were experiencing it, did you even know, at the time, that it was happening? Take a moment now to write below your initial thoughts on what this type of persona means.

_____

_____

_____

_____

Female Rivalry is Unbiased

When women share their stories with me, frequently the start of our conversation focuses on rivalry they've experienced within an organizational setting. Often, our discussions then evolve to their sharing other stories of rivalry they've been exposed to in everyday life. It's rare, you see, to only have dealt with one instance of it. Commonly, the other kind of stories they share are more personal. They originate from social settings, college, high-school, middle school, grade school, etc.

Continually, as they reflect and the memories surface, they can connect the dots of what happened then to how they react now. Let me tell you, as they look back in hindsight, the women are astounded by the impact. Rivalry does not differentiate between age, social status, size, demographics, or race. Its boundaries are limitless.

The Adolescent Brain

A young girl, tween or teen, will worry less about what her parents have to say and instead put more focus on what her peers think of her. A young woman is more susceptible to peer pressure. Because she is still discovering her own voice, she may or may not have the ability to speak up on her own behalf. Although this type of behavior is hurtful at any age, if it occurs during adolescent years or in college, it can have a huge impact on how she views herself, now and later. This is a crucial stage when self-esteem is forming. As a result, the projected negative mean girl behaviors can be especially harmful because they help to shape incorrect beliefs about herself.

To summarize an article I recently read, a teen's subconscious thoughts control up to 95% of her habits and behaviors which makes it challenging for her to make decisions. In an adolescent, add to that, the fact that her brain is still forming and will continue to do so until she's in her mid-twenties. Primarily the prefrontal cortex, the rational component of the brain that helps to influence emotional and impulse control, is still developing. It's the part of the brain that responds to situations with good judgement and awareness for long-term consequences. A maturity rate of development for females is around 21 years of age; the maturity rate for a male is around 25 years of age.

Girls in this age demographic frequently will doubt themselves. They will try to fit into certain groups, and in the process of this, morph into what "others think they need to be," to be accepted. My deep wish is for young girls at this age to be able to hold on to who they are as their individual selves, to know that who they are is good enough, strong enough, unique enough, and to be accepted fully, just as they are.

Grade School

Think back to the story I shared at the beginning of this chapter about being excluded in fifth grade. These types of mean girl behaviors can begin at such a young age. The impacts of negative behavior can stay with you and become a part of your story. These instances can then change your behavior, change your attitude, and especially if harmful in nature, cause you to have self-doubt.

Eva's Story. Eva, a high-school student, shared her earliest memory of mean girls from grade school.

> *"I was really good friends with a girl named Clare. In fifth grade, we were in the same class with another girl that Clare was also good friends with. After that, things changed, it was like the two of them just ganged up on me. At recess they'd invite me to play with them and then when we were together, they'd tell me that I couldn't join them and had to leave. In class, they'd instant message me on the computer and say really mean things. I'd ask them to stop but they didn't. They got mad at me when I said I was going to tell the teacher. They totally excluded me and then actually went and told our teacher and the school counselor that I was being mean to them and that I wouldn't leave them alone. I ended up getting in trouble and was sent to the counselor's office to have 'a chat.' The other girl's mom was president of the PTA and good friends with my teacher. I told my mom about it, but no one believed me at school. Finally, the instant messaging on the computers gave them away. Because it was school property, it wasn't erased, and it was proof of how they treated me."*

Tina's Story. *"When you're little, you know second, third, or fourth grade, everything is great. And then things started changing, at least for me, right around sixth and seventh grade when girls' bodies started changing. People started taking notice. It felt like once the boys started taking notice, the relationships completely changed with the girls. It seemed like everyone was kind of pitted against each other. Because everyone wanted the boys' attention and whoever got that attention was now the enemy.*

I went to a private boarding school and I had a green dress. There was nothing special about it but we had very strict dress codes. My dress met all the dress code requirements but I couldn't wear it, because I wasn't allowed to. My roommate, on the other hand, who was my height could wear it without being disciplined. I had curves. I didn't feel pitted against her because she was my roommate, you know. But it just makes you go, 'why is this?' It was the little things like that... just some crazy dynamics that happened naturally, bodies changing, etc... But as a result, relationships changed too. That really stands out to me, as I look back now on that age."

Kim's Story. *"I grew up in a small town where everyone knew each other. In sixth grade, a new girl, Rebecca, moved from the 'big' city to attend our grade school. Being new, all the girls flocked to her. After a point in time, I questioned the behavior as to why we were all falling all over the new girl. I wasn't rude. I just questioned the behavior because I was curious about it. Unfortunately, I expressed my thoughts to the wrong girl. She spread rumors, told all to everyone, and I was ostracized from all the other girls. I had to make new friends with (as I found out) the other girls who also didn't fit in. It made me realize at that time, speaking your mind got you into a lot of trouble and ostracized. I see the same types of behaviors today when women speak out... they are called a b*tch or are rude. When all they are really doing is having a voice."*

Jackie's Story. "*I grew up in the Midwest in a fairly large town. Large enough that I didn't know all of the kids at my grade school. My dad, who I was very close with, passed away unexpectedly when I was eight and that was really hard. As a result, a couple of my friends became more important to me as I leaned into them for support. One friend in particular, Kylie, became very close. For two years in a row, we were in the same class. We were constantly together and had sleepovers at each other's houses, talked about everything, played sports together... You name the activity and we were doing it together, connected at the hip. Kylie was one of those girls that even at a young age, always seemed to have a boyfriend. I had no clue about boys at that age and having a boyfriend was the last thing on my mind. And then things changed. Kylie started talking differently, about being a lesbian, and then she declared she was bi-sexual. One day on the playground, she told me she had feelings for me and wanted to be my girlfriend. I was shocked! As I look back now, I really didn't even know what that meant. I told her I cared about her as a friend but that I didn't have feelings for her in that way. The next day in gym class, she tried to hold my hand, and touch my hair and my body. It made me so uncomfortable.*

Over the course of several months, the behaviors escalated. She told other kids we were a couple. I was a quiet, calm kid who kept things to myself but at some point, I told my mom, who talked to her mom, who in turn, talked to Kylie. Kylie's response to her mom was, 'Oh! Well, that's awkward!' She alluded to her mom that it was all simply a misunderstanding and that of course it wasn't true because she had a boyfriend! The next day at school she was furious and totally went off on me. Yelling and asking, 'how could you tell that to my mom?' The more I tried to distance myself from her, the more she was always just there, and always saying bad things about me to other kids because I wouldn't be her girlfriend.

The clincher and very odd thing was, Kylie was so persistent about wanting to hang out with me, asking to do things together that I finally had had enough and got angry. I told her I wasn't interested, that I didn't want to be her friend anymore. In fact, I wanted nothing to do with her at all. I don't remember all of the details of the conversation from there, but she low-balled me and yelled, 'Well at least I have a dad!'

After that, the school year ended, and we were no longer in contact with each other. To this day, her behavior still confuses me. It makes me sad that such a good friend turned on me the way she did. In hindsight, I know she was dealing with things that I just couldn't understand at that age. I also now know that her extreme behavior shifts—nice/mean, bullying, anger, cruelty—were symptoms of other, bigger behavioral issues. And the interesting thing is, even though my mom escalated it, the school didn't really offer any help. The counselor even told my mom she didn't know how to handle that type of situation. In my mind, if it were a boy doing that to a girl, it would have had a different outcome."

Kendra's Story. *"My sister was several years older than me and hit puberty really early, in grade school. She had huge boobs. As a result, she was teased incessantly about it. Girls were mean to her and spread rumors that 'she was promiscuous and was a slut' because she'd developed early. She wasn't. But over time, she started to live up to what they were calling her, not in action but she accepted the names they called her. I lived in the shadow of it, watching her. It was an early memory to me of how mean some girls can be."*

Phoebe's Story. *"My daughter broke down this past year at age seven. She said, 'I want to tell you something that happened in preschool. There was a girl I wanted to be friends with but she didn't want to be friends with me.' She started crying. I knew those girls were not the right friends for my daughter but the behaviors they exuded... They* *were learning that behavior from their mothers. The moms weren't nice to me either. Sometimes behaviors like that happen because it's the only thing they know because they've learned it. I think the daughters compete and the moms just play along with it. My daughter's class had a whole bunch of alpha females in it. Not the alpha female sisterhood type, but the bossy female type. Boss girls. The very negative version, the ones not nice to each other. The word bully has been used quite a bit to describe these young women. It's really tough because I know this behavior starts so young."*

4.2: Your Turn. Dear reader, unfortunately, this type of behavior starts so young! Were you ever on the receiving end of a grade school vicious vixen? Take a moment now to write below, if one or more of the vicious vixen examples have resonated with you and why.

_____

_____

_____

_____

Middle School

The peer pressure for a middle schooler who is still learning who she is as an individual can be a force to be reckoned during this tween-to-teen stage. Especially in this era, where there is a strong social media presence in middle school. (Think back to Chapter 1 when I mentioned the concept of "keyboard courage").

Sally's Story. Sally shared her experience from middle school and reminisced how it still impacts her "trust factor" today as an adult, in her relationships with other women.

"In sixth grade, I was totally unaware of social things at that point in my life, but I think this was the moment I became aware of the kind

of social rankings that can exist. My experience was awful. It was worse than awful.

I wanted to be a part of the 'in/ cool' crowd, and so I tried to become friends with two girls who were the most popular in my grade at school. I did everything I could to mimic them and become their friend. I was never actually accepted into their circle, and it was so hard for me to understand back then and realize at that moment what was going on.

They'd invite me over to their houses, but they also did things together without me all the time. Then they'd come to my house and were really mean. They were also mean to other girls but that was never really talked about, outwardly. One time we went on a field trip. I was walking through the park by a creek on the rocks and they pushed me off. I got a gash on my shin. It was so mean and ugly.

Another time I was at one of the girls' houses, near the barn, and I was walking ahead of them and she sent her dog after me to jump on my back and she pushed my face in the mud. It was cruel emotional and physical behavior.

I was exposed to some cruel and unusual punishment, trying to get these girls to like me. For whatever reason, they both ended up leaving after seventh grade. By association, I then became one of the popular girls. That's the only thing that worked out in my favor from that. They were just mean girls, two peas in a pod."

4.3: Your Turn. Dear reader, as young girls get older, the behavior can tend to escalate, and become meaner. When you read the above descriptions about middle school did anything stand out to you? Were you ever on the receiving end of a middle school vicious vixen? Take a moment now to write below, if one or more of the vicious vixen examples have resonated with you and why.

_____

_____

_____

_____

High School

High school is different than middle school but there is still a lot of peer pressure of a different kind—driving, drinking, smoking, drugs, dating, sex, social acceptance, pressure for college, etc. But this is also an age where teenagers are on the cusp of adulthood. Their brains are still forming but there is also a greater awareness of knowing right from wrong.

In high school, I was friends with all types of kids: smart, preppie, popular, athletic, stoners, loners, etc. I was *really good* friends with a so-called group of "popular girls." I vividly recall mean girl types of behaviors occurring and originating specifically from this "popular" group of girls.

To gather research for this book and because I'm the first to admit that I have an awful memory, I've reached out to women I went to high school with to share their perspective and experiences from our school days. Sometimes, I also receive feedback, unsolicited. A female from high school reached out when I shared a post on social media,

> *"Hi Amber! I love what you are doing and think it's wonderful. Today's story can resonate with many. I'm sorry to ask, and forgive me in advance, but how does 'The Crew' fit in here? That was really some mean-girling at its worst!"*

She asked a great question. Not only were there mean girl behaviors at my high school, there were four young women in the popular group that targeted specific girls, and called themselves "The Crew." It wasn't clear then but now as I reflect, their "mean-girling" behaviors were very clearly extreme bullying types of behavior.

Looking back on "The Crew," if memory serves me well (which often it does not), the mean girls targeted one "main girl" who was a cheerleader. They also targeted other cheerleaders and their friends (guilt by association). It stemmed from one of the mean girls thinking the "main girl" and her boyfriend were colluding with one another. (They weren't). Cars were keyed, and threats were made, such as, "you better not go out alone or who knows what will happen." Two Crew individuals were terrifying because they were so viciously mean to a lot of girls at school.

A colossal incident occurred at school in twelfth grade, when "The Crew" attached printed flyers on all the lockers in the senior hall corridor that said awful things about certain girls. It was ugly behavior at its finest. Because I was friends with the girls in "The Crew," I was not prey to their awful behavior. I recall coming into school the next morning seeing the proof of what they did and feeling utterly appalled. I also remember having strong feelings of relief, guilt, sadness, and fear. Relief that it wasn't me. Guilt that it wasn't me. Sadness for whom the behavior targeted. Feeling fearful of these girls and worrying that if I ever got on their bad side, would I also become a target?

Maybe I am wrong, but the other thing is... as I reflect... I do not recall that there were behavioral ramifications for these actions from the school authorities.

> ***Maren's Story.*** *"In high-school two girls keyed my car. Their perception was something I had done warranted that type of behavior as a punishment. A school bus driver saw them do it and reported them. I don't recall if the school did anything about it but I did. I drove to one of the girls' houses, knocked on the door, and told her parents. All her dad said was, 'Kids will be kids.' As I look back on it now, I am surprised that I went to her house, by myself without my parents. I am also surprised at the reaction of her father. It showed me that he was okay with that type of behavior and there were no ramifications for it. And so yes, it very much continued."*

Because my memory is horrible, especially reaching that far back, I've done some soul-searching. In my heart, I sincerely do not think I played a part in executing those negative types of behaviors. I've asked several of the women I've interviewed in the present day and they also do not think I played a part in the malicious behavior, even though I was friends with all the individuals in the group. One gal said, "No, you weren't mean. You were friends with everyone, we all knew that." Whew!

I know, however, there were instances, even though I cannot clearly remember what they were, where I was a silent bystander because I was afraid of standing out or having the behavior turn on me. As I see it now, that type of behavior is just as bad as initiating it is. I'll talk more about this in Chapter 6, but a bystander is,

> *"a person who observes a conflict or unacceptable behavior. It might be something serious or minor, one-time or repeated, but the bystander knows that the behavior is destructive or likely to make a bad situation worse. An active bystander takes steps that can make a difference"* *(MIT, 2020).*

I responded to my high school acquaintance and said, "I've been thinking about 'The Crew' actually, and how to incorporate that into my book. I wasn't on the receiving end of, but I recall how awful it was." She said,

> *"Thanks Amber. I'd be happy to share some time. My main offender apologized years ago and I for sure am not grudging on anyone. I do remember at least one time you were there, though, when it was my turn to be on the receiving end and several of you showed up at my house. Not placing blame, just saying. I've been on both sides of the bully stick and have had to own up to my own stuff... I was an early elementary school offender."*

Her response floored me. With a heavy heart, I stewed on that knowledge for several days. The thing is, and let me say this loud and clear, YOU ARE NOT SUPPOSED TO BE AFRAID OF YOUR FRIENDS, EVER. If you are, is that really a true friend? No. Not. At. All.

So yes, I was a silent bystander and her comment confirmed it. I'll accept that. And I truly apologize to anyone reading this. If I was a silent bystander when horrible behaviors were targeted at you, I am so sorry. I know better now. And if something were to happen now, you bet your booty I'd stand up for you.

If you see it, it is your responsibility to take action. You are like a gate-keeper and have a social responsibility… To do something. To stand up. When people look the other way, it's not just looking the other way. It's aiding and abetting the negative behavior.

4.4: Your Turn. Dear reader, at this age young girls are turning into women and behaviors can be more cunning. When you read the above descriptions about high school, did anything sound familiar to you? Were you ever on the receiving end of a high school vicious vixen? Take a moment now to write below, if one or more of the vicious vixen examples have resonated with you and why.

_____

_____

_____

_____

College

The transition to college is a steppingstone. While typically in the college years, teens turn into full-fledged adults and brains are fully developed. There is a lot of unfamiliarity and newness that many at this age will experience such as, leaving familiar faces and places to venture off on your own. Granted, not everyone has a traditional college experience, but my point is—this is a new chapter. It's the gateway into adulthood and with that comes a whole different type of social expectations and peer pressure.

Melanie's Story. *"During my freshman year, I was in the freshman dorm with a bunch of girls and everyone was excited to be there. A bunch of us joined the same sorority together and we were all happy to be together and there was no drama. I know it's unusual but there were twelve of us and we really all had a great bond with each other. It really was wonderful.*

Our school was small and so you didn't really have a choice of who you were friends with. I mean it was good and bad. In many ways, I loved the small school atmosphere academically, but maybe it wasn't the best socially.

My freshman year, I became very close with Courtney. She and I were like instant best friends that just clicked. We decided to room together our sophomore year and then a new girl, Katy, transferred in across the hall from us. She was drop-dead gorgeous. She joined our sorority in the Fall rush. I can't even describe it, but I mean she just had this way about her... of clinging on to certain girls and sucking everybody in. She pretty much broke our whole dynamic apart. And it was sad because she used to pivot girls against each other. She was an instigator. And that's exactly what she did to me.

So my best friend, Courtney, was a great friend but she also wasn't the strongest of people, if you know what I mean. As I'm older and look back on it now, I can totally understand how this happened. Courtney and I were pretty tight that year, along with two other girls. Katy saw the four of us and I swear it was her mission to break us apart. She weaseled her way in and separated Courtney from us. The other two girls were closer to each other, and Courtney and I were closer so when Katy got involved it was hurtful. It was hurtful because I lost my bestie. At first, I was like, what in the heck? Katy, I was never really friends with. But I was friends with Courtney, and I felt so betrayed.

I finally got the courage and brought it up to Courtney. It was very hard because I didn't want to bring her any pain and a part of me also thought if I brought it up that would make it official, that it was really happening. Like once it's out, you can't take it back. I just remember telling her how I felt... I said, 'It's not like I don't want you to have other friends at all, it's just that this girl is very malicious to me. She excludes me from anything that has to do with you.' It ended up being a horrible conversation. Courtney got very defensive, which was not my intention. But a part of me wonders, when someone gets that way if they know they're being called out on their behavior and there's truth in it. I think she felt guilty because she knew how much pain it'd cause me.

I think the most painful thing for me was she didn't stand up for me even though I knew she saw it.

I guess I thought that once you get to college, you're old enough to all be friends together and it was very depressing to me. I really went through a very hard time. I think junior year was the hardest because I confronted her, and nothing changed. I thought for sure that when I talked to her that day, junior year, that you know, it would get better and then it really didn't. I think it was like a breakup. It was like a horrible breakup and it was awful."

Tina's Story. *"A painful instance that is still actually very painful, even to this day. It's so painful because it put my character into question. There was a guy I liked a lot and had for a long time. And we started dating. I was in my early twenties and there was apparently someone else that also really liked him. Well, she ended up telling him that I was prostituting myself and stripping. I was shocked! Fortunately, he knew me well enough that he didn't believe her. I'd gone to school with her since second grade. I'd known her for a long time. Her family lived in my neighborhood and we went to the same church together. She wanted to put me in a bad light so that he would stop dating me.*

Luckily, that didn't happen. A friend told me about it—what she was telling him and other people. He said, 'Hey, I think you should know what she is saying about you.' He was so nice about it.

I still vividly remember where I was working and what floor I was on in the hospital when that happened. I went into the stairwell and just started crying. I could almost cry now, thinking about it. I was just mortified."

***Julia's Story.** "I've known Cindy for almost thirty years. We met through our sorority freshman year in college and became good friends. I always tended to have a long-term boyfriend and Cindy always had a boyfriend too, but also always cheated on them. She always, to this day, thrives on having male attention. She even dated a married man, when we were in college. I didn't judge her then. Everyone was at school, partying, and having fun, but it gives insight into her character.*

A group of us in our 30's, all single at the time, went out to a club. I brought my friend Karly with me. Karly made a comment to all of us about a guy she thought was cute. We all mentioned to each other, the guys we thought were cute. Before you knew it, Cindy announced that she was going to talk to the guy that Karly mentioned she thought was cute. And sure enough, she did. She danced with him, had a drink, and flirted with him. It was just so blatant. Karly is quiet and didn't say anything, but I could tell it bothered her. I thought it was so rude and told Cindy so. Her response was, 'Why do you always take everything so seriously?'

Another time, I took my husband, whom Cindy had also known since college, to an ugly sweater holiday party. She flirted with him uncontrollably, and at one point, literally jumped on top of him and straddled her legs around him. Later on, he was standing on the deck, and she went up behind him and wrapped her arms around him and whole-body hugged him. It was just so awkward. It's that type of behavior that I'd just bypass, and not say anything about—but I stored it in the back of my head. I'm straightforward but then again, she wasn't really a threat to me. So that's maybe why I didn't pursue it more with her.

We're not friends anymore. As I look back, I think even though we'd been friends for so long, perhaps really, we didn't have a lot in common and we were staying friends only because we had a lot of memories together. I began to realize that when I was around her I always felt so down. She just wore me down and made me tired. That, and I didn't trust her. I don't trust her now and I'm not sure I ever did."

4.5: Your Turn. Dear reader, at this age females going off to college are women. Behaviors at this age and stage can be quite conniving and cruel. By sharing stories that highlight the various vicious vixen types of conduct from college, when you read the above descriptions, did anything sound familiar? Were you ever on the receiving end of a college-aged vicious vixen? Take a moment now to write below, if one or more of the vicious vixen examples have resonated with you and why.

_____

_____

_____

_____

Adult Female Rivalry Occurrences and Behaviors

Old behaviors, habits, and mannerisms can tend to resurface when you are back in contact with an originating behavior or circumstance. Think about when you are exposed to or surrounded by individuals in which the original behaviors stemmed from, like in high school. For example, if you were a Queen Bee during secondary school, as an adult it's easy to step back into that same mode of behavior when you are surrounded by people you once went to high school with. It may be a conscious (purposeful) or unconscious (totally unaware of) act, but nevertheless, it can be easy to step back into familiar patterns of old behaviors.

Here's a small example of what I'm talking about. Although my mom is from the Midwest, she spent a vast majority of her life on the West Coast, where I was born. Growing up, I never thought of my mom as having any type of drawl or Midwest accent. However, at family reunions or when my mom is together with all of her sisters, she picks up right where she left off when she lived with them. Certain words and dialects of speech become more prominent when she is back in comfortable and familiar surroundings. Is there anything wrong with this? Absolutely not. In fact, it's very common. This same theory can pertain to other types of behaviors too.

I've been to a couple of my high-school reunions. It's an effort because I live on the opposite coast now, but I do love going back. It's always so great to see people I grew up with. I vividly recall a memory from my 20th reunion when I was in my late 30's. Two women arrived late that were members of "The Crew." Other than saying "hello," I didn't really have an opportunity to chat with them. As the night progressed, I recall being shocked at their behavior. One of the women was upset that a fellow high-school acquaintance had given her a "dirty look." She wanted to take her out in the parking lot and physically "fight it out." Really. I didn't then, and genuinely don't now, have the words for how horrific that type of behavior is. If you are reading this you most likely are thinking, "did she grow up in the hood?" Nope. It's a small suburb about an hour south of Seattle. It's a great place to raise a family. But honestly folks, demographics don't really matter, as these types of behaviors happen everywhere.

I get that people change but there are times when mean is just mean. I felt like this particular "Crew" member hadn't emerged from the '80s. She was still residing in high school, glorifying her old persona of being a mean girl, and having power. It's a tragedy. Ultimately though, I think it's very sad. What is she going through personally that causes her to lash out at others and intimidate them in that manner? Is she so unhappy with herself that she must project mean, domineering behaviors onto other women just to make herself briefly feel better?

Connie's Story. A Perspective of Female Rivalry At Work: *"I work in the educational field and continually see 'mean girl cliques.' It happens between departments. For whatever reason, certain women feel superior to other women... and as a result, they are not welcoming. In one location, it's occurring in the office staff. Two 'mean girls' in the office have consistently driven out other women. They show favoritism by issuing privileges to whomever is in their clique and if you aren't in that group, it's an effort just to receive the required amount of 'normal' customer service that everyone should receive."*

Meredith's Story. A Perspective of Extended Family Rivalry: *"When I met Frank, we grew from good friends to life partners. He and his ex-wife Judy raised their children, who are now married adults together, but had divorced years ago. Judy also had a longtime partner.*

Judy was very used to having Frank 'on-call' as a secondary husband. Whenever she wanted something done, she'd say it was 'for the kids,' and Frank would jump to do it. It was a bad habit, and we could all see that she was taking advantage of Frank's good nature and generosity. Frank dated a couple of women in the past, but none of them put up with having Judy so constantly in the picture. When I met him, he'd been alone for 15 years.

Every year in mid-December Judy throws a huge, 'mandatory attendance' holiday party. The guest list includes several old boyfriends, that go as far back as high school and all of her 'social contacts.' It's a big deal. Frank is expected to attend because 'the kids' are there, and since I'm with Frank, I'm also invited.

At the end of one such evening, I made my way into the kitchen to say thank you. Judy with several of her friends turned to introduce me to them and said, 'Oh, this is Meredith... the woman who lives with my husband.' I was so stunned that I just stammered a 'nice to meet you' to the assembled company and backed out the door.

That one comment gave me so much insight into her character! To this day she still calls Frank whenever she wants something and uses 'the kids' as leverage to try to get him to do things for her. She still expects attendance and him to kowtow at her whim. She still hints that the only way Frank can have a relationship with his kids is through her. It's sad and pitiful, but Frank has learned how to say 'no' to her, most of the time.

I read something a while back about people who are misidentified as passive-aggressive when they are actually covert aggressive. That's Judy. She'll talk bad about her 'friends' to gain favor with someone she considers more important socially, as well as try to work behind the scenes to make other people look bad.

I'm sure Judy knows it bothers me, her being in constant contact with Frank. I figure the only way to keep her from owning me is to refuse to respond. It's not easy, not rising to her bait, but I try to not respond. Many times, I've wanted to call and have a 'woman-to-woman' talk, but I know it wouldn't help. She's a narcissist and that's just how she operates.

In the meantime, Frank and I are doing our own thing. I've finally convinced him that his children are individuals and love him all on their own. We're spending Christmas in Hawaii, so we'll NOT be attending Judy's Big Holiday Extravaganza! 'The kids' are coming over to visit after we get back. I'm looking forward to the holiday's this year for the first time, in a long time.

I don't know if this qualifies as 'rivalry,' because I don't feel that I'm in competition with Judy over anything. I think though, she is in competition with me... She has her life and I hope she's happy at some point. I just can't let her use me to make herself feel better, but it's not easy."

4.6: Your Turn. Dear reader, if you are out of college and in your mid-twenties or later, at this stage of the game you are dealing with a woman, not a girl. Unfortunately for some women, the ability to project vicious vixen behaviors is something they never grow out of. By sharing stories that highlight the various vicious vixen types of conduct from adulthood, when you read the above descriptions, did anything sound familiar? Have you ever been on the receiving end of an adult-aged vicious vixen? Take a moment now to write below, if one or more of the vicious vixen examples have resonated with you and why.

_____

_____

_____

_____

Now that you've read some specific stories you may be asking, "Ok, I can see how big this type of behavior is, but what are some specific behaviors to look out for, to be aware of, and to know if it's impacting me?"

Seven Signs You're Dealing With a Vicious Vixen

The following are seven key signs that you may be dealing with a "Vicious Vixen." These signs may also appear as types of personas as described in Chapter 3.

1. **She Purposely Excludes Others**. She uses relationship aggression to socially isolate someone while attempting to increase her own status at work and/ or socially.

Ruby. *"The first time I realized I was being excluded was when several of my close teammates got up to go to a meeting. A colleague said, 'It's our usual team standing meeting sent from Sonya's calendar (manager), just at a different time. Aren't you going?' I told her I wasn't invited. It was about that time that I realized a clear pattern was emerging and I began to document what was going on."*

2. **She Struggles With Envy**. She wants what others have and will go to any extent or extreme to get it—even if that means hurting you or someone else in the process. She cannot acknowledge good in other people due to her struggle with envy. She will take steps to destroy her target's character, work, or socially related projects if it gives her the edge up.

Debbie. *"There are just little things in which I feel she is trying to compete with me or is envious of me for some reason... And the funny thing is, I am so not competitive, nor do I care what she has versus what I have. It's just that 'gut' feeling that thing I can't really explain...I always feel like she wants what I have or is uber-competitive of me for things I do or get before she does. When my son was placed in the gifted program, by referral of his teacher, she immediately tried to push for her daughter to be placed in a similar program. She's also very professionally successful... I've always asked her why she doesn't branch out on her own with her own business, given she's so good at what she does. Until recently, she's always said no. But when I announced I was starting my own business, she suddenly announced she was starting her own business too."*

3. **She Steals Your Work**. Due to the strong desire to get to the top of the social or corporate ladder, she will do anything to get there, including riding on the success of your work. She may initially become your friend because of what she thinks she can get from you and your connection.

Sally. *"It was a volunteer job and I was in charge of a PTA fund-raiser for my son's middle school. The female PTA president, anytime anyone other than her would voice an idea, she'd verbally shoot it down. Later on, she would present it, rephrased, altered, etc., as her idea, one she wanted to move forward with. It occurred constantly. It was draining and I finally had to back out of the fundraising...simply because I just couldn't work with her. No one could."*

4. **She Will Lie, Gossip, and Spread Rumors**. She's fixated on what other people think of her and will attack you or anyone that may jeopardize her status in some way. These actions may consist of spreading rumors, making up lies about ethics or behaviors that aren't true, or other relationships, etc. She doesn't like to look bad in front of people. If someone does something to her where she feels that "she's been made to look bad," she will retaliate and make you or them pay in some form or another.

Patricia. *"My first serious rivalry experience was in high-school. I moved from a large private school on the West Coast to a small-town public school on the East Coast. Upon my arrival, I was accepted into the 'popular crowd,' something that was new to me. Of course, I had friends before, but I usually hung out with the 'smart' versus 'cool' kids.' Several months after living there, I voiced my opinion against something the 'Queen Bee' of the popular clique wanted to do. I could tell that while others also disagreed, no one else had the courage to stand up to her as she was such a dominating female.*

After our disagreement, I was out of school for a week with the flu. When I returned, I found out the Queen-Bee-Ringleader had told everyone, I'd been out of school because I was pregnant and had an abortion. None of my 'friends' stood up for me or warned me ahead of time about the rumor. It was a small school, and everyone was aware of the gossip. It got so bad, some of the teachers even believed the story and questioned my actions, in a humiliating and confrontational way."

Patricia shared how she coped and was able to navigate the negative experience.

> *"I was mad, sad, hurt, and humiliated. I was betrayed not by one, but by many—by people I thought were my friends. But I was also strong. I was a senior in high school and my time there was short-lived. I knew there was a bigger, better, broader world out there, that wasn't as small-minded as the town I was living in. I knew after I graduated, I would never have to see those people again. Had I not had that knowledge; I would have ended it all."*

5. **She's a Serial Bully.** She's a toxic woman who is systematic, calculated, and a controlling manipulator. Externally she may offer a persona that is sweet, charming, and captivating, but internally she is unemotional and scheming. She can inflict emotional pain on her victim over long periods of time. She will distort the truth to appear innocent and to avoid being chastised.

> *Mel. "I was the first female to work for an overseas private school as a superintendent. I worked very closely with a board that was all men, except for one woman—a parent-board-member, Kimberly, who had several children attending at various levels within the school. The board controlled the finances and had a say in many of the larger decisions the school made. Kimberly was always so nice and sweet... to my face. In board meetings, she'd offer up compliments, bring favorite foods, try to flatter the men by having it appear that she and I were a team. We were anything but that. I knew within my first month that she was a force to be reckoned with, that the image she put on in front of the men was nothing like her real exterior. She was venomous and a persistent liar about anything that suited her agenda. She*

spread lies about me to other parents, telling them what a horrible job I was doing by making up specific, false stories. She'd say she was voting one way for decisions and then change her vote behind my back. She'd alter plans when she knew it wasn't what I favored. The list frankly, is too long to relay. Ultimately, she tried to get me fired. For whatever reason, since the day I began working there, she didn't like me. Maybe it was because I was a female, or because I got along well with everyone else, or because I was educated and in charge. Perhaps it was all those things? I'm not really sure. I can tell you; she was one of the key reasons I left that position. I was tired of always having my guard up and never knowing what she was going to do or how she was going to do it."

6. **She Struggles With Anger.** She will undermine others with overt body language (eye-rolling, coughing, etc.). It's hard for her to restrain her emotions. She is frequently short-tempered. She will directly insult and name call, and can control conversations by arguing, being sarcastic, throwing insults, and openly criticizing others.

   Mary. *"I could tell she was always so angry. She was a bully and for quite a long time she'd gotten away with it, probably because she'd worked there for so long. But I took it up with my chain of command. At one point she tried to get me fired, but my higher-ups supported me and validated me. I was told not to confront her, so I didn't. But man did she have it out for me. She pretty much told me in not so direct terms that she had it out for me and wanted me to go.*

   She would spin things up, to almost out of control. Often, things that weren't true. I had evidence that I had shared with my superiors of her doing this. She'd go off on verbal tirades to my face always and sometimes too, in front of other people. She was good that way. There was a pattern with her. Once she'd gone over the cuff it was definitely emotionally bullying and it wasn't physical, but it was still very much a rivalry. Once she was mad, it was hard for her to contain it and not show it. We all knew to stay out of her way.

She'd also show anger in a very calm, condescending way. Very passive-aggressive. It wasn't tangible behavior. But you could feel her anger. It was boiling within her."

7. **She is Power Hungry.** She wants to hold command and be in charge. She'll use the power she already has to her advantage, versus collaboration and consideration for others. She frequently is disrespectful to others. She traditionally has a strong personality, authority, and verbal skills. She will use these traits to walk over the needs of other people.

Kim. "I started out, brand new at a new school, as a volunteer coordinator for the PTA at my son's grade school which meant even though I didn't know anyone, I had to find volunteers. It was a great opportunity for me to meet people. I was developing relationships. There was a female who'd led the PTA before my time and was still a board member because I am sure it was the same six people that kept rotating positions. There was conflict there, but I didn't think that affected me. The next year I ran for it and became the PTA president.

This group, this one woman in particular, had alienated people at the school. She was very strict in how she wanted the PTA to run, even though she wasn't the one in charge anymore. She also wanted to be in control of the sixth grade committee to take over the sixth-grade camp and allocated funding, which was super expensive to send these kids to camp for three days. And, this was a school where 50% of the students were on reduced lunches.

I think before I'd gotten there, people just acquiesced to what this woman wanted. This lady and her posse didn't think I was supporting her effort for the sixth-grade camp. Mind you, it wasn't just the camp that needed help. They didn't have an approved yearly budget, nor had they updated the standing rules in four years. It was a hot mess, nothing was in order, but she didn't see that.

Instead of addressing her concerns with me about the changes I was making, and finding out where she stood, she sent her husband after me who absolutely lit into me, saying, 'You are changing everything and all of the positions. And you shouldn't because we've all been here for a long time. You are putting too many new people into things and you shouldn't do that because the new people don't know how we want our PTA to run! You are out of compliance with what you are doing!' On and on it went. But no, his wife couldn't say anything to me even though she was super hungry to still be in charge and run everything. Even though she was not the president.

She'd send me nasty emails or have other people from the board come to talk to me, to do her dirty work. I never knew what to expect from her and it never was direct. At another public board meeting, normally we can't get ten people to show up. She set me up for an attack and the room was packed. It was standing room only. I walked into a completely hostile environment. She had me stand up in front of this group when usually we all mingled together. And there were teachers with super angry faces, she'd convinced them that I was the devil, that I was trying to take things away from their children.

I kept my cool in front of them but I cried at home. I called my husband and cried. I just didn't want to give her the satisfaction of seeing me upset."

4.7: Your Turn. Dear reader, by sharing the "Seven Signs You're Dealing With a Vicious Vixen," did that help to clarify some specific behaviors to look out for, to be aware of, and to know if someone like her, is impacting you? When you read the above descriptions, did anything resonate with you? Have you ever had or been on the receiving end of a vicious vixen? Or maybe, have you ever projected a certain type of vicious vixen behavior toward someone else? Take a moment now to write below, if one or more of the vicious vixen examples have resonated with you and why.

_____

_____

_____

_____

Validated Vicious Vixen Behaviors

Negative or positive occurrences that have a role in your life become a part of who you are. Real or not, over time you may begin to believe things about yourself that may or may not be true. You may have low self-esteem, feel like you're unable to make female friends, or second guess yourself, all because of what you've experienced at various stages throughout your life. This is all because of what happened to you in grade school, in middle school, in high school, in college, or even, in the present day.

I hope that by sharing these types of behaviors with you in a timeline and milestone format you can better understand how young the rivalrous behaviors can begin, how extreme they can be, and how they can influence your conduct, personality, or the way in which you interact with other females presently.

Just as rivalry comes in many forms, a "Vicious Vixen" may also appear in a variety of ways and personas. She can be someone at school, a family member, someone at work, or even the neighbor down the street. The shared stories in this chapter reveal everyday occurrences of female rivalry, and for the most part these types of females are peers. They are not typically someone that has direct control over you (so to speak)... so you learn how to avoid her. You learn how to recognize her. You learn how to run away.

But what if you are in a work situation and you can't run away? And you can't hide? What if a vicious vixen appears in a situation that makes your life more difficult? A situation where she isn't a peer? Where you may report directly or indirectly to her but ultimately, it's in a manner that impacts your job? A situation where you feel so, so very stuck.... but when all is said and done, she impacts your paycheck so you can't leave. What then?

That's when a "Bolshie Bully" Boss rears her ugly head. Stayed tuned dear reader, for I'm going to talk about her in the next chapter.

Chapter 5:

Battling With a "Bolshie-Bully" Boss

"There are two powers in the world;
one is the sword and the other is the pen.
There is a great competition and rivalry between the two.
There is a third power stronger than both, that of the women."
—Muhammad Ali Jinnah (Brainy Quotes, 2020).

Tori's Story

"When I worked for a fashion company in New York, I had an awful female boss. Her name was Lucile and she was very much like the boss from the movie, 'The Devil Wears Prada.' But even more so because she had this certain look about her. It was totally all her and it was her thing. She was very intimidating.

I was brought in to grow and change the direction of things. Of course, I knew I'd be met with some resistance. I knew there'd be situations where people were just used to doing certain things. It was an uphill battle to begin with, but then when you're younger than the people you are having to manage when they perceive you in a certain way...It just wasn't easy. And so I've said and thought this... I don't know if it's better to either be really young and have no authority, so that you are not really bothered too much about these types of things. Or to be very seasoned and old enough that no one will question you, because they are all younger than you are.

I worked for Lucille for almost three years. I found out about halfway through my time with her, that she'd been through almost 13 managers in 12 years. And I realized at that point, her going through people like crazy, that there was clearly a problem but I kept hanging on. I didn't think that I could change her, per se. I just thought it's the working world, it's tough out there, it's not going to be easy, but I am going to learn to make this work. I also couldn't lose that job because I needed every penny, I could get my hands on.

She was the type of woman when you walked into the room it could be anyone, not just me. She'd look you in the eye first. It wasn't a friendly look...but definitely a look. It was a visual scan, an assessment top to bottom, then up and down again. It was always a scan. Making sure that everything about you met her very exacting standards. And if it didn't, she would let you know. And when she did that, it didn't matter who was in the room with you, she'd call you out. And it was always appearance-based. Because when you worked for her, you had to look perfect. She called me to come in on my day off, to bring her something. I stopped by the meeting, showered, wearing makeup but was in yoga pants. I went to hand her the paper and of course, I got the head-to-toe scan. 'What are you wearing?' was her very loud, public response. Not a 'thank you' for coming in, just a loud condescending insult. It was hugely embarrassing to me and everyone else as well. I remember that when I left no one would look me in the eye.

She was very much from high society and had that 'couture look,' Armani suits, you name it. She was very made up and had several surgeries. She was very tall and thin. When you saw her from the back, often men would ogle and awe at her...but when she would turn, they would realize that she was much older.

She had married a very wealthy man and the business had pretty much been given to her. Come to find out, she didn't have a lot of business acumen, but she was perceived to have it because she ran in these very high social circles. The storefront, boutique location was in one of the finest fashion neighborhoods, surrounded by the best fashion retailers. Because of her perceived status, she was asked to speak at business schools to give talks on business, but honestly, she couldn't even read a spreadsheet.

We'd go to public events and people would be lined up to get her signature and they'd just be praising her, telling her she was ageless and so amazing, an angel sent down from heaven. My eyes were really opened wide in that environment. It was interesting to see how power, or perceived power, wealth, and fame... Fame in the fashion world that started from these social circles. To see those inner workings and all of that... because I was behind the scenes and it was amazing, in a disbelief type of way. Because truly, she was such an awful, awful person.

I've kept a few of my emails from then. One was from her secretary, the gay man, who totally enabled her behavior and would do things for her and not get any credit. He said, 'I know it's not easy, princess...' as he praised the work I was doing, how my numbers were up, all the while knowing, I wasn't getting any acknowledgment for it either."

Introduction

Rivalrous situations are not good in any circumstance but in a working environment, a variety of feelings can emerge that add to an already emotional condition. Work is how you make a living. It's your support system, a means to an end. Very frequently, it's not so easy to just quit one job and find something new at the drop of a hat. In this type of situation, the chances are high that you are dealing with a female who *isn't* your peer. This suggests that you are dealing with a woman who has some epitome of authority over you. Whether it's control of your paycheck and/or professional standing, this dear reader, is what makes this type of behavior a complete game-changer. This is when it escalates to a whole new level of rivalry. It's not just bad behavior—it's direct control over your livelihood. As a result, it's customary that a woman in this situation feels trapped with no way out like she doesn't have anyone to turn to or trust. She is stuck.

The "Bolshie Bully"

Like a "Vicious Vixen," a "Bolshie Bully" is the "bad actor" that exudes the many persona qualities of female rivalry that I described in Chapter 3. She is "h*ll on wheels" and I'm sure many of you have experienced working with someone like her. Likewise, any one of the previously described personas can apply to a bolshie bully, but not every bolshie bully will display all the traits of the personas. Before diving in too deep about this particular "type" of individual, let me define what a "Bolshie Bully" is.

bol.shie. |bōlSHē|. *adjective.*
"a person or attitude. deliberately combative or uncooperative. defiant. difficult to manage, rebellious" (Merriam Webster, 2020).

bul.ly. |bù-lē|. *noun.*
"a blustering browbeating person. especially one who is habitually cruel, insulting, or threatening to others who are weaker, smaller, or in some way vulnerable. to treat (someone) in a cruel, insulting, threatening, or aggressive fashion" (Merriam Webster, 2020).

As you may have gleaned, this chapter focuses specifically on female rivalry within the working environment. I am going to share examples of how it occurs, the ages it occurs (and let me tell you, no age is off-limits), what it looks like as it pertains to real life, and signs to be aware of.

5.1: Your Turn. Dear reader, have you ever worked for, or been on the receiving end of a "Bolshie Bully" boss? Or, have you ever worked with a "Bolshie Bully" colleague? How did that make you feel? What did you do? When you were experiencing it, did you even know, at the time, that it was happening? Take a moment now to write below, your initial thoughts on what this type of persona means.

_____

_____

_____

_____

Organizational Culture

Besides the fact that the woman you are dealing with could just be a bi*ch, there may also be other contributing factors that are influencing her behavior, and that of your colleagues. It's called "organizational culture," because the culture of an organization greatly impacts its social and psychological settings.

Let's take a quick dive into some historical information about the meaning of "organizational culture." I'll then highlight a few studies that support findings about *how* an organization can contribute to these types of underlying behaviors.

Organizational Culture Defined. Organizational culture broadly defined is, "the underlying beliefs, assumptions, values and ways of interacting that contribute to the unique social and psychological environment of an organization" (Gotham Culture, 2020). Organizational culture specifically, is,

> *"an organization's expectations, experiences, philosophy, as well as the values that guide member behavior, and is expressed in member self-image, inner workings, interactions with the outside world, and*

*future expectations. Culture is based on shared attitudes, beliefs, cus-
toms, and written and unwritten rules that have been developed over
time and are considered valid" (Gotham Culture, 2020).*

Study #1. An organization's culture can foster aggression, competition,
and rivalry, or likewise, it can promote solidarity and trust. Studies on aggression suggest the reason for the behavior of rivalry between women in a working environment relates to its organizational culture (Kanter, 1977; Ely, 1994;
Mavin, 2006a). This viewpoint examines organizational demographics, the
population and particular groups within it, and the corporate culture of gender,
the impact on men and women.

A study conducted (Ely, 1994), noted that in an organizational environment and in the social settings where women work, there are three primary
reasons for rivalry to occur:

1. Sex-integrated organizations,
2. All-female organizations, and
3. Male-dominated organizations.

Ely concluded that the angst that many women experience with other
women in the workplace can be the result of a male-dominated environment
with few women "at the top," in leadership positions. A "healthy" organization
can be looked upon as having a well-represented ratio of men and women, one
that includes female partners promotes healthy competition and also has the
opportunity for collaboration.

Ely's work suggested that male-dominated firms in which women are the
minority promotes negative competition with the "token" women, and will
ultimately foster problems between the females. If you compare organizations
that have many women in leadership positions versus women in organizations
that have fewer senior women in leadership positions—the company with
fewer females will not experience "common gender" as a positive basis for
connecting with each other. The women will be less likely to perceive senior

women as role models with legitimate authority, more likely to perceive competition in relationships with peers, and less likely to find support in these relationships (Ely, 1994, p. 203).

Study #2. In research targeting women in managerial roles, Mavin (2006a) conducted several studies that addressed the topic of Venus Envy, Solidarity Behavior, and the use of the Queen Bee label. From her work, I've surmised the term Venus Envy to be described as a woman of whom other women are envious of. Venus is defined as,

> *"A strong woman. Beautiful on the inside and out. She knows her boundaries. She is comfortable with her sexuality. She is grounded, and in the moment. People are attracted to her looks and personality. She is true, and does what she pleases, she likes to make a difference in the world. She knows who she is and loves life. She's in tune, brave, strong, and interesting" (Urban Dictionary, 2020).*

Mavin's studies focus on the complexity of female relationships, the effect of those negative relationships, and highlights how a gendered social order promotes and inflames the differences between men and women (p. 264). Her work explains the solidarity assumption between women as one, "that assumes that women view other women as their natural allies, regardless of hierarchical differences and that senior women should view the 'women in management mantle' as their individual responsibility" (2006). Solidarity behavior should, in a manner of speaking, bring women together to form alliances, share common goals, and collaborate with one another. This, however, is not always the case. As Greer (2000) stated, "Women are still more likely than men to be disloyal to their same-sex colleagues."

Mavin summarized that the construct of an organization's culture supports the notion that the environment in which one works can influence the behaviors of its workers (Kanter, 1977; Ely, 1994; Mavin, 2006a). In much the same way as the structure of an organization's gender placement impacts the social contexts in which women work, either negatively or positively, a healthy environment should have a good ratio of women and men at all levels within the organization.

Insight about rivalry in the working environment, why it occurs, and what the root causes stem from, provides awareness to the obstacles. Knowledge, as to "why" it occurs, can help the organizational culture and prevent the behavior from continuing. The topic of aggression, specifically aspects of behavior and differences in gender, especially as it pertains to workplace behavior, is very important for awareness of these behavioral obstacles. Ultimately how individuals behave in the workplace, either positively or negatively, impacts the work environment and culture.

> *"Nothing will kill a great employee faster*
> *than watching you tolerate a bad one."*
> —Perry Belcher (Leading with honor, 2020).

Organizational Culture Effects

A toxic work culture is no place for great workers. They simply don't survive because it is difficult to produce when a veil of toxicity shrouds the working environment. In all of the stories I've collected about rivalry at work, in some form or another, every woman described the environment in which she worked as having contributed to the behavior of the "other woman." The organizational culture, or lack thereof, was a direct reflection of the type of support these women in these situations received, from the company they worked for.

> *Corina.* *"My boss was mad that I had to take time off to have surgery. She complained to our director who was a male, and totally terrified of her too. So, he just let her do whatever she wanted. Ultimately, she ended up getting promoted. I just knew that wasn't the right solution. I finally found a new job and left. I loved my co-workers though and I went back and visited sometime later, and they were telling me all of the same stories. Absolutely nothing had changed. That organization didn't know how to handle her even though during the time I was there, they lost four good*

people from her team all because of her horrible behavior. All the women who'd left shared their stories and the reason why they were leaving in their exit interviews. The organization just didn't want to deal with it."

Beatrix. *"The organization that I was in was not only 80% plus male, they were career-focused in that business. And so, any woman, also in that business, was fighting an uphill battle, period, to get equal treatment from her male colleagues."*

Natalie. *"I think there should be ramifications for bad behavior. The more I've read Brené Brown, the more I realized that in my old office environment our female managing principal managed using shame and that is just no way to live. She didn't follow through with consequences. If somebody had done something bad, she'd rake them over the coals but not in an appropriate way. And then, she wouldn't follow through. So we had all these people feeling like they were not living up to some expectation that she said, that was absolutely impossible. And then the people who really should have been weeded out of there...they didn't do anything about them."*

Clio. *"It was all women in our office. The project managers were men, and they came and went. They didn't spend a lot of time in the office. The support staff were women. There was a lot of gossip and behind-the-back fighting because it was all women in a confined space. It was ridiculous."*

Lola. *"At some point, I've seen people walk away, nurses and other staff members, because they are not being supported. And really, that's just money walking out the door...and she'll put it in a non-nice way, saying it's other things. But it's not just money. It's good people, good women, who are leaving because of her."*

Grace. *"I think in a sense, there were instances where there were characteristics of the environment or contract vision and mission that* *she was able to manipulate. Sometimes the whole collaboration, inte-gration, and communication, which were key characteristics of this contract, and the team environment. She twisted or manipulated it all, to benefit her in ways that were not beneficial to the team."*

Sydney. *"I felt like when I went to HR I had no leg to stand on. They alluded that it was personal and not professional...and I knew she was targeting me. They listened to me but also talked to her separately and then decided they weren't going to do anything. It was really disheart-ening that they didn't have my best interest. They were just supporting her as a leader because she'd just been promoted. I was the victim, but they didn't see that."*

Faith. *"I worked at a non-profit family service agency during the time I experienced rivalry with another woman. It was with a woman whom I'd worked with for several years, and to whom I was initially her supervisor. This woman was very forward and aggressive in her approach of wanting my job.*

The on-going behaviors of the other woman caught the attention of the CEO and eventually led to her having a promotion. What evolved over the years is that she got promoted to a supervisory position, and she was really admired by the CEO, and they began to have an affair. The affair was known, but not known. It was like an unspoken thing, but there'd be rumors and people seeing them parked in cars making out. The CEO loved the attention. He was a guy who had three sisters. I think he really sometimes almost set it up to see the females squab-bling over positions or his attention or his promotions or his special perks of going to conferences, etc."

Selena. *"There was an on-going crazy type of behavior. I felt like I had nowhere to go. If I went to her boss or HR, also women, they were afraid to act against her. There were a lot of fearful women who* *wouldn't let their feelings out or tell you they were afraid. And so they just sidestepped everything.*

My same friend that I'd previously confided in at work who saw every-thing that was going on, stepped up and went to the director. She told him I was on edge and if they didn't do something about Tina's crazy behavior, they'd lose me. They didn't do anything. My friend was shocked. In hindsight, I see that the pushover boss was also threatened by this woman too, so he did nothing."

Food for Thought: So, let's think back to the beginning of this chapter and how the culture of an organization contributes to these types of rivalrous behaviors. Do you think there are other factors that I may not have addressed that could be key contributing points? Do you agree or disagree with the orga-nizational culture aspect?

5.2a: Your Turn. Dear reader, have you ever worked for an organization where the culture contributed to negative behaviors? Or, if working now, do you per-ceive your organizational culture to be aware of gender biases? For each of the previous two questions—How did/does that make you feel? Does/did it feel like a safe place to work? Did you like working there? Take a moment now to write below, if one or more of the stories about organizational culture effects have resonated with you and why.

_____

_____

_____

_____

5.2b: Your Turn. Dear reader, if you are in a leadership position, do you per-ceive your organization to be aware of gender bias? What are you adding to the conversation as a leader? Do you see this type of behavior occurring? Do you take gender differences into consideration? Do you see people within our organization stepping in to foster positive change? Take a moment now to write below, your thoughts, and why.

_____

_____

_____

_____

Psychological Safety

In addition to the culture of an organization having an impact on the social and psychological setting… There is another crucial factor that must be taken into consideration. How secure someone is in that setting, regarding to their ability to truly be themselves, will greatly impact how they feel, how they contribute, and how they are able to utilize their full potential.

That "feeling" is defined as "psychological safety,"

> *"Psychological safety refers to an individual's perception of the consequences of taking an interpersonal risk or a belief that a team is safe for risk taking in the face of being seen as ignorant, incompetent, negative, or disruptive. In a team with high psychological safety, teammates feel safe to take risks around their team members. They feel confident that no one on the team will embarrass or punish anyone else for admitting a mistake, asking a question, or offering a new idea" (Bariso, 2020).*

Google conducted a study in 2015, to answer the following question using data and rigorous analysis, "What makes a Google team effective?" Their findings concluded that psychological safety was hands down, first on the list. They discovered that in order for teams to work well together, team members must feel comfortable enough to be themselves (Bariso, 2020).

A psychologically safe environment is one in which team members feel safe to take risks and be vulnerable in front of each other (Rozovsky, 2015).

Emotional Intelligence (EI), is the ability to identify, understand, and manage emotions. It is a key premise for psychological safety in the workplace. I'll talk more about EI in Chapter 11. But as it pertains to building great teams it means the following:

> *"When working on tasks, all teammates get the chance to speak. No single person dominates the conversation. Teams have a high average social sensitivity which means... Individual team members can correctly interpret fellow team members expressions, tone of voice and nonverbal cues. Which ultimately leads them to be more sensitive to teammates feelings during conversations"* (Bariso, 2020).

You may be asking, "Ok, I get all that you are trying to say here, but really, how does this apply to the topic of female rivalry at work?" I'll tell you why dear reader, psychological safety hits the nail right on the head. It's the core, fundamental element of this issue as it pertains to women experiencing rivalry in a working environment.

If a female, or any other team member for that matter, does not feel safe in her environment... if she is scared of her boss, a fellow colleague, or someone in HR, she will not be able to contribute to her full potential. If a female doesn't feel like she can talk to or be listened to, as it pertains to a negative rivalrous type of behavior, she does not feel safe. And if she doesn't feel safe... what happens then? She walks.

When rampant toxicity is widespread in the workplace, good employees are unable to shine. If you don't feel safe in your working environment... would you stay or would you go? I would go. I did go. And the bottom line is (this is an extensive topic for a different book altogether), that women who experience rivalry between another woman at work, more often than not, leave.

This means two things:

1. The woman initiating the harmful behavior stays which means negative behavior is ultimately being rewarded.

2. The woman who is the recipient of the harmful behavior leaves which means talent, time, and money just walked out the door.

Bye-bye, Felicia! Don't let the door hit you where the good Lord split you because she is gone! Many leaders, because it's a topic not talked about, shake their heads in bewilderment because they have no idea why their turnover is so high and why such good people are leaving.

> *Maggie.* "*And after that transition occurred, I never really saw the other people from my team. I never spoke to them again. In fact, when I'd come into town to collaborate, they really just ignored me. Which was great. The old boss mostly avoided me completely and when I left the company she didn't say anything to me at all. I knew she knew that she had screwed up. That she didn't know what to say, or how to handle things. Instead of handling things, she was conflict-averse even when it didn't have to be a conflict at all.*
>
> *And when I sailed out that door for the last time, it was a beautiful experience. For a long time, I was mad how the experience unfolded. But now, I am just more saddened by the fact that the leadership group for this company will never actualize what they truly say they wanted to do. I mean they might be profitable, but they will never achieve the mission they're looking for because they don't empower their leadership. They need a culture shift and their culture was awful. The negative behavior was endorsed, and it was toxic.*"

> *Selena.* "*I'd had it and walked out of a job with nothing lined up. It was just a slow build-up, and hard to name because a lot of her actions were intangible. But they hit you hard emotionally and were so passive-aggressive. And sometimes, you are just knee-deep in and you're completely miserable and it just hits you.*"

5.3: Your Turn. Dear reader, have you heard of psychological safety as it pertains to the working environment? Have you ever experienced a situation where you felt unsafe at work? Are you familiar with Emotional Intelligence (EI)? Do you agree or disagree, about the concept of EI playing a fundamental role in psychological safety at work? Take a moment now to write below, if one or more of the stories about organizational culture effects have resonated with you and why.

_____

_____

_____

_____

Types of Workplace Rivalry

There are many different types of workplace rivalry scenarios. So many, in fact, that I know I will not be able to cover them all. Plus, each situation is quite unique and different. Frequently, rivalrous behaviors aren't just from a boss, manager, senior leader, etc. Sometimes it's negative behavior from a co-worker, colleague, or someone that in general, just feels threatened by you and the work you are doing.

First Job Rivalry. Think back to your first job out of college. You were young, naïve, and probably wanted to please. You were new to an organization and eager to learn. You may not have had much power but you were willing to grow, develop, and ultimately advance within the organization.

Edith's Story. *"It was my first job out of school and I went to work for a manufacturing company, and it was pretty cool. But the woman who was the accounting manager, and my boss, well, she was crazy. I mean everybody knew it, but it was my first experience with a micro-manager, so to speak. And that's when I realized that I wasn't going to be able to work for people like that. For example, no matter what it was, if there was a deadline or not, it was her hard and fast rule that once a month you had to work all day on a Saturday. We were already working long hours during the week. A really good friend of mine got married on one of the Saturdays I was scheduled to work, and she wouldn't let me go to the wedding.*

She was gone on vacation one time and one of our team members asked me how to do something because she was out of the office. I told her what she needed to do. The next day our boss came back to work and just tore into that poor girl because she didn't wait and ask her. She was my supervisor and needed to be a bit hands-on I guess, but she was ruthless. She had the need for control or was insecure or threatened. I am not sure what it was...but she felt the need to make somebody else's life miserable to feel better about herself. For whatever reason, it's totally messed up thinking, but I could tell she wanted to show me who was boss."

Wants Your Job Rivalry. It may be that you work in the same organization, but you got the promotion, not her. It could be that internally she was the best candidate for the job, but they instead hired you, an outsider. Whatever the reason may be, she wants your job, feels it should be hers and she deserves it.

Maggie's Story. *"My position was created for me... The president of the company said we needed this new type of position and mentioned my name, and said, 'go get this girl, she does really well.' And my boss seemed excited because I'd already done this type of work for another organization, and she said, 'Oh, I've heard nothing but amazing things about you.'*

But then with her, it was a personality conflict the entire time. She'd show up and say something to me but then go and do something else entirely with other people. She wouldn't follow through on common behavior. She wouldn't follow through with anything as it pertained to me. She didn't have time for me. She consistently cancelled our one-on-one meetings. I had no feedback from her at all. It turned out that I became the 'fall guy' or the 'fall girl' in this case.

I was on this team for three years. My first year there my boss gave me a sub-par performance review, something I'd never had before. One night she got drunk at a group dinner and said, 'Maggie, you could do a better job than me.' And I said, 'I don't want your job.' Because at that point, I knew there was no changing anything."

Hates You Rivalry. It doesn't matter what you do or say, chances are her opinion about you was formed the moment she laid eyes on you. Add to that the fact that you are now working in "her territory," it doesn't bode well for you that things will improve. As you continue to work together, there may be other factors that influence her decision but simply said, she just doesn't like you and she may never will. Just remember, it's her, not you.

Katrina's Story. *"When I first started working at a small firm, doing the exact same job but for different clients, Darcy had already been there 11 years, who had more seniority over me. Although we both were married, we also had a lot of differences. She was 10 years younger than me; a Jehovah's witness. I was a Christian. She was a little bit overweight... I wasn't. And to top it off, she was extremely self-righteous, very neat and clean, and very much into herself.*

I worked my tail off and my desk would look like a bomb went off and then I'd go in her office and her desk was always super clean. I made a comment once like, 'Wow, it looks like you're doing a whole lot in here. Your desk is so neat.' And I don't even remember her even look-ing at me, but she said, 'The proof is in the pudding, honey.' Oh, she was such a b*tch. I mean I hated this woman. In my head, I called her every name in the book and then went home and complained about it. She made my life so miserable right from the beginning. The first week

I actually thought she was nice and then all of that changed. We ended up working together for 3 1/2 years.

So, she was always ahead of me in fulfilling her quotas. She was always above me in our meetings. Even though I did a really good job, we both were always ranked number one and number two, as the top two consultants for our practice. Her number one. Me number two. I never really felt like I was in competition with her, I was just doing my job. But she'd been there long, and was threatened by me because I was right behind her. She was really good at her job. I was always amazed. I always had the utmost respect for her in the aspect of her job knowledge and how good she was.

But her personality, that was a different story. I truly thought that she was an evil person and I would hear her on the phone with her husband. And she horrible to him. She would say things like, 'Bob, I told you that I'll be home at five o'clock. When I get there, I expect you to have that car packed, us ready to leave for our trip, the house is in order and gas in the car. Do you have any questions?' That literally is how she talked to her husband and I'd be sitting in my office going, 'Holy cow, I'd be leaving her if I were him!' She was brutal. She treated me that way too, as well as the other office staff, who also were female. The only one that loved her was the head client partner, who was a man.

Because she always produced and always did such a good job, they never got rid of her. She truly though, was like a cancer in the place. The office manager had a hard time with her and couldn't stand her either. She'd confide in me saying, 'Katrina, don't let Darcy push you around and don't let her treat you that way. Stand up for yourself! I'm behind you.' She was always encouraging me.

I was in the job about two years when the client partner took Darcy, me, and two other women to L.A. for a conference... I didn't have to *share a room with her, but I had to deal with her closely in regard to meals, going to events, and showcasing our firm. She continually would roll her eyes at me, judge me and you know, just looking me up and down. Saying things like, 'Well that's an interesting choice of shoes that you are wearing.' She would do things like that all the time. I was like, 'Really, b*tch?' (to myself of course). I called her a b*tch more than anything.*

While we were there the client partner showed me some attention and made a comment about how beautiful I looked one evening. He wasn't flirting, he was just being a nice man and said, 'Wow, you look beautiful tonight, Katrina.' I said, 'thank you.' And I'll never forget, we were on a rooftop deck with various heights of seating watching the sunset and I wanted to get on the higher stool to see better. But I couldn't get up. I was trying to get myself up when he said, 'I'll put you up there.' And before I could say yay or nay, he picked me up and put me up on the higher stool. Oh, that pissed her off. She was rolling her eyes, sighing, and getting all huffy.

Darcy and I had to stay over one more night because the last day of the convention was just for consultants. Everyone else went home so I had to share a room with her. I was just dreading it but moved all my stuff into her room. We ended up going to dinner and having sushi. I drank a whole bottle of Saki by myself and thought, 'I'm going to get drunk because I just can't put up with this anymore!' She of course said, 'You're drinking a lot.' During that dinner, we had a very blunt and ugly conversation. She told me that she was highly disappointed in my behavior with the client partner, that we both were married, that I was flirting with him, and how dare I? I said, 'Girl, you are smoking some sort of crack because I was just being polite.' She was holier than thou and I didn't understand where her attack was coming from. I basically told her she was crazy. I said, 'I don't know what your problem is. Since day one when I first started at this place, you've been such a *b*tch to me.' We basically had it out that night during dinner and the whole time I was still drinking Saki. After our meal, I said, 'Listen, let's just call it like it is. I don't like you and you don't like me. And we are in L.A right now, it's our last night here and we're sharing a room. So we've got two choices, we can either go our separate ways, you go figure out what you want to do and I'll go do what I want to do, or we could suck it up because we're two single women in a new city and we shouldn't be alone. We could try to deal with each other and enjoy this beautiful night. What's it going to be?'*

She said, 'Well, I guess we'll stay together.' So, we did. We walked to the beach and it was a gorgeous night with a full moon and perfect weather. And there was, I kid you not, an amazing fireworks show. And I said to her, 'This is the most beautiful experience I think I've ever had. This is amazing.' She's like, 'I know.' It's like that broke the ice a little bit. We continued our evening and went and got ice cream. While we're having ice cream, we sort of came to a little bit of a truce that we would try to overcome our differences and that we would try to do the best that we could to, you know, get along. We made a joint decision that we were both going to try.

Tuesday morning however, back in the office, Darcy was back in b*tch mode. So, by then, I was just done. I chalked her behavior up to really that's just who she was and I knew I was just going to have to just deal with it... Fast forward several months, we hated each other personally but we actually had a very good working relationship. We were so opposite to each other, that we complemented one another. I didn't like her, but my strengths were her weakness and vice versa. We used to say we were yin and yang. I think that's the one thing that let us work together for so long.

We had to tag-team each other when one of us went on vacation, which ended up being double the workload. I got back after being gone for a week and said, 'Hey I'm back.' And she looked at me and just burst into tears. I was floored because she was so cold-hearted, she never cried. She didn't tell me what was wrong. She just said, 'I can't tell you. I know we don't even really like each other. But I'm asking you to give me some space, to support and cover me. Because there might be times I'm going to need to dip out of the office and I don't want anybody to know where I'm going.' I said, 'Ok.' I thought she was sick but she wouldn't tell me. This behavior went on for a week or two. She'd start crying and was really depressed. I gave her the space she needed and covered for her. Then I had to drop the news that I was moving and would be leaving the practice. She said, 'You can't leave. You can't leave me!' She was freaking out. I was freaking out. Finally, she told me what had been going on. Her husband of 12 years had just left her. I was thinking, 'It's about time!' But told her I was sorry. She was devastated.

On my last day in the office, I said, 'Darcy, it's my last day here, would you like to go to dinner tonight, my treat?' She said, 'I'd love to.' So, we went to sushi, which I chose on purpose for obvious reasons from our L.A. trip. We had a heart-to-heart talk and basically reinstated and reinforced everything that we'd been feeling the previous years when working together. We weren't each other's favorite person, but we'd grown to like each other towards the end of our time together, because of how we supported one another. We'd found a common ground. But I'll tell you this now, when I left, I was like, 'Sayonara b*tch, I hope I never talk to you again.' Even though we'd patched things up, I thought that would be the end of it. I'd never see or talk to her again, and that made me happy."

Jealous of You Rivalry. The big green ugly monster called envy consumes her as it pertains to everything about you. Even to the point that extends outside of the workplace...Your office, your looks, your life, your clients, your clothes, your children, your social etiquette, the car you drive, your performance reviews… You name it and she is jealous of you for it. This default in her behavior stems from something internal, that she is not happy with herself, but you end up taking the brunt of her wrath.

> ***Sydney's Story.*** *"She would insult me all the time. She would tear me down in front of other people. She was very demeaning, very hostile. It was awful. She sometimes was nice to my face but would then rip me apart behind my back and other people would tell me about it.*
>
> *She was about my age. I'm 58, she was 52. She was very frumpy and married to a much older man who was almost 80. I keep myself in good shape, have blonde hair, wear make-up, and enjoy picking out clothes. She never wore makeup and looked much older than she really was. Yes, so I think that was a part of it too…If we're going to get down to talking about women, we've also got to talk about physical appearances because I think she was threatened by mine and that's why she treated me as she did."*

Just Wants You Gone Rivalry. Unbeknownst to you, you inadvertently push all her buttons. In her mind, you make her look bad, you are better than she is, she will never be enough compared to you… so she just wants you to go. Come h*ll or high water, she will find a way to make that happen.

> ***Maggie's Story.*** *"I went to my boss and said, 'This just isn't working,' referencing how the department could be better structured. I then shared with her how I would restructure the department to make it more effective, so that we could have people at different levels to achieve our organizational goals, together. She said no.*
>
> *A year later, she told the team she was going to restructure the department and said, 'this is what I have planned.' And no joke, it was the plan I'd shared with her. The exact plan along with everything I'd*

outlined for her the year before. Then she looked at me and said, 'Oh by the way Maggie, we're eliminating your position.'

So, by this point, I knew her game and how to play it. I said, 'You're going to have to do it this way. Why don't you hire somebody here, and then have me here?' She asked, 'Who would be a good leader?' And I named a woman whom I'd hired on my team and said, 'I think this person would be an amazing leader. I think you should interview her.' And this person became my new boss. And it was amazing because she also recognized all of the cr*p that was occurring."

Threatened by You Rivalry. Because of your differences and her insecurity about herself, she is threatened by you. If she is in a position of control or authority over you, she will be the "h*ll-on-wheels" type of boss. She will go to great lengths to make you feel inadequate. She will make your life a living h*ll.

Selena's Story. *"I worked for a lady named Tina. She was about ten years older than me. She was the director and I was the associate manager. I'd come up with an idea and she helped me put it together but then she changed it and I didn't agree with what she was doing, and I told her so. I was very direct, opinionated, and confident and I know she didn't like that. I think it reminded her of what she wasn't. She doubted herself and I think she didn't want to be reminded that I was different than she was, so instead she took it out on me.*

She told me, 'I know you are a high performer and good at what you do but I would much rather work with someone who is not as high performing and easier to get along with. I'd rather have someone on my team who is softer, and easier to get along with than someone like you.'

I don't think she had an issue with the other women on our team, it was just me. Tina didn't like my energy as a person. I had a strong personality and she didn't like it. She didn't want me on her team if I couldn't operate like her, the kind of person who was soft and people-pleasing. There were a few times when I knew I didn't have any meetings but didn't want her breathing down my neck, I would hide in my friends' office. She'd search everything yelling, 'Where is she? Where is she?' There was no specific reason she was looking for me. We didn't have a scheduled meeting. She just needed her power. One time, my friend told me, 'That crazy woman is circling this whole building looking for you.' She would keep tabs on me via instant messaging and ask me what I was doing. She did not allow me to have any boundaries. She could have them, but I could not.

She would look at me when we were on calls and say, 'Do not speak until I tell you to.' I was supposed to be interacting with clients, but I couldn't speak. I was supposed to be having interaction with clients and I wasn't allowed to speak. I'd never experienced being somewhere where I wasn't allowed to speak or to interact. It was very new to me. She was controlling and it was crazy. I was no longer enabled to be a high performer. She didn't want me to be strong, but she wanted to use me, for her to thrive. My thriving though, was not in her major interest."

Other Workplace Rivalries. There are a lot of other types of workplace rivalries that I have not directly named or called out. Some women too, are just mean, catty, and have nothing nice to say. Here are some other examples.

Tina's Story. *"Being young in the workplace wasn't too much of an issue. As far as being young, as long as you weren't in a position with too much power, it wasn't too much of an issue. You know, some of the older ladies would notice you and then make comments about you... Or if the doctors noticed you, they'd really have something snide to say about you that wasn't nice."*

Lola's Story. *"So, I have very close relationships with our patients because I see them from the onset. And when they get to our unit, I've* *already formed these relationships with them. And I don't know if it's because these families trust me if she's threatened by that? She's like the Queen Bee. She treats people, women specifically, very poorly. There's always some type of turnover from nurses going in one direction or the other, based upon what they want to do. It's not uncommon. And when they give their notice to her, she is cruel and evil to them. I mean it's just awful. We once had a nurse that was sexually harassed by a doctor, and this woman took his side. He's since been fired for that exact thing. She just doesn't like women. Several nurses have left because of her. There's a pattern there but no one does anything about it. Higher-ups fear her or the retribution she'll cause because she's worked there for so long. For whatever reason, it just hasn't caught up to her yet. But it's there, the pattern, a theme of rivalry I can see it so clearly. But once it goes over the cuff, it's emotional bullying and it's not physical bullying. But it's still a rivalry."*

Melissa's Story. *"I look back now and see how Naomi treated other women. She abruptly hired and then fired them. Not even because they were doing something wrong but because she simply decided she no longer wanted them around. Shortly after the opening, she executed a big wave of firing people whom she thought were talking about her, to her sister. One woman who'd simply had enough of the egregious behavior and how Naomi treated the other women, quit... She legitimately resigned, giving two-week's notice. Instead of just letting her leave on her own, Naomi sent her a nasty email that said, 'I wish that you receive pain and misery in your future because this isn't how you should treat people.' Seriously, who does that? I was shocked."*

Bonnie's Story. *"I work with a woman a couple of years younger than me who I've worked with for about three years. I really don't know what I've ever done to her. I've tried to establish if she's immature or whatever, as the reason for how she treats me. We have very different roles but we work in the same department, and sometimes we have to* *work very closely with one another. I don't know if she's threatened by my number of years at the hospital, and the number of people that I know who will say to her, 'Oh, have you talked to Bonnie about this?' She will keep things from me to prove that she can do something on her own, but then it will ultimately hurt the patient's discharge. I usually find out about it either because: 1) my team is paging me that the patient is being discharged or 2) by conducting a simple chart review. She just won't come to me with anything. It's almost like she does the opposite of what should be done, just to spite me. And it really doesn't hurt me at all—it ultimately hurts the patient and makes her do more work in the long run.*

She's not rude to my face but she's rude behind my back. I know this because other people frequently tell me about it. I've got very strong ties at work that come from being there for almost 20 years. And the thing is, it just backfires against her. They'll say, 'Do you know so and so is saying this about you?' She was spreading rumors that I was responsible for her coworkers' removal from the unit which I didn't play a part in at all. I do think that's where this animosity from her comes from. She'll tell my colleagues that I'm mean, that I don't like her, that I withhold things from her, etc... Her co-worker was removed after a year and a half of working together. That's when it all started...I think she was bullied by another hospital worker. I believe she has a co-dependency type of working relationship with people. If I took her out to coffee and just tried to talk about it, she would deny it. She'd probably be mortified."

Corina's Story. *"I worked in an art museum and had a female boss who was a bit older than me and single. We had an all-female team, and I didn't realize how bad it was until we hired a man. I thought it was because I was one of the newer team members and perhaps just seeing things differently... She wrote an evaluation about me and sent it to the director before letting me see it. She'd tell me I didn't have* *an initiative, but she was having me do small, tasked, mundane types of things. I was used to running programs. I finally broke down to our marketing person who said, 'She's the biggest b*tch I've ever met. I've gone home and cried so many nights.' I was like, 'Thank goodness! I'm not alone!'*

There was one day when I was sick, I was throwing up in the trashcan next to her desk. She said, 'you're not going home, you have a shift to do.' Our HR person was a mama hen and said, 'Corina, grab your coat and go.' And they both went at it for a bit. My boss said, 'She can stay.' And the HR director said, 'No, you can't decide that.' All the women on our team got in trouble about everything from this woman. We were all afraid of her."

5.4: Your Turn. Dear reader, as you read the various types of rivalry that can occur at work did one resonate with you? Have you had this type of behavior from a colleague? If you haven't had it happen to you, have you seen it happen to someone you know? Have you ever projected a certain type of "Bolshie Bully" behavior toward someone else? Take a moment now to write below, if one or more of the "Bolshie Bully" examples have resonated with you and why.

_____

_____

_____

_____

Now that you're reading some specific stories and examples you may be wondering, "Ok, I can see how big this type of behavior is at work, but what are some specific behaviors to look out for, to be aware of, and to know if it's impacting me?" The following are key signs to be aware of that you may be dealing with a "Bolshie Bully."

Eight Signs You're Dealing With a 'Bolshie Bully" Boss

1. **Undermines Your Work.** She purposefully detains or impedes career advancement or impairs assignment or project success. She withdraws from promises or commitments and wavers from between being supportive and/or critical behavior.

   Ruby. "A couple of times she promised me an upcoming project, something she knew I was excited about... But when the time came to begin work, she always had an excuse why I was no longer going to work on it. She always had an excuse, 'Well yes, we did talk about that as a 'potential', but I feel your other workload is just too heavy right now.' OR 'I know you want to work on this, but Siena needs more to do so I am going to give it to her.' Likewise, if I voiced that there was something I didn't love doing, somehow that seemed to always land on my lap, 'Yes, I know you don't care for the communications aspect of this but you are just so good at writing that I feel this needs your personal touch.' It was so frustrating. It got to where I didn't voice my thoughts, positive or negative, because she always changed things and I knew the outcome would be unfavorable to me. I really just didn't believe anything she said."

2. **Creates Conflict.** She turns peers against each other with initiating "she-said/ she-said" types of conversations. (i.e. "Oh did you know that Lucy told me you said this?") She displays subtle actions to create conflict amongst peers or reports against a supervisor. She'll instigate behind-the-scenes scenarios of conflict versus collaboration, issued by a divide and conquer method, cultivating a culture of distrust.

   Grace. "The rivalry that I experienced with her was very insidious because she would always smile and grin to my face, but then I would find out after the fact that she was doing things to undercut the team and our camaraderie. She said to me, 'It should be me in your position, not you.' Because she felt she should be the one in the position of leading the team (not me) she would meet with clients without inform-ing me or the rest of our team about it."

3. **Removes Responsibility.** She'll assign work and then take it away. She may also assign the same work to a peer or different team member. She will remove enjoyable and interesting work by lessening your current workload to lower-level, entry-level functions with unclear goals and little instruction. She will do these things on the pretense of "helping" you.

Autumn. "She would assign me with a project or team to lead and then in a different meeting that I was no longer invited to, would turn around and purposefully give the same work to a different female in our group. This resulted in a duplication of efforts that was unbe-knownst to either of us. It happened a few times and always came out later in a joint meeting. On several occasions, we combined our efforts, and the team or assignment then went to another team member to lead, not me. Our manager always feigned ignorance that such a miscommunication had occurred and played it off that we were collab-orating, instead of doing the exact same work."

4. **Promotes Isolation and Exclusion.** She will purposely exclude you from certain meetings, or email lists, and refuse to share essential information that you need to achieve your goals. She'll provide mis-information about events, decisions, discussions, and intentionally not share feedback or follow-through on performance reviews. She'll con-tribute to lies, office gossip, and rumors to cause discomfort and anx-iety. It's also not out of the question that she'll relocate you to isolate you from the rest of the team.

Rachel. "I started a Corporate Affairs position that was a 'bucket-list' big deal to me because it was my segue to get to the State Department. I knew my new boss didn't like me from the onset. I could feel it the first day I joined her team. There was no like, 'Hi, welcome to work.

It's nice to meet you.' Nothing. Although I felt it, I just chalked it up to cultural differences.

After a couple of weeks, my boss said she didn't have an office for me anymore, so she had someone help me pack my boxes and move me to a vacant office space in the Economics building several floors away from the rest of the team. Two weeks later, she moved me to another vacant office. I had absolutely no contact with the rest of the team. I was trying to understand what my job was. I knew I'd been hired to write communications plans but I also had to understand the culture, who was doing what, and understand what was going on.

We had a weekly meeting that she would cancel, always right before we were supposed to meet. Since I'd started working for her, I never once had a one on one with her. Yet, she would tell people that she had no idea what I was doing because we hadn't met yet insinuating, I was to blame. Basically, nobody interacted with me at all until six weeks into my job, not even my boss."

5. **Employs Intimidation.** She'll use fear-based tactics to issue veiled threats about employability, future career trajectory, or professional reputation. Even though she says she will have your back or best interest at hand, she will conveniently "forget" or "misplace," and fail to support or endorse you for advancement or accolades.

   Beatrix. *"The door closed, and she came around the workstation, spun my chair around, leaned down face-to-face, and said, 'You have been told you're wonderful. I've heard so much about the great Beatrix and this is what I get. You are an idiot! You are so stupid! Everything you said in there was a complete embarrassment to you. I was trying to get you to shut up and you weren't even smart enough to take my signals. You just humiliated yourself. And if you want your career to continue, you better just shut up and let me do the talking!'"*

6. **Manipulates Through Rationalizing and Minimizing.** She will purposefully ignore reasonable concerns and minimize things to defend other types of behaviors, causing you to have feelings of self-doubt. You will feel like you are the problem but will have no clear insight as to how to remedy the situation because it's not something tangible that you can address.

Rachel. "It got to the point where we had check-in meetings every single morning with the entire team. And some days, she would just skip me, even though I was in person with the rest of the team and act like I wasn't there, like I wasn't a contributor. This type of random behavior continued. Then this past spring, she went to the Secretary and said we can't do all of our work unless we are a combined unit. He said, 'Ok, do what you have to do.' So, she organized a big reorg and combined the Public Affairs with another office. The coup de gras is, she completely wrote me out of it. Literally. She took my job, got rid of it, and never once told me about it. She froze me out of a job, cut me off emails and meetings, and didn't tell my team. I found out about it on the morning of my birthday via email.

I was very concerned and knew I had to find another job quickly, which I did. Unfortunately, I had to go through her to be transferred. When I told her about the new position, she said, 'Well, I'm not going to give this to somebody with your kind of attitude. Absolutely not!' At that point, I could not go into her office without having someone with me because her language had gotten abusive. I knew it was an uphill battle with her, and one I was never going to win."

7. **Acts Inconsistently.** She will portray unpredictable behavior and display varying shifts of emotion; you won't know which personality will show up or when. She'll provide unsupported criticism and errant blame for unfounded behaviors. She'll issue unreasonable requests to

work late or come in for early meetings, and instill impractical deadlines or cancel pre-planned vacation or leave.

Clio. *"And all of a sudden Laurie comes flying down the stairs screaming at me, 'Why didn't you tell me we were going to lunch, you b*tch! I said I was going to go get the birthday card, and you knew! And I can't believe it! I'm sick and tired of you trying to undermine me and make me look bad!'"*

8. **Withholds Recognition and Takes Credit.** She'll refuse to give recognition of work you've done and will take credit for, or give credit to, another individual for something you have accomplished.

Eleni. *"She took credit for all of the work I was doing and presented it as hers to senior leadership. And then when things started falling apart within the department, she started blaming me and throwing me under the bus for what was happening."*

5.5: Your Turn. Dear reader, did sharing the "Eight Signs You're Dealing With a Bolshie Bully Boss," help to clarify some specific behaviors to look out for, to be aware of, and to know if someone like her, is impacting you at work? When you read the above descriptions, did anything resonate with you? Have you ever had or been on the receiving end of a "Bolshie Bully?" Or maybe, have you ever projected a certain type of "Bolshie Bully" behavior toward someone else within the office environment? Take a moment now to write below, if one or more of the "Bolshie Bully" examples have resonated with you and why.

_____

_____

_____

_____

The Elephant in the (Board)Room

The environment in which a woman works should be a haven where she feels safe. In some form or another, these combined, shared stories mention an environment that contributes to, even supports, the behavior of the "other woman."

Rivalry exists and currently is an issue for many women in the workplace. Hopefully, these stories will open your eyes on a broader level to better understand why these behaviors are occurring at work. On a strategic level, there is an implied connection between workplace performance and organizational success. On a tactical level, there is overall employee success, which includes personal wellbeing, job satisfaction, and happiness. In the working environment of today, women need each other to succeed and advance. Female working relationships fluctuate and can vary from one extreme (positive) to the other (negative).

Whether it's a male-dominated organization, an atmosphere that prioritizes performance over competency, a passive environment that lets inappropriate behaviors slide, a psychologically unsafe environment, or a company that's simply unequipped to deal with improper behavior... the women who shared their stories were not appropriately protected. In several instances, these women were not perceived as needing help. Often the fear and apprehension of vocalizing the situation kept them silent.

Many corporations are not effectively dealing with the situation by failing to provide necessary support to females encountering rivalry at work. As a result, they are losing valuable employees. Trust me, I've seen it. These women will eventually reach their tipping point, get fed up, and leave. And leadership doesn't have a clue for the reason why.

The big fat pink elephant in the corporate (board)room sitting in her chair in the corner watching all of us. The one that we tip-toe around, wave and say hello to, constantly trip over but never actually stop and talk to, needs to be addressed. "She" needs to be brought out in the open and the negative behaviors dealt with, head-on.

Organizational communication needs to be transparent. Companies need to recognize the signs before, when, and not just after it occurs. When there is overall cultural awareness about what it is and what the outcomes of indirect aggressive and passive-aggressive behaviors between women in the workplace are, preemptive measures can be instilled to address these behaviors in a positive manner. Until it's talked about, the elephant in the (board)room will not go away.

For the most part, rivalry is viewed as negative. However, in some instances rivalry can be viewed as positive, especially when it creates awareness for change. A "healthy" organization can be looked upon as having a positive ratio of men and women, one that includes female partners which promotes healthy competition, and encourages collaboration.

5.6: Your Turn. Dear reader, maybe you haven't experienced female rivalry personally, but have you ever witnessed an "Elephant in the Board(Room)" in an organization you've worked at? What other thoughts come to mind? Take a moment now to write below.

_____

_____

_____

_____

Closing

Regarding this type of behavior, organizations appear to be "just coping." The environment in which women work is a direct attribute of the behavioral outcomes. The "catfights" affect more than just the two women directly involved. It affects the culture as a whole. The negative behavior is infectious; if left unaddressed, it will influence the morale of the entire group.

Each woman who shared her story and gave voice to this topic felt lost in the organization in which she worked. In addition to being rejected by the "other woman," she was neglected by her company. Her environment should have been a safe haven, but it failed to support her. Ultimately in order to find solace and peace, many of them left the environment in which they worked.

After reading all of these stories from the last few chapters, you may be thinking, "Ok, I get that there are lots of types of rivalries, personas, and situations for it to occur... but why in the world don't these women fight back? What's wrong with them?"

That, dear reader, is a great question! I had very similar thoughts until I dove deep into the research. And then of all things, it happened to me and I too, lost my voice. There is actually a very good, scientific reason why many of these women don't speak out. Now I bet you *are* curious! Read on... You'll learn more about "why" in the next chapter.

Chapter 6:

The Freeze Factor

"Fear of a bully; fear of a volcano,
the power within you does not distinguish.
It does not recognize degree."
—N.K. Jemisin (Goodreads, Inc., 2020).

Lindsey's Story

"One day, first thing in the morning, out of the blue my female boss showed up unannounced. She knew I had a big meeting with one of our main clients because it was on our mutual shared calendar. She arrived and said, 'I'm going with you because I need to see how all of this is happening.' I said, 'Okay, they've spent $6M will us this year and I expect it will be the same next year and grow actually because we've met all of their metrics and it's been very positive.' I

153

firmly believed what I'd told her because up until that point, it had been very positive.

When we arrived at the meeting she literally screamed at the supply/ procurement contact who was in charge of that division which included vendors and contingent workers. She said, 'You need to just stop blocking us and let us get all the way to the executives because clearly we've done good work. So why can't we just advance? Why are we still in whatever bucket we are in when we've been doing great work here? This just needs to go away and you just need to deal with it!'

My relaying it doesn't do it justice because honestly, she just totally went off on the guy. He'd initially been contentious and very hard to deal with, but he was also someone who up until that point, I'd developed a good working relationship with. While she was openly yelling at this guy he said, 'You know what, this isn't working, and everybody just needs to step out and we're going to figure out if there will be a next step.'

So as the meeting ended and as she went storming out, I tried to talk to our contact and said, 'I'm really sorry how that went down. I know that got completely out of hand. Can we follow up another time and start over?' He didn't say a word, shook his head, put up his hand, and walked away. I never saw him again.

When I got outside, my boss started yelling at me, 'What did you do? How did it come down to this?' I said, 'Everything before was fine, we were going in there to talk about contract renewal.' She said, 'I think you've really done damage to this relationship. I am hoping that he calls me when calmer heads prevail so that we can talk through this, but I don't think you should be involved with this account again. This is a HUGE problem. It's our biggest account and I'll be taking it over now. How can you manage anything? How can you even lead this practice?'

It was her yelling and extreme crazy behavior that was the downfall of that meeting. She never acknowledged it, that she had anything to do with it. It was all on me. And I just sat there, stunned and quiet, looking at my laptop, thinking, 'this can't be happening to me.' She was on a bender, and I didn't say anything to her or anyone else because she was my boss, and I was powerless to do so."

The Urban Legend

The simple force of the female dynamic in female-to-female relationships can be powerful. Whether it's divulged via negative or positive behaviors, there is truth in this one-on-one relationship between the so-called, "gentler sex." Are we gentler? As you've seen through the earlier stories that I have shared, there is evidence that we are harsher, more conniving, and more contemptuous but in a less blatant observational way. It is in more of a "behind the scenes" manner.

There is a common myth that women are harder on each other than they are on men... Is it really a myth or stone-cold truth? I think it's not a myth. I agree with it. I've seen it. I've heard it. I've studied it. And because of my gender as a female, I've experienced it.

In the research I've done and the work I've conducted on this topic, it often appears that this judgement, rivalry, and detachment between women stems from a wounded place inside of the "other woman." She feels she is not enough, is not *good* enough, inadequate, and insecure about herself. Enough so that she has an intolerance for women who are secure and confident with who they are. It is this intolerance that feeds fuel to the fire. Dr. Chesler (2001) reaffirms the power between women and the diverse types of relationships that women have with one another.

Indeed, the primary target of women's aggression, hostility, violence, and cruelty are other women. As most women know, a woman can make life h*ll, on a moment-by-moment basis, for any other woman whom she envies, fears, or with whom she must compete for resources. For example, older women and all-female cliques tend to bully girls *and women into submission; cliques shun any women whom they view as prettier, smarter, sexually freer, or 'different.' Female rivalries tend to support, not disrupt, the status quo. Thus, in order to survive or to improve their own lot, most women, like men, colluded in the subordination of women as a class (p. 37).*

Startling Behavior

Have you ever been in a situation, either at work or personally, where you felt verbally attacked or bullied? Did you feel paralyzed with disbelief, shock, or fear? Did you feel like you had lost your voice? Did you feel ashamed because when the incident occurred, you didn't stick up for yourself, respond, or fight back? Did you think there was something you could or should have done differently with your own behavior that would have prevented the negative experience from happening? Did you think, perhaps if you had changed your behavior or said something else, the confrontation would not have transpired? At some later point after the conflict took place, did you think of all the things you could have said, or done in which to regain your power or find your voice? Later, were you also angry... at yourself, at the other person?

The aggressive acts of behavior, indirect or direct, portrayed by the other woman are often so startling to receive that you are caught off-guard and unaware of how to properly handle the situation. As a result, the behavior is frequently left unaddressed. This lack of self-acknowledgement adds to the confusion and rollercoaster of emotions that women experience in this type of situation.

> **Hannah.** *"I never wanted to even bring it up because it was uncomfortable."*

> **Tina.** *"I was just mortified. I wish I'd been a bigger person to be able to confront her about it. Instead, I just let it go."*

> **Melanie.** *"I tried to bring it up to my friends but it was just so uncomfortable to talk about. I knew they'd seen it but maybe too, they also felt*

bad for not doing anything about it. So, in the end, it wasn't something we discussed even though we all knew it was there, hanging over us."

Rubi. *"I didn't tell anyone when it was happening because it was hard to absorb all of the passive-aggressive actions to make them tangible actions, to then in turn, tell someone else about what it was I was experiencing... I also didn't know who to turn to or who would believe me. And at that moment, it was hard to digest everything that she was doing. It wasn't really until I was out of the situation that I was able to clearly see it and by then, there was no way I was going back to tell anyone about it."*

6.1: Your Turn. Dear reader, have you ever been on the receiving end of extreme behavior, projected at you verbally or physically, and you froze? Have you had times when you simply had no means in which to respond? How did that make you feel? What did you do? When you were experiencing it, did you even know, at the time, that it was happening? How did you feel about it after the fact? Take a moment now to write below, your initial thoughts on what this type of behavior means.

_____

_____

_____

_____

Female Bullying

I recently read an article (Houlis, 2018) about female bullying in the work environment. It stated that 70% of high-performing females in leadership positions feel bullied by other women at work. These women also felt that by being the recipient of a workplace bully their professional growth was negatively impacted. Additionally, it was reported that someone who has been bullied is more prone to bullying someone else as a result of what they have experienced.

While these insights are staggering, sadly, I am not surprised. Professional and personal female competition has no boundaries. When it comes to a rivalrous attack, nothing is off-limits. And when it escalates to a constant, repetitive, ruthless rivalry, it is bullying. Rivalry and bullying types of behavior have the same effect on the victim and perpetrator. In both types of behavior, the victim feels powerless, intimidated, and out of control. In rivalry and bullying types of behaviors, it is not uncommon for a victim to lose their self-confidence, their voice, and their passion.

If you've been the recipient of rivalry, bullying, physical, or aggressive behaviors, empirical evidence claims there are factual reasons why you lost your voice and may not have been able to defend yourself. If any of these types of behavioral responses resonate with you, you are not alone. There *is* a reason why you responded as you did. It is not uncommon if you are bodily attacked or feel verbally attacked or bullied, that your brain will take over and you physically freeze, becoming unable to respond as you normally would.

Victim Blaming

When indiscriminate acts occur, people don't feel safe. It's human nature to look for causes as to why harmful incidents take place. In a crazy way, it makes us feel safer to have a reason why versus the unknown.

One natural, although destructive and often incorrect, way to respond is through victim-blaming. Victim-blaming is holding the victim responsible for a crime they did not commit. It's defined as occurring when, "the victim of a crime or any wrongful act is held entirely or partially at fault for the harm that befell them" (Wikipedia, 2020). Victim blaming is real. Victim blaming can be projected toward someone. It can also be projected inward, toward yourself.

As a result, it's not uncommon to end up doubting our own behavior and questioning our actions, to find blame within ourselves… "I must have done something to make her mad." OR "She misinterpreted my behavior." OR "She's ignoring me because I spoke out of turn during the meeting." OR "She must have emailed or texted me about going out, but I never got it." And so on, and so on. And while victim-blaming most definitely occurs, there is *also* another side.

Fight, Flight, or Freeze

There is also a basic internal protection mechanism, the physical sensory side. The fight, flight, or freeze response, also called "hyperarousal," is a level of stress in which you decide whether to face the situation or walk away (Wikipedia, 2020). It's a biological response that humans and other animals have to severe stressors and is defined as, "a physiological reaction that occurs in response to a perceived harmful event, attack, or threat to survival" and was first described by Walter Cannon in 1932.

When someone feels attacked or bullied in any fashion, they freeze. The human brain has a defense circuitry system that triggers bodily reactions when you are perceiving danger. The amygdala is a part of that system and includes the flight, fight, or freeze center. When an individual is bullied or feels attacked in any manner, the amygdala, the brain's fight, flight, or freeze center, is triggered and sends a message to the hypothalamus. The hypothalamus acts like the brain's command center.

Can you think of a time when someone confronted you and you completely froze up? Let's look at what was happening to your body when that happened. Your amygdala sends a distress signal to the hypothalamus. Your hypothalamus then communicates with the rest of your body through your autonomic nervous system. This controls such involuntary body functions as breathing, blood pressure, heartbeat, and the dilation or constriction of key blood vessels and small airways.

I won't go into all of the medical details but essentially, your adrenal glands activate and pump the hormone epinephrine, also known as adrenaline, into your bloodstream. This promotes psychological changes in your body such as increased heart rate, pulse rate, blood pressure, and rapid breathing. Your hearing, sight, and other senses become more alert.

These changes occur so quickly that you probably aren't aware of them or even have the ability to process what is happening. That's why people are able to jump out of the path of an oncoming car even before they think about what they are doing (Harvard Health Publishing, 2020).

When this happens, the logical thinking part of your brain shuts down, preparing your body to save itself. When an attack occurs—emotionally, verbally, physically, sexually—it's frequently *not* possible to fight back. You simply cannot respond to your attacker. The backlash or response to the traumatic event may not materialize immediately. It *could* surface within a matter of minutes, a few hours, a couple of days... or *even* years later.

The Trauma Recovery Center (2013) shares a list of fight, flight, or freeze responses, possible signs that one is no longer feeling safe and might need to stop what they are doing. It's not a complete list but may help to identify what you should be watching for:

Fight	Freeze	Flight
Crying	Feeling stuck in some part of the body	Restless legs, feet, numbness in legs
Hand in fists, desire to punch, rip	Feeling cold, frozen, numb, pale skin	Anxiety, shallow breathing
Flexed, tight jaw, grinding teeth	Holding breath, restricted breathing	Big, darting eyes
Fight in eyes, glaring, fight in voice	Sense of dread, heart pounding	Leg, foot movement
Desire to stomp, kick, smash with legs, feet	Decreased heart rate (can sometimes increase)	Reported or observed fidgety-ness, restlessness, feeling trapped, tense
Feelings of anger, rage	Orientation to threat	Sense of running in life, one's activities
Knotted stomach, nausea, burning stomach		Excessive exercise

Yes. It's that intense. Combine "victim-blaming" with "flight or fight" and you have a real doozy of a mess on your hands in terms of freezing up. The aspect of "the odds being against you" in how you respond to a traumatic situation is real. And it's not generally in your favor. So many people have no idea that these things, these human qualities are real and that they truly do exist. Instead, they blame themselves, they get mad, and they feel remorse, shame, and guilt that they didn't speak out.

6.2: Your Turn. Dear reader, have you ever experienced "victim-blaming?" Have you ever blamed yourself or mentally kicked yourself later for not responding to a situation? Have you ever experienced the "fight or flight" feeling? How did you feel when it occurred? How did you feel about it after the fact? What other emotions do you recall when this occurred? Take a moment now to write below, your initial thoughts on what this type of behavior or reaction means to you.

_____

_____

_____

_____

When I Lost My Voice

This topic makes me think of an altercation I experienced several years ago when I was confronted by an infuriated female. She was a peer from work that I interacted with, not daily,but at least several times a week. In this situation, I wasn't bullied but I was verbally attacked. She was shaking, livid with emotion and anger, as she accused me of things that were untrue. In her rage, she also brought up incidents from the past that she was upset about; things that were totally unfounded and quite frankly, ludicrous. Her impression had several partial truths which very much distorted the facts. Mind you, this is someone who frequently gave me the cold shoulder for weeks at a time. So should I have been bothered? Absolutely not, but I was.

Traditionally, I am a very vocal person but in that instance, I wasn't. I did deny what she was saying but I was so caught off guard that I didn't challenge her any more than that. As a result, I was mad at myself for freezing up in the moment. I felt ashamed for not further countering what she had to say, for not sticking up for myself. I was alarmed that this type of conduct had occurred in a professional environment. Even though we were not direct reports to each other, I was anxious that the negative behavior would impact me professionally. Shocked at her anger, I was in absolute disbelief that something that had happened was so greatly misrepresented. It was an attack on my character, but I said and did nothing. I simply walked away.

I later thought to myself, "How in the world did all of that come about? What could I have done differently? What could I have done to make amends?" But in all realization, the answer was nothing. Had it progressed, I certainly would have escalated it to HR. But I know now, that even if I would have found my voice, it would not have been believed. Her mind was made up and there was absolutely nothing I could have done in that situation to change it. There was absolutely nothing I could have done either, to change her behavior.

As time progressed, I self-reflected. Also, I sat back, watched, and listened. I began to understand that it was her, not me. I'd witnessed her project similar actions to other females. Her behavior was nothing I had control of, nor did I want to. I knew what really had occurred. I knew myself, my character, and what I stood for.

Additionally, I realized that someone who intentionally ignored me for no apparent reason and treated me as she did was not someone I wanted in my inner circle. She was not someone who truly knew me well at all. And quite frankly, that is okay. If you listen carefully enough, if you watch closely enough, someone will always tell you exactly what kind of person they are. It is what it is. I haven't seen her in several years, but I wish her well.

Hazel's Story. "*I was at an off-site location working a government contract. The relationship I had with the lead on-site female, Maureen, was rocky at best. She didn't like me from the onset. There were also a lot of other dynamics going on. The associates had given feedback again and again to us as well as their own leadership, that hadn't been addressed. They were fed up with the department and a complete lack of change. One 'call-center-super-user' gave us insight about what Maureen was like and what had happened over the years. It was just crazy. We'd given feedback to Lisa, Maureen's leader and she just said there was nothing that could be done about it. I think the call center person, giving the insight to us and not her, ultimately put Maureen over the edge. She'd have instances in conversations where she was boiling over with rage. It was the strangest thing...I've never seen anything like it. I was shocked at how much anger she had and I never even 'poked the bear' to instigate her anger. It was the overall situation, it was me, it was her lack of power... all of it.*

We were doing some 1:1 testing about user experiences when Maureen popped her head up and started screaming, 'Where are you going? What's going on? You can't go do that without me! We forbid you to talk to any users!! That's OUR job. We're your customer and you're NOT supposed to talk to users!' What followed was a series of conversations where she would just yell at me. It was so disruptive, and it no longer made any sense to me. I remember her tone and the feelings she made me feel when she went off on me. She was so pissed off that she was shaking with rage. She brought up things from the past. I thought it was ludicrous. Even in hindsight, I recall thinking that she had a few marbles loose. But I couldn't deal with this type of crazy, I couldn't say anything to her. I sat there and kind of let it roll off my back and said, 'I'm sorry.'

And the strangest thing was, after she left me with all that rage inside her... not two minutes later, she was back on the floor with all the users and she was giggling, totally laughing, and it wasn't forced. It was real. It was beyond strange to see her shift so suddenly. If I were that mad, I'd have needed an hour-long walk to calm down. It really didn't make sense because she was legit pissed."

Shannon's Story. *"I was in a graduate group working with a woman who was in her mid-twenties. Most of us were in our late twenties to early thirties. She was a bit young for being a graduate student, which I think was part of the issue as to why she was so difficult and seemed to take everything personally. She constantly talked down to me as if I were stupid, like she was my superior. She'd try to explain very basic concepts to me, but I already had a*

Master's degree in Bioscience, so it wasn't really relevant. She was so condescending, mostly to me, not really to the other women. It was a rivalry, competitive type of thing, like 'I want to be better than you.'

She and I worked together a lot and with other groups. But she always would take sole credit for all of our work we'd done together. She'd always go to the professor first, as the bearer of good news, and literally say, 'This is my idea.' She'd leave everyone out as if she did all of the work on her own. And the professor believed her, he truly thought she was doing everything. She literally would swoop in and have meetings with him and act like she did it all by herself. I am sure the professor had no idea that they were also my projects. Projects that I also worked very hard on.

I was hurt and would think, 'Oh, no she didn't!' It was such shocking behavior. I had moments in hindsight where I knew I should have said this or done that. In those moments though, I was so upset and in shock that I couldn't do anything without causing a scene. It began to be a breaking point for me, I was so distraught over it."

6.3: Your Turn. Dear reader, have you ever lost your voice in this type of situation? How did you feel when it occurred? How did you feel about it after the fact? What other emotions do you recall when this occurred? Take a moment now to write below, your initial thoughts on what this type of behavior means.

_____

_____

_____

_____

Other Contributing Factors

Whether it's in a social setting or at work, a lack of support is a direct result of the environmental influences and silent bystanders that impact the behaviors of rivalry.

Depending upon how long these types of situations last, the control of the other woman will often escalate and get worse. In the stories related to me about rivalry in work and social settings, several women described being subjected to acts of direct aggression, often resulting in demeaning behaviors and public humiliation. As reported, when the behavior of the other woman intensified to direct aggression it was occasionally witnessed by other acquaintances or co-workers. Often, however, the acquaintances and co-workers were silent witnesses to the onslaught of the degrading conduct. In some instances, such as the one reported by Clio below, these individuals even sided with the other woman.

> **Clio.** *"So even when it all blew up and she got mad at me, and they all turned their backs on me, they did it out of self-preservation because if they didn't side with her, they would get it too. They knew that I would leave just like everybody else did. So, if they took my side, after I left, she would do the same thing to them."*

> **Jennifer.** *"I remember feeling awful for Melissa while at the same time feeling safe because I knew she wouldn't come after me. My parents were friends with Sarah's parents. Sarah treated me well that entire time; we even had a few classes together. We'd gone from daycare all the way up through high school together. Sarah obviously knew I was friends with Melissa. I remember being irritated and upset for the girls Sarah was going after but also feeling safe because her behavior wasn't directed at me. But I also felt really guilty too for feeling safe and not doing anything about it."*

6.4: Your Turn. Dear reader, have you ever been in a position where the environment contributed to this type of negative situation? How did it make you feel? What other emotions do you recall when this occurred? Take a moment now to write below, your initial thoughts on what this type of behavior means.

_____

_____

_____

_____

Silent Bystanders and a Lack of Support

In Chapter 4, I introduced the concept of a silent bystander as someone who watches an unacceptable behavior occurring yet does nothing to stop or prevent it. Whether they know it or not, by doing nothing a bystander supports the bullying behavior. The bottom line is, bystanders have choices: they can either be part of the problem, by staying silent; or part of the solution, by helping (Reach Out, 2020).

Although many people may have insight and awareness about this type of negative behavior, many women also expressed to me that in several occurrences at work, senior management or individuals in leadership roles were *also* aware of these inappropriate behaviors.

While bystanders frequently expressed awareness that the behaviors were wrong, they still chose to not get involved and were passive in their response to the individuals needing help. They were aware of the inappropriate behavior but chose to not get involved.

In one situation, being asked to change her behavior to accommodate the offensive other woman only furthered her feelings of isolation.

> **Amy.** *"I was chastised, of course, by the principal even though she thought that I probably was doing something good. She couldn't let things like this happen because she didn't want parents back in her office anymore complaining about me."*

Clio. *"Management didn't support my position; they just ignored it. They felt sorry for me, but they didn't deal with it."*

Dana. *"No, no (there was no support), not by management at all."*

Faith. *"I don't know this for sure, but a friend that had worked there that kind of drifted away because I think that she didn't want to hear about it, or she didn't want to deal with my frustration or depression. So, I also felt like I lost a close family/friendship because of this experience."*

Grace. *"The senior management team was trying to appease the parent company, which then just meant that I had to grin and bear the difficult situation because of political reasons that were out of my control. Then when it all came out, it was like, 'Oh, well we feel sorry but for political reasons we have to kind of smooth this over,' which just made it stressful for me the entire time."*

Shannon. *"Our professors had no idea about her and me specifically, but according to them, this was academia and you had to deal with it. Rivalry is part of it because some students are there on grants and it was a very competitive environment. The strong survive. The attitude was, 'If you can't handle it, leave.' It was an old school attitude, but the culture pretty much endorsed the negative behavior."*

In one situation portrayed by Eleni, being asked to change her behavior to accommodate the offensive other woman was further cause for her to feel isolated and alone.

Eleni. *"Yes, I went to HR at one point and basically it was extremely unhelpful, and the HR rep was a woman as well. It was just like they were taking her side. As basically they said, I needed to change, and they didn't know or understand why I had the problem."*

Clio. *"They knew. The owners were cousins, a man and a woman. I went to the female. She was technically the owner so that we could be a 'Woman Owned Business.' She's the one I went to, thinking she would help. They were kind of hands-off though. They didn't like to get involved in that kind of stuff. As long as they were making money, they didn't want to deal with management issues."*

In most of the stories, women have shared with me about female rivalry at work, management teams or human resources departments were passive in their response to the women needing help. It is not uncommon that HR will do what they can first to protect the company. It is also not uncommon that HR may not be fully equipped as to how to best handle this type of situation. In most of the stories shared with me, HR offered no direct acknowledgement of the situation by openly discussing it with either of the women involved.

In Beatrix's experience, although HR was aware of the behavior of the other woman, they did not directly address the behavior. Rather, they let the other aggressive woman stay in a job she did not like.

Beatrix. *"Supply Chain jobs, in general, will wear you out. And so a role like hers, you're two, three years max before you're just completely burned out. And they've just left her there. And physically, when you look at her, she has aged. I mean just in the time that she's been in that job, it wears you out. And it is wearing her out. And they've basically said if you can find something better, fine. And so, they haven't withheld support from her, but they haven't promoted her to a different job either."*

In many of the working environments as relayed by the women who shared their stories with me, it appeared the HR personnel did not want to address this type of behavior or simply lacked the appropriate training to do so.

Selena shared her story of how her HR department was willing to help, but not necessarily in a direct manner.

Selena. *"I chose to leave and also gave an exit interview. There was*

*another woman in a different department that was known as a trou-
blemaker, but I got along with everyone, including her. We had lunch
one day and she was trying to help and counsel me. She said, 'Selena,
you're not supposed to be coached on it but you have to say these
words when you go to HR. 'I'm suffering from a hostile work environment. Unless you say that to HR they are not obligated to help you. So
you must say that to make it have an effect legally with HR.'*

*In my exit interview, I said all the things she'd suggested. HR actually
said they wanted to get rid of her too. Because I think by then, everybody was realizing how terrible she was. But they also said, 'you know
we need to protect the company.' Essentially, it was so backward. HR
wanted me to be the bait and throw me under the bus. They anticipated
the lady would go off on me and retaliate and then they would have
something on her, to fire her because the company had a zero-retalia-
tion policy, and they could get rid of her then. I guess in an odd way it
made logical sense, but it really didn't feel good to me. The company
was trying to protect themselves from liability, not really protect me per
se and that felt very backward and disempowering. It just felt wrong and
even though I was the victim in this, I felt like I was being victimized.
So, I just went in and resigned and let them do their own dirty work."*

Beatrix provided an example of what it was like to work in a male-dominated environment with a passive HR department.

Beatrix. *"The company I was in was not only 80%+ male, they were
also on the career track in that business. Any woman in that atmosphere was fighting an uphill battle, period, to get equal treatment
from her male colleagues. As a woman, it felt like you could only get
somewhere by stepping on someone else. You were having a rivalry
with the other women in trying to be as good as the men were. If you
were going to be the only woman who could survive, then you obviously could only do that by stepping on someone else and this organi-*

zation never really addressed that type of behavior."

Silent Bystanders and Lack of Social Support

Similar to the workplace, many women also expressed to me that in many occurrences in social settings, friends or other acquaintances were *also* aware of these inappropriate behaviors yet did nothing to stop them. Their fear that the negative behavior would also be projected toward them made them choose to not get involved. As a result, they were passive in their response to the individuals needing help.

> ***Melanie.*** *"You couldn't not see all of the hateful behaviors. Other girls told me they saw it. And hurtful was that our other two good girlfriends saw it and didn't say anything either. No one stood up to Katy and I felt like no one went to bat for me."*

> ***Melissa.*** *"And she told me, 'Unfortunately, I don't like all of the drama around this. I don't think it's a good idea for you to be here. It's a bad representation. It's bad energy to this budding new program.' She saw all of the negative behavior that was directed toward me...I was the victim in this case, yet I also paid the consequences for something I did not do. I paid the price for someone else's behavior that I did not have control over."*

6.5: Your Turn. Dear reader, have you been in a situation where someone did not stick up for you? How did that make you feel? Have you ever been in a situation where you may have in fact been a silent bystander? How did it make you feel then, and after the fact? What other emotions do you recall when this occurred? Take a moment now to write below, your initial thoughts on what this type of behavior means.

_____

_____

_____

_____

Closing

Whether it's victim-blaming and thinking you did something wrong to deserve this type of behavior... Or a "fight or flight" situation when you are frozen, and have no means physically, in which to respond. Or it's a silent bystander, someone who's watching and does nothing to help you... Whether it occurs in a social setting or work environment, this negative type of behavior is infectious. When left unaddressed, these actions influence the morale of an entire group.

Many women who've shared their stories with me expressed that they felt fear and apprehension about vocalizing their situation. They didn't know if they would be believed or who to turn to. So instead, they just kept quiet.

What happens when and why you "just keep quiet" about something? It can eat you alive. "How," you may ask, "does that happen?" Emotions take over and will eventually manifest in a variety of ways—physically, psychologically, mentally, and internally. Dear reader, brace yourself for what all of this entails, as that's what I discuss in Chapter 7, "When Your Tiara Tilts."

Chapter 7:

When Your Tiara Tilts

"When we feel anger and hatred toward someone else,
it becomes very hard to let go.
Every action breeds a reaction, and negative feelings only escalate.
Our inner light becomes obscured in a vicious cycle of negativity."
—Carlos Warter (Walter, Carlos, 2020).

Marjorie's Story

"I felt like I was in prison.

It had gone on for quite some time, my being in that negative situation.
Then when Sunday rolled around, on Sunday evening I would get this
terrible feeling in my stomach...

At the same time because I was experiencing so much anxiety, I developed gastroesophageal reflux disease (GERD), a long-term condition where acid from the stomach comes up into the esophagus. I ended up in the hospital one night, not being able to swallow, and they had to put a tracheotomy down my throat so that I could breathe. I've been on medication ever since. There's no question in my mind that the anxiety I experienced because of working with her initiated the GERD. Now, since I'm out of that environment, I'm off prescription meds and am beginning to wean myself off of over-the-counter meds too. I also don't have the anxiety that I once had.

Even though I'm not an expert in it, I do feel like I experienced some sort of post-traumatic stress disorder (PTSD) from experiencing what I did. After being at the company for eighteen years, after completely breaking away from it, I was grieving because I'd also lost a job and a good (male) friend. Additionally, after getting out of being a vice president and the security of my job being gone...I really had second thoughts about my abilities. I started thinking, 'Well maybe it was me. Maybe I jumped off this cliff and now I am hitting the ground.' I had all sorts of thoughts going through my head like, 'I'm not worthy.' I felt like I was cheating because I got out."

When Your Tiara Tilts

That is a true summary of how Marjorie felt emotionally and what she experienced physically after dealing with a "Bolshie Bully" boss for several years. It doesn't matter if you experienced this type of behavior at work, socially from a family member, or a parishioner from church... The impacts of the behavior are all very similar in nature. They will make you feel like you have lost yourself, that you've lost your shine and sparkle.

I know from personal experience that it completely sucks when your tiara tilts. What do I mean when I say, "your tiara tilts?" Here are several of examples:

- You can't find your voice
- You've lost your joy
- You lose your shine
- The world is grey

There are so many influencing factors. All the impacts you feel from this type of behavior can result in your tiara being tilted and tarnished, for quite a while.

Never fear, dear! I have no doubt that you will be able to turn this around. You may be asking yourself, "what makes one woman a target versus another woman?" There's no black and white answer to this question because as I have mentioned previously, this type of behavior does not discriminate. It's completely situational. In no way will something you've experienced mirror the experience of another female. Two experiences can be similar, but chances are they are not the same. What I can share with you, to give you a tad bit of insight into that question, is the following synopsis from the small population of women who've shared their personal experiences with me.

Common Attributes of the Women Who Shared Their Stories

All of the females that I've spoken with about their experience with the "other woman" have different professional, personal, and cultural backgrounds. Collectively as a group, I've discovered similar likenesses and commonalities amongst them, in some form or another, regardless of if their experience occurred socially or at work. They've been very frank and direct in their demeanor. They are competent and confident. They have a strong personality and are out-spoken in nature. They are intelligent, they are bright, they are forthright, they are attractive, they are nice, and they are bubbly.

Often when the experience occurred, they were young and likely younger than the "other woman." Frequently, at the time of the experience, the women considered themselves to be naive. For the most part, at the time they experienced rivalry with another woman, these women had similar jobs or had been in a situation where they challenged the other woman. They exude positive traits and are generally people that other people like or like to be around. Whether based on appearance, personality, or competence, they felt they were a perceived threat to "the other," jealous woman.

7.1: Your Turn. Dear reader, have you ever been in a situation where your tiara has lost its shine? Have you ever felt like Marjorie did? When you read her story, did anything sound familiar? Have you ever been on the receiving end of these types of feelings due to interaction with a "Vicious Vixen" or "Bolshie Bully" boss? Take a moment now to write below, why this resonated with you and why.

_____

_____

_____

_____

Now let's talk about what's going on when you're stuck in the thick of it. You are going to feel a lot of "feels." To be fully transparent, for the most part, at least for a chunk of time, it'll feel really crappy. It may even feel that way, as Marjorie described, for a chunk of time after you are out of the situation, as you step away and process it all.

> *"Don't take anything personally.*
> *Nothing others do, is because of you."*
> —Don Miguel Ruiz (Goodreads, Inc., 2020).

Stages You Experience, When Your Tiara Tilts

This type of behavior traditionally happens gradually over time and in stages. As a result, when you finally figure out what is occurring, you may realize that you aren't as strong as you used to be. The following stages may not progress sequentially or in a distinct series of steps. They may in fact overlap to a degree. All the stages, however, will reflect distinct emotional and psychological states of mind.

Stage 1: Disbelief. You'll question her behavior towards you. In turn, you'll question your own behavior. You may say, "I must be imagining things. Of course, she didn't do that!" You'll doubt behaviors, and then brush them off as just being abnormal, weird, odd, "She must be having an 'off' day, which is why she's acting this way."

> **Tina.** *"Over the years, I've experienced different things where women are pitted against one another. I'm not sure if those women begin to lose their integrity or if in fact, we were never really friends to begin with. Then you start questioning, was there ever even a friendship there, or were they using me to get closer to something they wanted?*
>
> *For example, I was still learning in the new environment I was in. I was so excited about this job. I really wanted this job. I really thought it was a good thing for me... But you know, after you got there and strange things kept constantly happening, I just started questioning it all. Was it just me? Did I miss something here? Did I misunderstand? Did I miscommunicate?"*

Stage 2: Defense. You begin to defend yourself against the behavior "she" is projecting toward you. For example, if the behavior occurs at work, you may tell your boss you feel something has changed, there's a rift between you, and you feel the communication is not as it used to be. Asking, "What can I do on my end, to make it better?" She may laugh and respond, "You are imagining things. I think you are being too sensitive."

In this example, she does not directly answer the question about the altered communication. She deflects it instead, to refer to an emotional state. You may justify your feelings to her (rightly so) but ultimately during this phase, this type of conversation will drive you crazy because you aren't receiving a concrete answer as to "why" things have changed. Think back to Chapter 2, and the "gaslighting" persona I highlighted. This is a form of that behavior.

This type of dialogue portrays the kind of relationship you have. Her demeaning response will bother you that "she" sees you in this light (imagining things and being oversensitive). You know it's not true, but she is your boss and ultimately yields power over you.

> **Beth.** *"The anxiety would just bubble up in my stomach into my chest. I felt like I was going to throw up on the spot and I don't usually get nervous. But, I didn't know what it was. I didn't know what part of what I was saying was right or wrong or what. I didn't know what was going on."*

> **Shannon.** *"Finally, I started talking to her and would say, 'What is wrong? I can tell you're upset with me.' And always, she would say, 'No. Nothing is wrong.' Then it'd get better for a few days and then the behavior would resume. And we'd do the whole thing all over again."*

> **Sydney.** *"I did try to confront her. I walked in and said, 'Do we have a problem? Because I'm getting the feeling that you don't want to work with me.' She said, 'No, there's no problem.'"*

Stage 3: Depression. When this stage hits, you may feel like you've hit rock bottom but can't clearly identify why. You have no joy, your friends or family think you've changed, and you don't recognize who you are either as your behavior feels foreign. Along with the depression, you:

- Feel confused, crazy and second-guess yourself
- Frequently apologize to people, even if you've done nothing wrong
- Withhold information from family and friends so you don't have to explain or make excuses
- Don't understand with so much good in your life why you aren't happier
- Have trouble making simple decisions

- Alienate yourself from those closest to you and don't really talk about what's going on.
- Believe your poor behavior caused the situation (Stern, 2009).

> *Faye.* *"I think I felt depression, frustration, feeling stifled because I would usually try to fix a problem. I was confused because I wasn't sure how to fix this problem. I felt bad, in retrospect, for my family because I think that there was a lot of depression, just tiredness, lack of joy during this period. In retrospect, I should've left sooner for my personal health."*

7.2: Your Turn. Dear reader, have you ever experienced any of the three previously mentioned stages, either in a social situation or at work? Did any of the stages hit home? If so, how did you feel when you experienced it? Or did it take leaving the situation for you to even realize what had occurred? Take a moment now to write below, why this resonated with you and why.

_____

_____

_____

_____

Plethora of Emotions

If you are a recipient of this type of behavior, the range of emotions you'll feel can be utterly overwhelming. The effects of all these emotions will have an impact on you mentally, physically, socially, and psychologically. Sometimes, you may not even be aware of the ramifications until much later... until after the situation is behind you.

Here's a quick overview of why emotions matter and how they impact us as written by Marc Brackett, Ph.D., Founder and Director of the Yale Center for Emotional Intelligence (EI). His research focuses on the role of emotions and emotional intelligence in learning, decision making, creativity, intelligence, health, and performance. His findings reveal that emotions influence:

- Attention, memory, and learning
- Decision making
- Creativity
- Mental and physical well-being
- Ability to form and maintain positive relationships
- Academic and workplace performance (Bracket, 2020).

When I conducted formal research on this topic for my dissertation, every woman I spoke with had these emotions in common that they were feeling when they were knee-deep in an unfavorable rivalrous situation. Not one emotion was positive. Every single emotion was negative. There are more I could add, but the following nine words sum up what they all were feeling:

- Confusion
- Fear
- Anxiety
- Self-doubt
- Anger
- Frustration
- Despair
- Stress
- Hopelessness
- Disbelief
- Sorrow

Upon reflection, after looking at all the stories I've received then and now, the combined narratives create an interpreted meaning of the phenomenon of rivalry between women as a whole. And let me tell you, it isn't pretty. It's harmful, negative, and definitely not the simple, petty "catfight" that people chalk it up to be. All of the women I've spoken to have directly described the variety of emotions they've experienced in their situation of rivalry with another female.

> ***Amy.*** *"And it always left a big question mark in my mind and in my heart why Karen found it so necessary to put other people down in order to boost herself up when she was an accomplished teacher by her own right." (Confusion.)*

> ***Amy.*** *"And I would look at her, and I would wonder why she'd even want to do that or behave like that to me?" (Disbelief.)*

> ***Amy.*** *"Yeah, it was f***ed up." (Anger.)*

> ***Clio.*** *"I was stuck, at least it seemed like I was. I needed to get out, but I hadn't the slightest idea how to do it. I was getting sick more often, had chest pains, was sleeping poorly, and had a pit in my stomach every day when I pulled into the parking lot." (Despair, hopelessness, and anxiety.)*

> ***Dana.*** *"I probably didn't sleep. And I probably lost 35 pounds. Because there was so much stress." (Stress.)*

> ***Eleni.*** *"I felt isolated, paranoid, crazy, desperate, worthless. I felt like I was out on the edge and nobody was around to support me. I feel that I kind of withdrew from my job more than anything else. That I wasn't spending as much time working when I was at work. You know, probably doing personal things or leaving or something like that. I cried a lot before I went to work every day." (Isolation, sadness, paranoia, crazy, desperate, and worthless.)*

> ***Grace.*** *"So that was a challenge because you always had to put on a face as if you were a cohesive group, but then you never felt...I never felt comfortable in not being right there on the spot or breathing*

because I felt like, at any moment, she could pull something and I never knew what it would be." (Anxiety.)

Hannah. *"Not to say that I'm some glamazon here, but it was one of those things where you don't ever want to feel like...Is the attention you're getting, and the respect you're getting, and the accolades you're getting, or the promotions, or the raises, or whatever you're getting...Are they for the right reasons? And I think that it's always been a little bit of a theme. If I look back at these situations, I wonder if people thought that that's why I was getting, what I was getting. What I had really earned."* (Self-doubt.)

Ilene. *"Well, I will be honest you know it is not the same kind of fear that you would have when you have a near-miss in a car or going to the war zone. But there is this kind of undertow of fear that you know at some point is going to cost you a critical assignment, a critical promotion. And you feel helpless because with the way the system works you don't always know who is in the realm, saying things about you. You just don't know if it is rational and real or when it's just kind of this rivalry playing out."* (Fear and helplessness.)

Roller Coaster Ride of Emotions

For every woman I've ever spoken to about this topic, every single one of them lived through a variety of negative emotions as a result of their experience. This ranges from feeling frustrated and confused as to why the incident occurred, to doubting themselves about what they'd done wrong to bring on the unwanted behavior.

Melissa. *"I don't know... Maybe I am attracting this type of behavior somehow?"*

Natalie. *"It's made me wonder what is wrong with me. Why has this happened? Why am I such an awful judge of character?"*

These women encountered despair coupled with disbelief that someone they had initially trusted, either a friend, someone at work, someone in a mentoring, social, leadership, or supervisory position had treated them with such animosity.

Many women I've interviewed about this phenomenon spoke of feeling trapped, hopeless, and helpless in a situation they perceived as having no control over. Several of the participants expressed they had feelings of fear in anticipation of what the other woman would do. They revealed feeling anxious and stressed out. A number of the women articulated intense feelings of anger toward the situation and the "other woman." However, many also proclaimed immense anger toward themselves, simply for being in the situation, for not standing up for themselves, for not doing anything sooner to change the circumstance, and for not taking actions to eliminate the situation.

Frequently, when we are hurt by someone, the first thing that is easy to do is point blame at ourselves and ask, "Why did we let that behavior occur?" The fact of the matter is, giving someone the benefit of the doubt doesn't mean we let them hurt us. It just simply means we trusted them not to. Initially, all these women were in situations, in some form or another, where they trusted the other female or were placed in a situation of "assumed" trust. It's very easy, in a rivalrous situation, to place the blame internally, instead of extending ourselves the grace we deserve. It's always harder to show ourselves grace than it is to other people.

The women who shared their stories with me experienced rivalry personally and professionally, not to mention the rollercoaster of emotions they dealt with which was extreme. Initially, the subtle negative actions toward them were confusing and there was a lack of understanding as to why. How could someone in a mentoring or leadership position, someone they trusted, treat them with such animosity? Also, their self-esteem was shot.

Some women became subject to demeaning behaviors and public humiliation. Some women began to believe what the other woman was saying and doing to her.

> **Amanda.** *"Oh, it affected me personally all right. I think when she spread the rumor and accused Caroline, my neighbor and me, of being lovers, which wasn't true. It hurt really bad. Other people were made*

aware of this, and they lived in my neighborhood. So, it became very personal. I quit the PTA after that."

Clara. *"When my boss came back, she did not respond well to the fact that I had succeeded in her absence and this confused me greatly. She was very angry with me, even though we'd received kudos from several senior leadership teams. She consistently asked me, 'Why did you do that and what in the h*ll were you thinking?' She accepted the honor but then didn't include me in that circle. I didn't understand what I had done wrong and started to doubt my own competency. It was an awful feeling."*

Shelby. *"We moved into a new neighborhood that at first seemed amazing. We instantly clicked with neighbors down the street who had kids similar ages to ours. The thing with new neighborhoods is, it takes a while to truly understand what the social dynamics are... For whatever reason after several months of hanging out socially with them, she completely ghosted us. She stopped calling and wouldn't let her kids play with ours. It was very hard to understand. I later found out from another neighbor that the wife was telling people crazy stories about me, that I was boastful about all the money my husband made and that I drank too much and couldn't hold my alcohol. It totally wasn't true. If anything, she was describing parts of her personality. It was hurtful and made it hard to trust other people in the neighborhood."*

Beatrix. *"Well, I think she figured that out, that I was over-analyzing my behavior because then she started over this 12-month period, this systematic tearing down of my self-esteem. And the thing is, I started to believe her."*

7.3: Your Turn. Dear reader, have you ever been in a situation where you've similarly experienced this rollercoaster type of an emotional state? Did any type of emotion mentioned evoke a memory for you? Did you realize what was occurring when you felt this emotion, or did it take leaving the situation for you to even realize what had occurred? Take a moment now to write below, why this resonated with you and why.

_____

_____

_____

_____

Losing Your Voice

Throughout this book, I've mentioned losing your voice. Let's explore what this means. When this type of behavior is directed at you, it's confusing and hard to pinpoint the exactness of it. This type of rivalry is frequently not tangible enough for other people to notice. The other female, although often controlling in nature, can be quite passive-aggressive in her approach. Therefore, this one-on-one type of behavior is frequently discernible only to the recipient. Women exposed to this type of behavior often feel hopelessness and despair from being caught in what feels like a never-ending circumstance. Frequently, they do not voice to others what they are experiencing. If they do, it traditionally is after the fact and not during the experience. It's like living in a hall of funhouse mirrors not knowing where to turn or whom to trust. So instead... it's kept inside making an already lonely situation, lonelier.

As demonstrated by the abundance of stories I've collected, women who've experienced rivalry from another woman socially or at work are individuals that did not speak up when the rivalry occurred. Yet when asked, many of these women viewed themselves as traditionally outspoken in nature. During their experience, they remained silent, primarily due to fear. This type of behavior provokes immense fear. Fear of:

- What the other woman will do
- How she will be received and perceived by others
- Not being supported
- Not having a job and/or fear of not having friends

- Being excluded or left out
- Not being accepted

And because of the fear, you slowly begin to wear down. You are weighed down. And under all this heaviness, you ultimately lose your voice.

> **Natalie.** *"I went through a period where I just stopped talking. I just shut down. I isolated myself from everyone."*

> **Sydney.** *"I thought about getting out because I had a feeling, they were trying to push me out and I had been looking around at other jobs, but there were no options. You know, I'd had a couple of interviews, but I couldn't find anything. It's tough when you get to a certain senior level to find a position equal to that with equal pay. I also was in such a bad place that, no, I don't even think I could have gone on an interview and portrayed myself in any kind of positive light. Even in the weeks after I got laid off, I was just so angry. I went on a couple of interviews and I really wasn't myself. I knew I wasn't presenting my best self because I wasn't my best self, at all."*

7.4: Your Turn. Dear reader, have you ever been in a situation where you've lost your voice due to negative behaviors that were cast your way? Did you know when you were in the thick of it that you had the inability to speak? Or did you instead experience other negative ramifications? Did you realize what was occurring when this was happening, or did it take leaving the situation for you to even realize what had occurred? Take a moment now to write below, why this resonated with you and why.

_____

_____

_____

_____

Emotional Encumbrance and Life Impact

Emotions help guide us through life. They aid us in decision-making and are a filter for our thoughts and feelings. When they become extreme, however, they can become an encumbrance. Per the APA Dictionary (2007) emotion is defined as, "a complex reaction pattern, involving experiential, behavioral, and physiological elements, by which, the individual attempts to deal with a personally significant matter or event" (p. 325). Per the New Oxford American Dictionary (2005) the term encumbrance is defined as, "a burden or impediment" (para 1).

As mentioned by Landy & Conte (2007), "Emotions experienced at work affect *both* work behavior and non-work behavior" (p. 378). Lazarus (1993) stated that emotions are a response to a relational meaning and identified them in terms of positive and negative,

> *"There are nine so-called negative emotions: anger, fright, guilt, shame, sadness, envy, jealousy, and disgust, each a product of a different set of troubled conditions of living, and each involving different harms or threats. And there are roughly four positive emotions: happiness, pride, relief, and love. What gives this multiplicity of emotions great analytic power is that each emotion arises from a different plot or story about relationships between a person and the environment" (p. 12).*

As a result of experiencing rivalry from another woman in any situation, the emotional toll these women encountered is vast and burdensome. My findings revealed that women who experience this phenomenon undergo a plethora of emotions that are extensive in nature. Although they vary for each woman, the inner toll is burdensome all the same. This vast array of emotions further exacerbates an already stressful situation.

The women who've shared their stories with me about this type of harmful rivalry have only ever spoken of negative emotions they experienced. During each of their individual situations, **not once** has any female identified experiencing a positive reaction. This negativity impacts *everything* she does. As a result of the "other woman," the negativity is experienced personally, socially, at home, at church, at book club, professionally, on vacation... It's experienced everywhere.

It's evident that all the women I've spoken to about their experience felt a huge amount of frustration when the rivalrous experience transpired. The behavior of the other woman is, to say the least, confusing. Combine confusion with frustration, and then add doubt. Although traditionally confident in nature, they began to doubt themselves, and felt stressed out and anxious. At some point, all of the women endured hopelessness and despair at how the situation would end. Women who endured this type of bullying behavior long-term summarized the following. They felt:

- Vulnerable and afraid
- As if they were not enough
- Unworthy and "less than"
- Disconnected from their inner "true self"
- Numb and detached (when they normally were not)
- As if they could not put their guard down

Women who experienced this phenomenon spoke of feeling hopeless, trapped, and helpless in a situation over which they perceived they did not have any control. They expressed feelings of fear, never knowing what the other woman would do. They felt anxious, stressed out, like they were walking on eggshells never knowing from one minute to the next what would happen. They were emotionally drained and tired from having to keep their guard up simply to protect themselves. Some women felt depressed and an overall lack of joy. Many women have articulated intense feelings of anger toward their situation and the other woman. However, many also proclaimed anger toward themselves simply for being in the situation, for not standing up for themselves, and for not acting sooner to change the circumstance and make it go away.

> **Jennifer.** *"Every weekend I had a 'Sunday pit in my stomach.' When my husband asked me what I wanted to do for the weekend, I'd get mad at him. Because to me to think about the weekend meant that I*

had to think about Monday and I didn't want to make plans for Saturday because that meant that got me closer to Sunday, which got me closer to Monday. I know that sounds crazy. It was crazy. I was crazy… but I couldn't stop how I was feeling or change the situation.

Because I wasn't getting any solution at work, I talked to my husband about it. I was talking about it at home nonstop probably to the point where I was making him crazy because I was obsessing so much. I've been at my new job for a year now and I don't hate the weekends anymore."

Health Ramifications

There is another huge side effect of this type of emotional encumbrance and that is the physical side. Some women simply shut down and retreat into themselves, but many women also experience unknown health issues.

Negative emotions and feelings just don't disappear on their own, especially if on-going and not talked about. If they are kept bottled up inside, they eventually will come out in some sort of physical form, ailment, sickness, or disease.

I know this type of reaction all too well. While my encounter doesn't pertain to a female rivalry situation, it does have first-hand relevance about what keeping emotions inside and not talking about them will do to you physically.

My Story. "During my late twenties, I lived in Seattle with two fabulous roommates, had a good job, and was dating a guy named Jack. To say it was a rocky relationship is a nice way of putting it, but really, it was dysfunction at its finest. Nothing crazy had happened to trigger it, but out of the blue, I began to experience crazy awful back pain. No matter what I did or took, the pain persisted. I had an MRI, went to a few specialists, drank too much, got pain prescriptions, tried exercise…. I experimented with absolutely everything I could think of to relieve the pain.

I decided to try acupuncture. When I filled out the form to describe why I was there, I wrote, 'back pain' but did not specify where. In the office I laid face down on her table while she did some energy work and all of a sudden she pressed a finger to my spine in the middle of my back and said, 'this is where your pain is.' It was, indeed, the exact spot. What she said next floored me, 'You have a sad heart. Because you are not expressing your emotions, because you keep them inside, the pain must find an escape in a different form. It must find a way out. That is why you have back pain.'

I was shaken to the core by her analysis. And sad, yes, I was very sad... I was beyond sad because I knew it was true. Something needed to be fixed, even though at that moment, I wasn't exactly sure why or what it was. That very week I found a counselor and began intense therapy sessions to deal with what was going on. Jack went to the wayside. And while I'd initially gone to therapy for a broken relationship, it didn't take me long to realize it went much deeper than that. I actually ended up dealing with childhood trauma and pent up emotions that had been held in, and not talked about for years."

At the beginning of this chapter, Marjorie's story addresses the health impacts she suffered as a result of such a negative emotional experience. Other women have also shared what they experienced.

Clio. *"At the time, I kind of went into myself. There were a couple of times during that period of time that I had health issues that I couldn't explain, nor could the doctor."*

Amy. *"Anger, frustration, hurt...in order for me to survive the situation, I had to live in my own environment in the classroom. I rarely left my classroom. Basically, I didn't associate with anybody except the school psychologist and the speech teacher."*

Beth. *"To me, the biggest thing was this constant feeling of anxiety— like wondering how someone was going to respond to you. And I prob-*

ably, I can't clinically diagnose myself, but I can't imagine that I didn't experience some level of depression."

Eleni. *"Isolated, paranoid, crazy, desperate, worthless. I cried a lot, every day before I went to work."*

Natalie. *"I stopped taking care of myself. I was eating like crap. I was drinking too much. Because I was mad and I just, I literally, shut down. I stopped going to the gym. I was like, this is not happening again. And so, I think I was kind of in denial at the same time that I couldn't stop talking about it. Also, when you've had that type of experience happen previously and when it happens again or something similar to it, you go back to that how you were at that time, you know what I mean. You go back to that girl or how you felt or how you reacted at that other time too."*

Lola. *"I felt like I had PTSD. I was sick to my stomach. I had crazy physical, mental, and social feelings. After one patient case, I thought I was going to be fired... because she'd planted that thought in my head."*

Selena. *"It got to a point where I didn't even realize how bad it was getting. I was so miserable that I didn't even know I was miserable. I started to resent my husband for not making more money. So, then I considered divorcing him and marrying someone with more money. I just felt crazy. I confided to a friend at work and she said, 'What? This isn't like you. You are on the edge. This is not normal. You are unhappy and you need to change things because you feel stuck in a situation where you are not able to change the situation, you are thinking about taking it out on someone else.'*

I couldn't even see it all. I was confiding in my friend and blaming it on my husband. She said, 'Your marriage is great. This is an exam-

ple of someone having a nervous breakdown.' I simply let go of all my self-awareness. My husband was actually very supportive and felt sorry for what I was going through and how I was feeling."

Sydney. *"I was angry, had a lot of anxiety, was very stressed and couldn't sleep. My husband noticed it. My son noticed it. Everybody knew how stressed out I was. It sucks the joy out of you. It wasn't just impactful at work. It encompassed my life and I brought it home with me. I was miserable."*

Reflection

Hindsight offers the ability for deep reflection. As time passed, many women were able to think about their experiences. They shared the guilt they felt for having put up with such hostile behavior, often for long periods of time.

It's common that women who are recipients of this type of behavior often do not speak about their experience until it's behind them, or near to being over. Because they've lost their voice, they feel they can't talk about it, or feel it is too passive-aggressive to verbalize. It simply might not be "digested" enough yet for them to be able to share. It is common that women in this type of situation will withdraw from others and experience deep feelings of isolation. They often hide circumstances from others, as they are embarrassed by it. While there frequently may be awareness about it by others as it's occurring, traditionally it's not overtly dealt with until after the fact, if ever. It's simply swept under the rug. The experience typically ends when the targeted woman removes herself from the situation.

Maggie. *"Three years to live with this... it was not a good feeling. I felt for a long time that I was stupid. That I was missing the point, and things like that. I definitely doubted my abilities. I'd think to myself, 'did I ever really have the success that I'd thought I had in my other positions?' I thought I wasn't communicating right, especially as someone who is a communicator, who makes a living off helping other people to communicate. It didn't mean I was perfect but that* *was my skill set. So, my behavior at work, I believe always in showing up as myself at work, and in this case, I felt like who I was, my person was not accepted."*

Corina. *"I couldn't let it roll off my back because I couldn't live in fear going to work every day. I hated it. I felt so miserable and encountered depression. It just took over my body. I did not want to go to work but I had to. And it was so hard too because several of us at work were feeling the same way. But she was that one person, right above me, making my life h*ll. I tried to be optimistic and cheerful at work. She said something to me once, and still, to this day I can't recall what it was, but I went into the bathroom and just broke down. And my co-worker Melissa came and said, 'Oh, no, not you too.'"*

Shannon. *"She wanted to be in control, to micromanage, to receive all of the credit for what we did as a group together. It did create a lot of stress on me. And when those types of behaviors occurred, they didn't just stay in the lab, the experience also went home with me. I remember I felt so angry at her and how she would talk down to me. It was embarrassing and I felt devastated after. I remember feeling upset, like I was worthless. Especially because it was in academia and intelligence is everything and to put you down like that was essentially saying, 'You're not as smart as me.' On top of it, she took credit for my work. It was just so, so very frustrating. And a lot of times, it felt heartbreaking too because I was really proud of what I'd accomplished and she just took that moment away from me."*

7.5: Your Turn. Dear reader, have you ever felt so emotionally loaded down due to the behavior of another female that you felt vulnerable and afraid? Did it escalate to the point where you felt like you were not good enough or were unable to put your guard down? Did you realize what was occurring when this was happening, or did it take leaving the situation for you to even realize what had occurred? Take a moment now to write below, why this resonated with you and why.

_____

_____

_____

_____

Rivalry Ramifications

Various encounters throughout your life shape who you are, stay with you, and ultimately become part of your story, a chapter from a certain point in time. You may have dealt with the situations when they occurred, but they still reside in you. Your experiences always shape who you later become.

If you've been bullied or dealt with an intense rivalrous situation, scars from indirect aggressive mean female behaviors can cause pain and life-long negative effects. If you've experienced similar types of negative behaviors as a younger girl, even though as an adult you have moved on and are stronger, present day situations can elicit those negative experiences and bring them back up to the surface. Those previous harmful encounters can undermine you, trigger anxiety, instill a lack of trust, and impact your self-esteem.

Perhaps because of your flight, fight, or freeze response to situations you've experienced as mentioned in the previous chapter, you've never been able to fully comprehend the after-effects of bullying behavior. You may not understand that your trust was taken and that the negative behavior changed who you are as a person. This can make it hard to move on.

It's not until later, after you are out of it, after your nervous system calms down, that you can digest it. It's like you must step outside of yourself to truly see yourself and let the whole experience sink in. There may be guilt and shame. You may be hard on yourself and don't see yourself in the light that you truly should. But my dear, don't throw shade on the tiara. Let that bad boy shine!

Previous harmful events can greatly impact your present day mindset. Frequently, if you've been the recipient of previous negative bullying, aggressive, and rivalrous behaviors from another female, it will have an influence on:

1. If you choose to work for or with a female boss (again).
2. Who you select as friends and if you are hesitant to make new friends.
3. Who you trust enough to let into your inner circle.

> **Sydney.** *"And you know, if I must decide between two jobs, one reporting to a woman, one reporting to a man, I don't even think I would consider the one reporting to a woman again. There's no way I would consider it right now... it's just too soon. I think if there's a choice, of reporting to a man or a woman...There are men that are screamers, but again, it's not personal. They get over it and five minutes they don't hold it against you. They don't come after you. With women... well, it's just not like that. What she did to me has carried over socially, in general to how I trust, or don't, other women."*

7.6: Your Turn. Dear reader, have you endured ramifications of rivalry with another female to the point that you... 1) Won't work for a female boss again? 2) Are hesitant to make new female friends? 3) Are beyond cautious of who you let into your inner circle? Can you pinpoint a time to a specific instance when this type of behavior occurred, resulting in why you feel this way now? Have you ever thought that you, although not knowing why, were the cause of these types of projected behaviors? Take a moment now to write below, why these points resonate with you and why.

_____

_____

_____

_____

Closing

I've had many women say they will never again work for a female boss and that they are very hesitant about joining a team composed primarily of women. I've had many women voice that due to being the target of a Queen Bee or being the receiver of excluding, b*tchy behaviors that their faith in female friendships has been broken. I've had many women share that they think they did something to cause the behavior, that it could have been avoided in some way, that they feel broken and sad. I've had women share the deep sorrow they've felt because they were unable to comfort the girl they were back then. I've had many women say they do not have a circle, sisterhood, group, squad, community, or tribe of good female friends. I've had many women say they are afraid to make new friends because they do not know whom they can trust.

I've had many women say they no longer trust themselves... that is because they are continuously the target of such mean and spiteful behaviors they must be doing something inappropriate, they must be doing something to attract it, or that there must be something wrong with them.

And if that doesn't break your heart, I don't know what will. It saddens me greatly that these women blame themselves for something that happened to them, for something they fundamentally could not control, for something calculating and slippery... the Machiavellian behavior of the "other woman."

What is very clear in my research and that of others is the role that emotions play in an individual's overall well-being. It's no wonder if a female who is experiencing this negative behavior is unable to confide or talk to someone about it, she will endure and experience anger, self-doubt, isolation, social consequences, and physical complications. It's little surprise that the aftermath of this type of behavior will govern everything she does. It will impact her ability to perform well at work and navigate social relationships. It will influence her decision making, attention, creativity, memory, and learning. And ultimately, it will shape her mental and physical well-being.

When your tiara tilts, there are a lot of influencing factors that contribute to it being tarnished. However, ultimately... regaining your sparkle back, is up to YOU! Are you ready, dear reader, to learn about how to do this? Turn the page to the next chapter and you'll find some very insightful tips.

PART III:

The Victory

vic·to·ry. /ˈvikt(ə)rē/ *noun.*
"An act of defeating an enemy or opponent in a battle, game, or other competition" (Merriam Webster, 2020).

"Tell me about the light that you are trying to find.
Tell me where you are searching for it.
For all the places you had been and for every moment you failed.
You forgot to look around and realize
that everyone you meet, is doing the same.
The day you realize that the light,
which you always searched for, was inside you.
And you are the home, for all the answers to
every question you ever had.
The time will freeze at once for you.
You become the light that you always searched."
—Akshay Vasu (Goodreads, 2020).

Chapter 8

Regaining Your Sparkle

"Some periods of growth are so confusing we don't even recognize that growth is happening. We may feel hostile or angry or weepy and hysterical, or we may feel depressed. It would never occur to us, unless we stumbled upon a book or a person who explained to us, that we were in fact in the process of change, of actually becoming larger, spiritually, than we were before."
—Alice Walker (Goodreads, Inc., 2020).

Ilene's Story. *"So, I've taken the lesson and basically turned it 180, and said, 'Okay, I am not going to let that rivalry become the way I treat women.' And it also has made me apply an extra filter. When I am in a promotion panel, if I find myself thinking, 'Oh, I would never promote her, I would never select her, I would never... do this or that.' I always step back and say, 'Would you, if she were sitting side by side* *with another guy, would you be holding him to the same standard? Are you holding women to a standard above the standard you hold men to? And if so, how do you rationalize that?'"*

Natalie's Story. *"I texted my sister a quote the other day that I got out of one of Brené Brown's books and it was something about… 'If you parent with shame, you end up with kids that are maladjusted,' or something like that. And I sent that to my sister and said, 'Mom needed to read more books like this because our mom parented with shame.' I know that now. But I didn't then. There are always these things that I'm able to recognize retroactively. That helps me understand what's going on around me, even at work, and it helps me now understand and go, 'Oh, I see you and I'm not playing your game.'*

My mom would do the, you know, 'You should be so ashamed for what you've done. You should be embarrassed.' She'd just drill it in us and when you're a kid you don't know that that is not okay. But we did recognize it when my sister started having kids. We couldn't label it because we weren't, we still didn't know what it was, but we knew it was wrong. But I totally recognize it now. And that has helped me recognize it in others too, especially at work."

And Still, She Perseveres

I'm always in awe of all the women who have shared something so personal, so emotional, so fragile with me… awe that they trust me enough to feel comfortable doing so. It helps me on my path to showcase what this phenomenon really means. But I also know it helps them too. It helps them cope and ultimately move on. It helps them adjust their tiara right back to where it needs to be, upright, strong, and shining bright.

I don't know many of these women personally, but when we talk, many of them have completely bared their souls to me. It's always an emotional conversation. Frequently, it is the first time these women have ever shared their stories about this behavior with anyone. As a result, they have built up so much unreleased emotion that has to come out. Because there is a rawness in relaying such hurt, regularly there are tears with the release of pent-up emotion comes a cleansing and an ability to reflect. Perhaps it's the questions I ask. But often, there are realizations that occur when they share... that solely come from them. They can see more clearly the entire picture of what transpired, which includes their own behavior as well as that of the "other female." They are able to reflect. This reflection also brings an unbiased approach to their thoughts and feelings:

1. They want awareness about this type of behavior highlighted.
2. They want to help other women.
3. They want to prevent this type of behavior from continuing.
4. They want to foster a community, a work environment, a neighborhood, etc., where this type of behavior does not occur.

After we talk, many women thank me. Some have been completely bewildered... simply by the fact that they never really knew how much their experience impacted them, or their friendships with other women, or their ability to work for another female, or their wherewithal to ever work on an all-female team, again. These conversations have been eye-opening. Eye-opening to me as to how they all have persevered.

I know from my own experience; female rivalry is not an easy thing to get through. It is difficult to be able to come out on the other side untarnished. When I was going through my experience, I was so frazzled, unhappy, and "unseeing" of what was right in front of me that I was unable to appropriately voice anything that was occurring. In hindsight, and now that it's a few years behind me, I am glad I went through it because it made me a better, stronger person.

Like me, these strong-spirited women have learned and ultimately grown from their experiences. It is their combined stories of coping that give hope and insight on how to overcome and regain your sparkle.

8.1: Your Turn. Dear reader, have you ever experienced something that resonated with you so deeply that you knew what you did not want to be? Did you know how you did not want to behave? Did you know, in your soul, what you had to overcome? Did you know with every inch of your being, that you wanted to take a negative and turn it into a positive to help others? Take a moment now to write below, your thoughts and why.

_____

_____

_____

_____

Effects of the Experience

A lack of trust, having her guard up, and more closely following her inner voice is a direct result of the experience of rivalry with another female. What a woman has encountered and experienced is life changing. She is more cognizant and on guard than she was before this incident occurred. She tends to set additional boundaries and have an increased sensitivity to other females when embarking upon a new situation. This type of situation influences individual behavior, modifies self-esteem, and in general changes the view she has of herself.

When the exploit took place, she dreaded the unknown behaviors from the "other woman." She felt like she was walking on eggshells, living in fear, and unsure how to find support. She stopped having a voice. She is angry at the situation. Additionally, she is angry at herself, because who puts up with this type of treatment and doesn't say anything?

Numerous women speak of the effects the experience has on them. Even though the situation may have occurred years ago, these effects are still with them today.

> ***Beatrix.*** *"It has made me more alert to looking for those situations around me and being an advocate for people who can't advocate for themselves. And it has made me—I think good leaders integrate things into their leadership styles and so it was the best example I have of a leader that I don't want to be."*

Clio. *"Now, if I feel like someone is headed in that direction, I am big about setting boundaries right up front. I let somebody know right away that something isn't acceptable. And sometimes, I'm almost too quick to judge a situation and might think, 'uh, oh, here we go again.' So sometimes, I'll lay down a boundary when maybe I didn't need to. But most of the time, it's appropriate."*

Dana. *"I really felt like I have trust issues, definitely trust issues, which I thought I like to give people the benefit of the doubt and I typically do give people the benefit of the doubt. But at any signs of weirdness or things that, to me, don't seem right, I keep track of them now."*

Eleni. *"I won't ever when I'm interviewing for a position if I don't feel an immediate connection with the individual, I don't think I'd even go there. Especially if it is a female because I need to feel that I can really trust that individual."*

Faith. *"I don't know if this applies, but I have a daughter and a daughter-in-law, but the daughter-in-law I knew when she was 16. She's been part of our family for a long time, so at times, she can feel like a daughter as well. So, I have to watch that my daughter doesn't feel left out because the 'new' daughter is getting attention, recognition, and participation in the family to an intensity that is more unusual for an in-law to have. So, I'm trying to be more sensitive to that."*

Grace. *"It's made me a lot more cognizant of following my instincts a little more. Like, listen to that inner voice that women are not nice all the time to other women."*

Natalie. *"So, this has happened to me a couple of times. I'm mad that it happened more than once, but I think now that I've been through it a couple of times and I see it now, I see it coming, and I put my hand up. It's bold to say I don't think it's going to happen again, but I think that I know what to look for now. I look back on the first time I dealt with this behavior. I was 23 or 24 and now I'm 48. The funny thing though is when it happened again, I didn't see it for that right away. It's interesting."*

Shannon. *"I've experienced both types of situations with women, negative and positive. I think the negative things are also drivers of what you don't want to have happen. But unfortunately, you may also need both to happen, to fully understand it. A lot of it is attitude. If somebody is really after you and they're negative, you don't have control over that. It's hard, but you really only have control over your own behavior."*

Self-Awareness

I would characterize all the women I've spoken with as having strong personalities and a strong sense of self. Perhaps, it is in hindsight or due to their having had such a negative experience behind them. Maybe it is simply their personality. Most importantly to note, these are not weak women.

They all portrayed themselves as having dynamic, direct, and forthright characteristics. Although not naming it directly, many of the women alluded to the concept of "an awareness of self." They were aware of how their personalities changed during the experience, how the experience continued to affect them after the fact, and how it still affects them in the present day.

Self-awareness is defined as, "having a clear perception of your personality, including strengths, weaknesses, thoughts, beliefs, motivation, and emotions. Self-awareness allows you to understand other people, how they perceive you, your attitude, and your responses to them in the moment" (Merriam Webster, 2020).

These women, traditionally so strong and outspoken, lived through an experience that, to say the least, was life changing. That experience broke them to the point of being a cracked shell of their former self. While many women who live through this overcome their story, this chapter in their lives remains ever-present. She always has a memory bubbling beneath the surface. It is always in existence on her radar as an undercoating of protection to ensure it doesn't happen again.

Beatrix. *"Yeah, it was interesting because I think for me, I've always viewed myself as a very strong and independent person. But I think through all of that, through me getting torn down and then having to build myself back up, you realize—I mean I counted on who I was because of what people said about me."*

Clio. *"Now, it has taught me, when I'm around kids whom I see struggling, I point them in the right direction. It's made me want to mentor people, and to prepare them because I was not prepared, at all."*

Faith. *"I was silent as other people were, and I'm not a person who's typically silent. I'm usually the one who's blunt and outspoken and gets in trouble for being that way. It just, for whatever reason, I'm not sure I understand even, I didn't challenge its existence or criticize that it was happening. I was worn down."*

Ilene. *"I am a very cards-on-the-table, handle things head-on, kind of person. So, to me, that was a very frustrating dynamic of the work because there really was no head-on way to take that type of behavior. You just had to kind of suck it up, like you are tiptoeing."*

Natalie. *"This experience has made me more aware of how I am when I interact with other women. I've also realized it was a real culture shame at my last office. They just didn't do anything about all of the bad behaviors. It was awful. It was after reading Brené Brown that I realized that this is what it was… I wouldn't have come up with that, or to that conclusion on my own. And I don't know… They say the closer you get to 50 the less you care. I'm like, yeah, 'Whatever.'"*

Phoebe. *"This behavior… it's real. I feel like I am moving forward in terms of these female rivalries, but for me, they will always be there as long as I'm in a patriarchal culture and discriminated based on race. For me personally, I've learned just simply to not take any-*

thing personally. When I see these women, I'm cordial but I also don't say anything else and that's a skill. Getting to where I can understand that, has been a lot... I know there were some things I didn't need to know how painful that experience was for me. But on the other end of it—I am thankful because it taught me so much. And isn't that amazing?"

Josie. *"What I'm learning... and I've always seen this. But you know, there are all sorts of these types of rivalries that are out there. It's the people not being able to step out of their heads or their life to understand or accept that other people are doing things different than they are. And what the people are doing that is different than them, is not wrong. You know what I mean? I'm like, 'What made you the expert?' You do you, and that's great. Don't judge me."*

I've seen remorse from all the women who've shared this aspect of their situation with me. There is always an element of defeat and confusion, even if the situation is years behind them. When internalizing this type of behavior, it is so hard to understand how a situation like this can have such a momentous impact. It causes them to alter their behavior so drastically that they lose their voice and are unable to stand up for themselves. There is deep regret and shame in this aspect of reflection.

Wendy. *"It was very much a painful time in my life. This experience really changed me. I've felt shame toward myself in the sense of, 'Why did I let it happen?' But I know now, there really wasn't much that I could do while I was in it... Because I just wasn't myself then... I wasn't the woman I am now.*

I do still feel very much like I have to have my guard up... These women were trying to undermine me. That stays with you in a certain sense. I was able to survive by being resourceful and continuing my education and certifications. I have to remind myself that I am talented and that

I shouldn't doubt myself. That is what gets me up in the morning and what I've tried to stay true to."

8.2: Your Turn. Dear reader, have you ever experienced a situation where you were able to clearly see insight about yourself and how that experience may have altered you? Perhaps this insight occurred more so after the fact of this experience taking place? Take a moment now to write below, your thoughts and why.

_____

_____

_____

_____

Coping

Traditionally, females who deal with this experience eventually find a manner to cope and/or ultimately leave the situation. In her coping, she can find a reprieve and escape. Rarely do women confront the situation while they are experiencing it. Speaking out induces fear that doing so entails the risk of potentially losing a job, friendships, social standing, etc.

From my experience, it is rare that a woman who is involved with this type of behavior will ever confront the "other woman." However, over time, and once it is behind her, she is able to self-reflect, learn, and grow. This may take years but ultimately, women who have shared their stories with me are more aware. They have the ability and insight to support other women encountering a similar circumstance.

Coping means to "invest one's own conscious effort, to solve personal and interpersonal problems, in order to try to master, minimize, or tolerate stress and conflict" (Wikipedia, 2020).

Utilization of Coping Mechanisms

Coping manifests an individual's character and is a personal process that is very different for each woman. Either simple or complex, its many facets are what helps each woman I've talked with tolerate this type of situation. Coping mechanisms developed as a response to situations that the women could not control. Whether the experience lasted several weeks or a span of many years, coping is a process that helped each woman endure.

> *"Coping shapes emotion, as it does psychological stress, by influencing the person-environment relationship and how it is appraised. Coping involves both (a) attempts to change the person-environment realities behind negative emotions (problem-focused coping) and (b) attempts to change either what is attended to or how it is appraised (emotion-focused coping)" (Lazarus, 1993, p. 16).*

In order to bear what they encounter, women developed coping skills to survive and deal with this type of experience. The type of coping mechanisms my research as a whole on this topic revealed is primarily two-fold in nature:

1. **Coping at the Scene:** is an immediate means of escaping the experience as it occurs. It manifests during the situation and appears often, not to incorporate a deep internal reflection. Rather, it is reactive in nature and simply a way to break free. It's an, "*on the surface, exterior type of coping mechanism*" and is not accomplished through direct confrontation with "the other woman."

2. **Coping After the Fact:** is a mindful effort to deal consciously with the behavior and incorporate deep internal reflection. For the many women with whom I've spoken, it manifests after their experience and is a means to move on with their lives. It is an "*internal, interior type of coping mechanism*." (I will introduce you to the concept of "coping after the fact" as the next chapter will focus more intently on this method).

Coping at the Scene

Coping at the scene can be likened to "reactive coping,"

"a stress-management strategy that involves efforts to deal with a past or present stressful situation (e.g., marital dissolution, losing one's job) by compensating for or accepting the associated harm or loss. Reactive coping may also involve efforts to readjust goals, find benefit, or search for meaning" (APA, 2018).

From gathered stories, my research gleans that coping at the scene entails the following coping mechanisms:

- Leaving the situation
- Therapy/counseling
- Exercise
- Confiding in/seeking advice from family and friends
- Religion
- Legal counsel
- Education as an outlet
- Wine/food/substances
- Conversing with other women in a similar situation

Women have recounted the way in which they were able to cope with their incident.

Amy. "I stayed one year, and then I took the only option that was available to me, and I left the building after being there 36 years."

Beatrix. "And after I was gone about six months, and I did go to therapy and get over all of that, to kind of get myself back. Once I put two and two together to see what had happened, I went back to the HR person in that business and just sort of replayed the whole thing because even when you're going through the process of it, there was some fear involved. I was afraid if I shared too much, I wouldn't be able to get out."

Dana. *"I mean, I just pray. And it is faith—a belief in God. I have a strong belief in God. Faith. Quite frankly, I was raised Catholic. I went to church and I prayed to God. And I said, 'God, I will go to church every Sunday for the rest of my life if you help me through this.'"*

Eleni. *"I told a couple people that I was feeling it necessary for me to tape my conversations with her just to protect myself."*

Faith. *"I'm a person who does cope decently using exercise to reduce stress, reaching out for help from my husband or special friends. I would cope in that way."*

Grace. *"Yes, I talked a lot to family members and friends about it in terms of what advice they would offer, or how they dealt with situations like this. So, that provided some support, reprieve as well. So, yes that was good."*

Hannah. *"I don't know that I had the best way to cope, other than possibly a few glasses of wine."*

Ilene. *"Not that I am terribly proud of this but I would say that probably the best coping mechanism was to sit around with other women that I knew were feeling that very same thing, coming from this particular individual. And we would just kind of laugh about it, and make fun of it, and say that when we were running the place we would be very, very different."*

Sydney. *"I was drinking a lot more. I would go home and sometimes wouldn't even take my coat off and I would just drink. Yeah... I would just drink. I would do a shot of tequila right when I walked in the door, which is so not like me. I'm like, yeah, a glass of wine at night type of person. I was just drinking more because I was so very unhappy."*

Shannon. *"I had a friend from the program I could confide in. I'd say, 'Am I being too sensitive? Am I misreading this circumstance? Am I being too insensitive?' Talking to her was validating. It let me know I wasn't crazy for feeling the way I did."*

The emotional impact of this type of experience can be all-consuming. An on-going negative incident with a female leader, supervisor, person in a role model position, or social acquaintance provides a good example of what these women do not want to be. They understand to not take what they've experienced personally and have learned from the situation.

8.3: Your Turn. Dear reader, what type of mechanism do you turn to as a reactional way to deal with something stressful? Do you ever face a situation that is so painful that it's easier to compartmentalize it and push it away to deal with later? Take a moment now to write below, your thoughts and why.

_____

_____

_____

_____

How She Coped

Amy. To cope and deal with the experience as an outlet for relief, Amy found solace in her educational assistants. "The only thing that helped to minimize the experience was the success that I saw in the classroom, and the comfort I had working with my assistants because they were so supportive of me." In order to break the cyclical behavior and move on, Amy ultimately had to leave a working environment she loved.

"I think that along with the rivalry from Karen and her team, it was one thing that I had kind of pushed far enough away so that I was managing to survive. However, with a new incoming principal and

Karen already camped on her doorstep, I could see the writing on the wall. That the stories were going to start all over again with the new principal and that she was already in there explaining to her what a bad person, as well as teacher, I was.

It still has an effect on me because even though I'm at a different school with a completely different staff, a few staff members that I knew. I'm still closed off. I'm still closed off because I don't trust anybody."

Beatrix. During her experience with the other woman, Beatrix was mistrustful of other co-workers but was eventually able to find an outlet and some support from a male colleague.

"I think as my expression and my demeanor and things about me started to change, he would frequently say, 'Are you okay?' And for a long time, I wouldn't say anything. But then when I finally sort of—you know how you kind of tiptoe into something just to see how somebody is going to respond? To see if it's safe or not, but he was really good. He helped me."

The only way that Beatrix knew how to cope with the experience was to leave the situation.

"But it wasn't really until the process of being able to go look for a new work opportunity—I mean I had to physically escape it. And after I was gone about six months, I did go to therapy to get myself back. After that, I could kind of put two and two together and see what had happened. I went back to the HR person in that business and replayed the whole thing. But even when you're going through the process, there was some fear involved. I was afraid if I shared too much, I wouldn't be able to get out."

Clio. Exercising was one coping mechanism that helped Clio find a bit of release from the experience.

> *"I would exercise. Pretty much the only thing that got me through it at the time was my best friend from college lived in the area. We would meet after work every day to walk on this local path. We would walk for four miles. The two miles down, I would vent about my day, and on the two miles back, she would vent about her day."*

Additionally, the support of close friends and meeting her soon-to-be husband helped to provide relief and was also a means of survival.

> *"My best friend's roommate went to college with us too, so the three of us socialized a lot. They knew my situation, so they just really supported me. During that time, I met my husband, so at some point during that time, it was probably just the last year, he became someone that I could talk to also."*

Dana. Dana was quick to acknowledge that religion was an outlet that helped her cope with her experiences.

> *"Faith. Quite frankly, I was raised Catholic. I went to church and I prayed to God. And I said, 'God, I will go to church every Sunday for the rest of my life if you help me through this.'"*

Eleni. Eleni said that at that time, the only way she knew how to protect herself and cope with the situation was to privately record their conversations, to have proof of her female supervisor's indirect aggressive behaviors.

> *"So, I talked with a couple of attorneys who had professional legal experience and asked them if it was legal for me to start taping our conversations. Because I was, I wanted to have the proof that I was*

asking and bringing things up to her and she was not supporting me on what I would bring up."

Although it was evident that the experience affected her and who she was as a person, today, she bore no resentment or malice at being fired from her job.

"So, where I was wrong in how I acted was that I needed to check my facts—the attorneys that I talked to had not practiced this type of law in our state. In my state, it was against the law to actually tape conversations without the other individual knowing so that's how I made the mistake."

In fact, Eleni was very matter of fact about the situation and took it as an experience she could grow and learn from. "I learned a lot in terms of what I look for in whom I report to in the future and the importance of that relationship." As she self-reflected about being fired as a result of experiencing rivalry with another woman within the working environment she had this to say,

"I feel that being fired is a bit of a black marker or failure I see in terms of my career. But I also know that most people that are successful, have been fired one time or another from their job. And I guess in some ways, I take solace in the fact that I wasn't fired for my lack of doing my job, but of, you know, I guess you could say bad judgment, which maybe that's even worse, but I wasn't fired for being incompetent."

Grace. A main outlet for Grace and a way to verify the experience was to document the behaviors of the other woman.

"I just documented things and having the experience of her being dishonest and deceitful with senior management also provided some reprieve."

Hannah. A way for Hannah to cope and deal with the rivalrous situations was to talk to the women from which the behaviors were occurring.

> *"In telecom, because I was there for such a long time, having some head-on conversations with one woman in particular, I think helped because it gave us a chance to understand each other's perspectives."*

Ilene. As the experience continued Ilene found that a means of distancing herself from the situation was to leave headquarters for a period to work overseas.

> *"...Because you are so close to the very mission of the organization when you are working overseas you are able to care less about things like political battles and rivalries that are really headquarter based. So getting back out in the field in my case allowed me to walk away from it and not really, not really have continued issues."*

8.4: Your Turn. Dear reader, in reading these poignant stories of how each woman coped, did anything resonate with you? Did something they shared trigger a memory or similar experience that you also lived through and dealt with? Take a moment now to write below, your thoughts and why.

_____

_____

_____

_____

Closing

We don't have control over the actions of other people. We may impact it, we may trigger it, but control it... no. Ultimately, it's always their choice to act, behave, and do, as they do. At any age, this can be a hard lesson to learn and understand... especially, if you are the recipient of something so harmful and damaging.

When the claws come out, what you do in response to that is up to you. It can be very challenging to not take things personally, to ignore them, and let things slide. Ultimately though, that ends up being a positive reflection about you. Sooner or later, negative actions and people will always reveal themselves and their true colors.

What you do have absolute control over, is your own actions. It is in that action that you have the ability to regain your sparkle. Because my dear, regaining your sparkle is completely something that you have the ability to regulate. Are you ready to straighten your crown, remove the rust, and find your shine again? Chin up my fair lady... the next chapter is all about that.

Chapter 9:

Chin Up and Straighten Your Crown!

"Healing is freaking messy. It's alienation.
It's detachment. It's batsh*t crazy.
It's jet-black inky darkness.
It makes you ache for the void or the mundane.
You want to quit everything, but you can't.
You won't. Not now. Not ever, baby.
Because even though it aches the mother of all aches, you've changed.
Underneath all the bullsh*t there you are. Brand new. Born again.
An angel awakened to her cosmic mission. And you aren't going back.
There are more out there, waking up in the dark.
So, don't worry about fixing any part of you and let your
wicked shambles raise the d*mn roof on this whole thing."
—Tanya Markul, The She Book v.2 (Mind Journal, 2020).

Shannon's Story

"I was in my mid-twenties, working in academia on my Master's program in Europe. There were a lot of international students from all over the world in our program. I was in the same program with several women. We took all our classes together and socialized together, too.

A Greek woman and I, when we initially met, rubbed each other the wrong way. We hated each other. It was very bad because we had really similar academic interests and would constantly get grouped together because our interests were the same. As a result, we always had projects together, even though we really just didn't get along. We argued constantly. We spent almost six months doing this, constantly arguing, which was very stressful to both of us.

The following semester it was the same, only more intense because we were also living together. We worked together for the entire semester doing the same research, and both questioned why it was happening because we knew we hated each other. It was also pretty obvious to everyone else too, as everyone knew we didn't get along. I think it was about that point that we both realized that we had to work together. I tried very hard. We still argued a lot, and she still got mad, and it was very draining. I felt like I was walking on eggshells... It was awful.

Those first semesters were very stressful because we were in a new country. It was also winter and there was no sunshine, so it was pretty dreary... The courses were hard, and everyone missed home. In general, I think a lot of us were really unhappy, were out of our comfort zones, and encountering great change. It was huge.

She flat out yelled at me in front of everyone in the middle of class one day. We didn't talk for weeks. There were also a lot of passive-aggressive behaviors too. Petty things like not inviting each other to group functions, ignoring each other, etc.

But what ended up happening was, we each gave a little, and after a while we started to get more patient with each other. A big moment for me was when she was on the phone having a very heated conversation, speaking Greek to someone. I thought to myself, 'This sounds so stressful.' When she got off the phone I said, 'Are you ok? That sounded so bad.' She said, 'What are you talking about? That was my dad. I was telling him about my day and how much I loved him.' And that's when it hit me. I thought, 'So much of this is because she is Greek. She sounds so forceful but she's not trying to purposefully be mean or angry. It's just how she speaks.' I became more patient after and saw her in a different light after I realized she really wasn't yelling at me at all.

What I found was, I needed to have a shared understanding of her culture and she of mine. I think the other thing that contributed to our getting along is that we both wanted it to work. It took a lot of effort from both of us, but we also knew that we were the only ones that could change it. It turned out that she and I became really good friends. She actually was one of my best friends by the end of the program. We found out that we had a lot in common and really liked each other."

"There will be very painful moments in your life that will change you.
Let them make you stronger, smarter and kinder.
But don't you go and become someone that you're not.
Cry. Scream if you have to.
Then straighten out that crown and keep moving!"
—Erin Van Vurin (Daily Inspiration Quotes, 2020).

Regaining Your Sparkle is up to You!

Since this behavior is insidious, it's hard to confront it head-on. You may physically feel its aftermath from head to toe. It may impact everything you do, your energy level, your outlook, and your perspective. It's difficult to speak out about it because the behavior is so perplexing to place or pinpoint. This makes it exhausting to address or tough to find support. The stories I hear, the stories I've read, the social media comments, the responses expressed in the audiences when I speak... These voices all carry a deep-rooted pain when discussing this topic.

And the thing is, if you do not address it, it will eat you alive. It will completely consume you. It will suck you dry until you are nothing but a shriveled shell of the woman you once were. And ultimately, this means "she" still has power... over you.

In all the narratives I've heard, I've only interacted with one female who was visibly unable to let go of her situation. It makes great sense that this experience was a part of her life and a large part of her personal story. Unfortunately, her sparkle remained dull because she was never able to regain it. Her experience crippled her, and she physically could not move on or get past it. As a result, she became socially introverted, had few female friends, and pretty much withdrew into a smaller non-social world of her own with her pets.

She became a victim of the situation.

I believe it's the variety of stories in your life that shape who you are and who you become. You can grow from them or you can let them consume you. To regain your sparkle, you must let it go. You have to carry on. Forgive. If you cannot forgive someone or the situation, years after it has occurred, then the fault is not on them, but on you.

To get over these types of negative behaviors, don't get even—do better. Rise above. You may not be able to change the other person's actions but letting them know they are getting to you gives them control. Rising above and becoming engulfed in your own life and your own successes will help you leave the negativity behind. And fundamentally, that is how you win.

Selena shared what happened towards the end of her situation at work and how rejuvenating it felt when she started getting her voice back.

> **Selena.** *"So, I'd given three weeks to a month's notice and was working in an open space in the office when Tina came back in after traveling out of town. She said, 'I heard that you resigned. Can we talk?' I stood up and responded to her in the open space in front of everyone, 'Tina, if you need anything for professional work, I'll work with you. If*

we have a meeting, I'll be there for you. But I will not respond to you from here on out in any form of communication except email.' And she said, 'Email?' And I said, 'Yes, thank you.'

I turned around and I remember feeling, 'This is who I am! Holy Sh*t!' I felt so good! And she stayed away from me because all of a sudden, I think she realized she no longer had control over me. And what pisses me off about the whole situation is that suddenly all at once, everyone else saw it too, her behavior. After I left, two weeks later they fired her. They then called me and asked me to come back. I said no. It felt like, you know, when you are dating a boyfriend all these years and you always think he's going to come through and then you find out that he's never going to come through. I knew we needed to break up immediately because I was done."

Phoebe shared how she handled her "h*ll-on-wheels" colleague, Cassie, who hadn't spoken to her in over a year and who was the ringleader of negative behavior with all the other women in their office.

Phoebe. *"On Cassie's last day, I left a pair of cute earrings on her desk. I heard Cassie going around desk to desk, talking to everyone, and asking if they'd been the one to give her the gift. Finally, it was my turn. I felt this presence behind me and as I turned around, she said, 'Did you give me something, these earrings?' I said, 'Yes, I did.' 'Thank you,' she said. 'No, thank you,' I said. 'You taught me how to be a better person, more patient, and compassionate. So good luck and thank you.' And it was true, she did. I knew exactly the type of woman I did not want to be, because of her awful behavior."*

"I learned that courage was not the absence of fear, but the triumph over it.
The brave man is not he who does not feel afraid,
but he who conquers that fear."
—Nelson Mandela (Goodreads, 2021).

Self-Reflection

Knowledge is power. Once you can identify this deceitful dynamic with the "other woman," you can work on changing it, either by getting out of it or using it to your advantage. A key component to getting more enjoyment out of your life and relationships is self-reflection.

Many women I've spoken with have revealed that as a result of such a negative experience, they now also examine their own behaviors and how they treat other women. To say they are hyper-aware in this regard is an understatement.

At the time their experiences occurred, every woman who's shared her story said it was without a doubt negative. However, for a chunk of the women, especially as it pertains to the working environment where it's easier to see a visible outcome, the longer, lasting effects are positive in nature.

Taking an unfavorable situation and turning it into a productive one is not done lightly. It's not easy. Over time, many of these women were subject to deep soul searching and intimate reflection about the situations they endured. Rather than dwelling on the adverse, most of the women ensured their personal and professional behavior was not like that of the other woman. Having a negative occurrence with a female leader, female in a role model position, friend, family member, or other female socially, etc., provided a good example of who they do not want to be.

As it pertains to the working environment, most of the women I've talked to maintain managerial or leadership positions. As a result of being more cognizant, when a similar situation exposes itself as experienced by another female, they can offer support and insight. Additionally, many of these women are in positions to implement change and awareness within their own working environments, home environment, social environments, etc., This yields them the ability to foster effective working relationships between women. They want to become a representation of what the other woman is not. They want to be champions for other women.

> ***Melanie.*** *"I guess I never knew how much that time from college impacted me. How much it invaded my trust and impacts me today with women I trust or don't...In the aspect of not having that many*

female friends because I'm afraid of what they'll do. That they'll do the same thing to me as my 'friends' from college. Thank you. Talking with you about this has helped me to see things in a different light."

Jessica. *"I've stopped internalizing it so much. I realize it's not me. I'm not the problem. No one has ever asked me the questions you've asked me before about my experience. It opened my eyes... It's talking about the 'unsaid,' so people feel less alone. It's also a very difficult subject to attack directly."*

Wendy. *"This has been so therapeutic for so many women like me, to see the research you are doing. It's a real problem. I appreciate you taking the time to listen and to also listen to the other women... It hurts my heart that other women are also going through this."*

As it's much easier to do in hindsight, I've had many women reflect about potential external factors that may have influenced their own behavior during the time the rivalrous experience occurred.

Clio. *"I was also very naive when at college. I thought the career center was for the business students only. Since I was a music major, I assumed those services weren't available to me so I did not pursue them. I missed out on valuable information about interviewing, the job search, and coping in the workplace. I regret my ignorance."*

Betty referenced her mother, and how as a young inexperienced woman she emulated similar behaviors she observed when growing up.

"Some of what plays into this and I responded to it is, my mom. My mom always tried to please her mom. So, when you grow up in an environment and you see that we then worked to please our mom. So that, then, translated for me with women in the workplace. I would try to please women who were older or further along than me."

Hannah mentioned her work ethic and how it affected other women within her working environment.

> *"I'm very goal-oriented. Just because other people weren't like that, I think that's in part why I stood out and so I felt bad because other people didn't have the same drive as me, that they were being measured against me in that aspect."*

Wendy reflected how her behavior helped to ignite the "other woman's" behavior to her because she did not succumb and "play the game."

> *"She would brag about things and I just wouldn't respond. Other people would say, 'Oh that is so fabulous or you're awesome.' I think she really needed that type of positive endorsement, but I didn't do it. I had already earned my respect but she had to run down the hall for it. Her earnestness was just so amazing."*

9.1: Your Turn. Dear reader, have you ever experienced something that caused you to sit back, take a deep breath, and self-reflect? Although it was hard, was it something that after some reflection you knew you had the power to change? Have you ever experienced this after a negative interaction with another female? Take a moment now to write below, your thoughts and why.

_____

_____

_____

_____

> *"Opposition can be your friend. Opposition can be the fire that tempers the better sword, as well as the ice that cools a fiery temper. Don't ever run from it; learn from it!"*
> —Jack R. Rose (Goodreads, Inc., 2020).

Coping After the Fact

As mentioned in the previous chapter, for each woman interviewed there are two types of coping mechanisms that helped them get them through their negative experience:

1. **Coping at the Scene:** is an immediate means of escaping the experience as it occurred. It's manifested during the situation and appears often, not to incorporate a deep internal reflection at the moment in which the experience occurs. Rather, it is reactive in nature and simply a way to break free. It's an, "on the surface, exterior type of coping mechanism" and, as portrayed by these interviews, is not accomplished through direct confrontation with "the other woman." Coping at the scene is a reactive means to cope while still, very much, involved in the situation.

2. **Coping After the Fact:** is a mindful effort to deal consciously with the behavior and incorporate deep internal reflection. For the many women with whom I've spoken, it manifests after their experience and is a means to move on with their lives. It is an "internal, interior type of coping mechanism."

Coping after the fact can also be likened to "proactive coping,"

> "a stress-management strategy that reflects efforts to build up resources that facilitate promotion toward challenging goals and personal growth. Proactive individuals are motivated to meet challenges, and they commit themselves to their own high standards. They see demands and opportunities in the distant future and initiate a constructive path of action toward meeting them. Stress is interpreted as eustress—that is, productive arousal and vital energy—and coping thus becomes goal management instead of risk management" (APA, 2018).

Coping after the fact centers on mindfulness and is a proactive approach to dealing with the negative behaviors after they have occurred.

Mindfulness

While they did not directly name mindfulness as the specific action, most of the women I've spoken with talked about utilizing a determined type of thinking or internal outlook to help change their situation. They did this as a type of coping mechanism to prevent the situation from having control over them. The method they utilized is mindfulness, defined as,

> "awareness of one's internal states and surroundings. The concept has been applied to various therapeutic interventions—for example, mindfulness-based cognitive behavior therapy mindfulness-based stress reduction, and mindfulness meditation to help people avoid destructive or automatic habits and responses by learning to observe their thoughts, emotions, and other present-moment experiences without judging or reacting to them" (APA, 2018).

My research findings on this topic suggests that coping after the fact included all but one woman whom I've spoken to about the act of forgiveness. Forgiveness does not mean condoning the experience or situation at all. It does not, that I am aware of for any of the women, mean direct forgiveness of the other woman. It simply means the ability to forgive *the situation*, which provides the capability to release the negative experience. It is the difference between "staying stuck" emotionally in a situation, versus learning to cope, let go, and ultimately carry on with their lives.

> **Sydney.** *"I finally let it go... The anger. I went to Florida for five days with my husband and my brother and sister-in-law. We had a nice little spot on the beach with a great Tiki bar and great weather. And I just let myself go. The ocean is my happy place. I just sat there and I said, 'I'm letting this all go. I'm not bringing it home with me.' I sat and relaxed and I had fun. I saw some friends down there and then... I left it there.*
>
> *I've also been doing a lot of positive affirmations. I've been doing some meditation at night. I use the Calm App. I've been going to the*

gym. I've gone to the gym every morning since I got laid off and the positive stuff is really very powerful. I really believe it changes your brain chemistry and I've been doing all of those things. And then when I went to Florida, that was a transformative trip.

I just sat there and had a great time. I know that sounds crazy, but it helped me. I stared at the ocean and said, 'This is not going to win. I'm going to win. I'm going to come out better because of this.' And when I came home and I said, 'That's it. I'm done. The pity party is over!'

Those people suck. Yes, I wanted to end my career there. They took that from me. But I believe that whatever happens to you is going to lead you to someplace better. Whatever that is... I'm going to believe that the universe is going to take me someplace better and I'm going to be open to it and I'm just going to listen to what the universe says. You've got to let it go though, because when you're just walking around with all this anger... It takes up so much energy.

You know, I'd kept a lot of notes about all the things I'd documented. I had hired a lawyer after it happened. I thought maybe I would sue them. And ultimately, I just said, 'I don't really want to litigate because I don't want this to live any longer.' I got rid of a lot of those documents because I don't want to look at it again. I don't want to relive it. I know what happened. She was very mean to me. She tortured me. She had a plan and she executed it. She came in every day with the agenda to just destroy me bit by bit. And she did. She got rid of me. And even after I was gone, she was still going around bad mouthing me and destroying me. And I felt like you got rid of me, 'Why can't you give it a rest? Was I that threatening to you?'

I had to find a way to put it behind me. Everyone kept asking me if I was ok and I'd say, 'I'm fine. I'm fine.' And then one night I just wasn't fine. And I imploded. I broke down and I said, 'I'm not fine.' I think once I finally let it all out, I was able to start my road to recovery.

I do believe something better will come. I just want to put this behind me. I have never been treated so horribly and deliberately. I guess I felt a little relieved when it was over because I wasn't being treated so badly anymore. I don't miss it. Believe me.

Everybody who has seen me since has remarked on how incredibly relaxed and unstressed I look. I've said, 'I feel it. I am relaxed and much happier this way. If I didn't work there ever again, I would be very happy because I never have to go back to what I consider to be h*ll on earth.' I never want to speak to that woman. I never want to see her again. I just can't even believe that that person can sleep at night knowing that she's just destroyed other people. How do you just deliberately go in and destroy someone's 32-year career? I'm glad I'm out of there, but you know, I had really hoped to retire from there. I only had a few more years to go."

9.2: Your Turn. Dear reader, how have you used coping after the fact versus coping at the scene to overcome challenges? Have you utilized mindfulness to center yourself, to cope, to reflect, or to move on? How does that make you feel in the moment? After the fact? Take a moment now to write below, your thoughts and why.

_____

_____

_____

_____

"I forgive people but that doesn't mean I accept their behavior or trust them. I forgive them for me, so I can let go and move on with my life."
—Unknown (Daily Inspiration Quotes, 2020).

Unresolved Trauma and Forgiveness

Did you know that once we heal from physical pain, it ends? Emotional pain is different. We are able to relive and feel that same emotional pain, in the same manner, that we did when it occurred, all over again, even years later. That type of hurt can stay with us much longer, possibly never decreasing in intensity (Rock, 2011).

Research suggests why rejection hurts as much or more so long term than physical pain.

> *"People who experience events like this (being unfairly treated at work or being attacked falsely by a rival in the media) find that the pain from these events can take years to recover from. A study of social pain in 2008 found that social pain comes back when you think about it again, whereas physical pain does not. Giving someone a thump on the arm as punishment for a mistake may, in theory at least, be a 'kinder' punishment than attacking their ideas in public and/ or in front of others"* (Psychological Science, 2008).

I've seen this show up in the women who've shared their stories with me, regarding the pain they've experienced from female rivalry.

Healing requires us to be honest with ourselves. It's the ability to see and understand that some things we may be holding onto are harming us. Although it's hard, it's ultimately a choice to decide to let go of it. Emotional feelings can linger years later. They can affect you personally, physically, mentally, and socially.

> *Certain events may even involuntarily trigger reactions in us that we haven't thought about in years: guilt, shame, fear, or anger sourcing from something earlier in our lives. Attachment research suggests that it isn't just what happened to us that impacts us. We're also affected by the extent to which we haven't been able to feel the full pain of, or make sense of, as it pertains to negative experiences and emotions. And so we compartmentalize them instead. When we don't deal with*

our trauma, it stays with us. We haven't made sense of our story, and therefore, our past is still impacting our present in countless invisible ways (Firestone, 2018).

Understanding unresolved trauma and how it impacts you emotionally, mentally, physically, and what that looks like in your life now is the start to dealing with it. It's instinctual to avoid pain, to not want to think about past negative events. However, accepting what has happened and separating the past from the present can lead to healing. Facing trauma is not easy, but it helps you recover. It makes you feel stronger and more secure within yourself. You have to understand and face the trauma in order to forgive it.

Negative resentments evolving from past experiences can hold you back and cloud the enjoyment of your present. This can impact you in some of the following ways:

- Kill your enjoyment
- Affect relationships
- Hold you back from experiencing love
- Live in your body and cause illness (physical, mental, emotional, etc.)

And you know what?! The absolute beauty of forgiving a situation, even a person for that matter, and contrary to an actual popular belief… two people are not required for it to work. Read that again, please. *Two people are not required for it to work*! This is all about YOU.

Deciding whether to hold onto anger or releasing it, is a choice you consciously have control over. How do you want to feel? What do you want to have taking up space in your brain and body? It's your choice. Forgiveness is not condoning the actions of the other party! It's not giving consent to what occurred. It's not rolling over and giving up. It is not giving in or losing...anything. It's letting go of hatred so that it doesn't consume you. Forgiveness frees YOU from what I call "resentment prison." Ultimately, forgiveness is for the forgiver, and that is YOU. Not the other way around.

9.3: Your Turn. Dear reader, have you ever dealt with unresolved trauma in your life? Have you experienced physical pain? Have you experienced emotional pain? What pain lingers with you longer? Do you feel that forgiveness of a situation or a person or an event in your life helps you to move on and let go? Take a moment now to write below, your thoughts and why.

_____

_____

_____

_____

Forgiveness in the Working Environment

Dr. Fred Luskin (2010), Director of the Stanford University Forgiveness Project, talks about forgiveness in the working environment.

> *"Forgiveness has been shown to reduce anger, hurt, depression and stress and lead to great feelings of optimism, hope, compassion and self-confidence. Few of us have had as many models for forgiveness in the workplace as we have had for negative competition, gossip, and retaliation" (para 10).*

Think back to Amy. She felt trapped in a career that she could not circumvent because to escape the rivalrous situation she had to leave the environment she once loved. Although she verbally said she'd "let it go," as Amy spoke, there was still an obvious, physical raw pain that continued to connect her to the 14-year-long experience.

> ***Amy.*** *"You know, I have let it go, but there are times when I look back at the fact that I spent 36 years of my life working with children in that school and it bothers me that I feel like my only option for survival to finish out my career was to leave that building I had given so much to."*

Michael Stone (2002) talks about the importance of forgiveness when applied in the working environment.

> *When we do not forgive someone for his or her actions, we are left energetically holding on to something from the past. In other words, we can never be fully present or move forward with that person because this constant reminder of the past robs us of our energy, attention and awareness. To encourage the greatest contribution, commitment and professional mastery in someone, we need to operate in the present. The failure to forgive keeps us stuck in the past, producing an endless cycle of recurring events which continue to spiral downward towards greater and greater alienation, separation and explanation (p. 279).*

In contrast to Amy, the rest of the women I've talked to over the years about their experience have also referenced "letting go." What is obvious in their demeanor and way in which they relayed their story is truly the fact they have forgiven the situation and are able to move on.

> **Dana.** *"And I think that I feel very blessed and fortunate to know a lot of people that I have professionally that have helped me and things like that. But you just have these few eggs that you run into. And I just say, 'Oh, dear God, help me through this.' And, somehow, He does. And it's hard when you go through it. But you just have to."*

> **Grace.** *"It's also made me realize that I can't take things like this personally because, at the end of the day, it's not—it had nothing to do with me, or what I did or didn't do. I don't take things personally because it's not about you. It's really what the other person's reality is, or lack thereof."*

Recall the other women who've opened up to me. When their experiences occurred, they certainly encountered their share of similar, gut-wrenching emotional pain. However, in present day, none of them appear to have the same type of distress toward their experience as Amy has.

> *When we face suffering there are two main avenues out of that—coping or forgiveness. Coping is when we say I will simply 'get through this with the passage of time.' We move forward with bitterness, and some degree of 'I've just got to battle through this.' This is basic coping as we stay with the old strategies. Another response is to learn and become aware of new forgiveness skills you can bring to bear now and on future problems. You can cultivate forgiveness and that gives you a greater efficacy and likelihood for handling more skillfully the next thing that comes down the pike (Luskin, 2010, para 4).*

What my findings of this phenomenon reveal is that forgiveness is a favorable means of coping that has enabled many of the women I've spoken with to take a negative experience and turn it into a positive one.

> ***Clio.*** *"It was a learning experience. If you'd asked me 16 years ago if I'd do it again, I would have run away with my hair on fire. Now I can say that it helped. I mean, I've actually learned a lot from it."*

> ***Wendy.*** *"I feel stronger now and more resilient. I feel like I can do what I can do, and I can get through. It's made me tougher and it makes me feel like I can last in this environment until I retire which is my goal. I've been here 19 years...I know this is a bump in the road but that I can keep on going."*

> ***Jennifer.*** *"I've had a couple of evil female bosses in between these other incidents, that have had their own issues...and I was like, 'Oh, I see your game. I'm not playing. Next!' You know, so yes there were a couple of other jobs in there that I just like, 'Nope. I'm going to skip this! On to the next job.' Sometimes, that's the only way to self-preserve. You have to be in control of you. Yeah. That's easier said than*

*done for some women that I know, who are stuck in a job or don't
have flexibility."*

Rather than dwell in the negative, these women are constructive in ensuring
their professional and personal behavior is not like that of the "other woman."

> **Ilene.** *"I think it turned me into even more of a feminist and I was not
> a feminist when I joined this organization 25 years ago. But it sure
> turned me into one. And so, I am hypersensitive, perhaps even to a
> fault, to want to look out for other women and others who just seem to
> be having a harder time of it. And I just have to believe it is because of
> the difficult experiences that I had early on."*

> **Beatrix.** *"It has made me more alert to looking for those situations
> around me and being an advocate for people who can't advocate for
> themselves. And it has made me... I think good leaders integrate things
> into their leadership style. And so, it was the best example I have of a
> leader that I don't want to be."*

> **Faith.** *"I'm the CEO now, for about 12 years now, and I have 20 staff
> members. About 17 of them are women. What I work hard at is trying
> to protect them from each other around some of the rivalry by working
> to treat them fairly and as consistently equally as possible and to jump
> in to calm down some of them—it's more jealousy I would say, rather
> than the word 'rivalry'—that can happen in the workplace. I think it's
> being sensitive to knowing what happens at times when there is a high
> number of females in the environment."*

> **Wendy.** *"Someone once asked me, 'Do you think this problem with women
> will get better once the baby boomers retire? And the new generation of
> women come along?' I thought about it but had to disagree... Because no,
> I don't. The woman in my situation was much younger than me. I think
> there needs to be more education, or a movement to address this.*

I think it's part of your story and you know... I do think stories can be changed, most definitely. I think you can find a group... your tribe, your sisterhood, whatever your circle, whatever you want to call it. But I do think there are a bunch of kick-ass women out there that do lift up and empower. But there are also some that are certainly the opposite of that too.

All we need is just to have someone to listen and to understand and really let each other contribute and provide value. Ultimately, it's about having respect for each other."

Sydney. *"You know, people say that two queens can't live in the same house, but I don't believe that. I believe that good, strong women who want to work together and be collaborative can do so. Because for a very, very long time, I ran a really great team. We were productive. We worked well together. And when push came to shove, we put aside everything, and we got the job done."*

9.4: Your Turn. Dear reader, have you ever experienced a situation where you had to apply forgiveness in the working environment? Was the other person or people involved in the situation aware of this? Did you forgive the situation and move on? Have you ever had to do this in social situations? Take a moment now to write below, your thoughts and why.

_____

_____

_____

_____

What Circles Do You Belong to? Who Has a Seat at the Table?

If you were to walk away from your circle, how would the conversation at the table turn? What types of tables do you sit at? Do the conversations, the tables, vary depending upon who you are with? At some tables are you afraid to get up for fear of what will be said when you are gone? If the answer is yes. It should be no… Make that a big fat NO.

No matter where you sit, you shouldn't have to worry about being the topic of conversation when you get up. Ever. If that is the case… you are not amongst true friends. I'd rather have one small table with fewer companions than several tables surrounded by those who are inauthentic.

It's time to build your own table. If you are not getting a seat at your current table, build your own. Build your own circle, seek your own sisterhood, find a new tribe. There are women out there who empower, include, uplift, and expand each other.

9.5: Your Turn. Dear reader, take a good look at who you are spending your time with and how they make you feel. Do you feel safe, empowered, uplifted? Take a moment now to write below, your thoughts and why.

_____

_____

_____

_____

Tips to Address This Type of Behavior

Never assume that other people are aware of or see the behavior and what's going on between women in a rivalrous situation. Chances are, they do not. Also, chances are, if this individual has been around for a while at work and/or socially, she's done it before, but others may be keeping quiet about it.

The following points (Houlis, 2018) give advice on how to address rivalrous behaviors. For the most part, they apply to both social and work environment settings. Please note, however, not all the points apply directly to social types of rivalry in the aspect of escalating the behavior to HR or senior management. Additionally, these points may not always be addressed in contextual order. They are simply points you can use. How you use them, depends upon your individual circumstance.

1. **Document. Document. Document.**

These types of behaviors are frequently intangible. Documenting what has occurred will help to show and produce a pattern. Take notes. Keep an account of what has occurred, how and when, to have proof of the behavior in case you need to escalate it to your manager, leadership, HR, or someone else (if outside of the work environment). Save voicemails, emails, social media posts, and texts. If applicable, take pictures. Don't record a conversation with her, take video, etc., without having her approval, unless you know the law in your state for doing so.

2. **Recognize Your Rival's Intent.**

To better understand her behavior, first try to tackle the underlying cause. The behavior could stem from a difference in personalities, or because she's insecure about something and wants to be heard. Maybe she's lacking certain social skills and is completely unaware of how she's coming across. If the behavior truly is unintentional, there honestly could be a variety of reasons for why it's occurring.

Initially, take the approach of "It's me not her," with thoughts of, "How can I put this back on me, so she doesn't get defensive, and we can work or get along better, together?" You can address it openly:

- "I hear what you are saying. Maybe we can work this out together?"
- "I feel like we could communicate better. What can I do on my end to make sure that happens?"

In a tense moment, the use of humor can deflect an interpreted, unkind or uncomfortable situation. Calling attention to something perceived as not nice or rude by making a joke of it addresses the behavior in a light-hearted manner. It also shows, by calling it out, you are not going to tolerate the rude conduct.

Maybe though, and trust me this type of female is out there, she is just mean and is fully aware of what she's doing. Calling out her behavior and bringing attention to it, publicly if need be, addresses her actions, puts it out in the open, and lets her know you see what she is doing:

- "You hurt my feelings."
- "That was rude."
- "What you just said was inappropriate."

When that doesn't work, as mentioned previously... Document. Document. Document. Always keep track of when the negative behavior occurred and how. This will provide proof in case you escalate it to other people.

3. Address the Situation One-on-One.

Invite her to speak privately, go to coffee, take a walk, or schedule a meeting. Whatever works, use it to have a one-on-one conversation. If it makes you feel more empowered and confident to confront the situation, write down what you want to say prior to meeting with her. Practice too, if that helps get your courage up.

Think back to point #2. Initially taking the approach of "It's me, not her," with thoughts of, "How can I put this back on me, so she doesn't get defensive?" Frame your concerns by stating, "We have the same goals for the neighborhood," OR "We are on the same team/project," OR "I want us to work or get along better, together."

She may agree with you. On the other end of the spectrum, she may also deny there's anything wrong. Be prepared for that. This one-on-one conversation does not guarantee a positive outcome. It does, however, guarantee to you that YOU are doing what's in your control to take the first step to try and modify a negative situation. If the behavior continues or she denies it's occurring, continue to... Document. Document. Document. This way you will have proof of the behavior in case you need to escalate it.

4. **Stand up for Yourself.**

It may be hard to do, but you must defend yourself. Especially if the behaviors are not visible to others, you may be the only one who is able to protect... YOU. When hurtful, humiliating, mocking types of behaviors occur, call the perpetrator out on their conduct and communicate how it makes you feel.

Extremely rivalrous behaviors should not go unacknowledged because they can lead to more harmful bullying actions. Additionally, all these behaviors, especially if on-going, can have serious physical, mental, and emotional consequences—illness, depression, anxiety, lack of sleep, avoidant behaviors, PTSD, burnout, etc.

5. **Establish Community and Advocate Inclusion.**

Implement team-building group activities. Open communication helps to reduce rivalrous behaviors because it provides opportunities to learn about one another on a personal level. This in turn builds stronger relationships and improves overall morale because people are invested in each other not only for the task, work, or goal at hand but personally too. Regular and frequent participation of this type helps to maintain a bond.

Provide an outlet of support that promotes inclusion. Create a circle or an environment of teamwork and trust that elevates, uplifts, and empowers each other. Call to action, "collaboration over competition." In this community, create a feeling of belonging where that type of negative behavior isn't tolerated. Once you start showing up for her, she will in turn show up for you. That my friend is the secret to the sisterhood.

Address negative types of behavior openly and ensure support systems are in place. Make sure that leadership, including men and women, are aware of the negative behavior signals. Guarantee that ramifications will be given for those that harass and bully. If you aren't getting it where you are, find other avenues of support and networking.

6. **Implement Education.**

Change the culture. Each person within an organization or social group needs to know they all equally share intervening responsibilities when witnessing bad behavior. Implement a bystander intervention program. As defined by the University of Michigan, it's a "type of training used in post-secondary education institutions to prevent harassment and unwanted comments. The bystander then takes on personal responsibility and takes action to intervene, with the goal of preventing the situation from escalating" (2018).

Having an agreed-upon "ready" word and strategies in place for intervention puts accountability on everyone, not just the targeted individual. Many times, because she has lost her voice, a victim may be unable to respond. Having a strategy in place will help to mediate a potential situation as it's witnessed and not "after the fact."

7.   **Share Your Experience With Others.**

Report and reveal. Previously I discussed losing your voice, your sparkle, and that sucks big time. Sometimes you may be so immersed in the situation that you are unaware it's occurring. But at some point, you will see it... and you just can't keep this whole messy thing to yourself. First, you will go crazy. Second, everyone needs an outlet to get things out. I promise this will help you feel better and not so alone. And third, by sharing your story you can be an advocate for someone else experiencing a similar type of situation. Sharing your story may help someone else find her voice.

If the speaking one-on-one approach doesn't help, then it's time to escalate it to someone else. If it's occurring in a working environment, take the appropriate steps you need to report the behavior to a coworker, manager, leadership, HR, etc. This all goes back to... Document. Document. Document. Because trust me, they will ask for proof.

If the behavior is occurring personally in your family or socially in your community, share it with a friend, someone in the same club or sports team, etc. Promoting awareness about it puts it out there for others to see and support you.

8.   **Maintain Control.**

Rivalrous situations can be intense and on-going. They can wear you down, cause you to lose your voice and your sparkle. It's important to be firm, maintain control, and hold your power. Always remember to... (say it with me) Document. Document. Document.

Don't let her know how she is impacting you or how her projected behavior makes you feel. Let her become bored with you. She wants a response. Don't give it to her.

9. Leave the Situation.

Sometimes the only option to escape a toxic situation is to leave the environment in which it's occurring. After the issue has escalated, if the social environment or workforce continues to tolerate the vindictive and bullying behaviors, it may not just be a problem with the bully at hand. It means the culture as a whole accepts this type of behavior as "ok." Since the behaviors are accepted, most likely they will not be stopped or addressed. Therefore, they will continue. Chances are, nothing you will ever try or continue to do will make it change. To maintain your dignity, self-worth, and respect, you have to leave. Find a new job. Find a new group. Find a new circle.

9.6: Your Turn. Dear reader, if you've ever dealt with these types of behaviors personally or in the working environment, what steps have you used to help alleviate the problem? Did you utilize any of the previously mentioned steps? Did you do something different? Did you ultimately have to leave the situation, environment, etc., to stop it from occurring? Take a moment now to write below, your thoughts and why.

Closing

If you don't own the story, you can't write the ending. If you can't write the ending, the story owns you. To prevent this from being a stain on your overall life outlook and fundamentally defining you, you must know now that regaining your sparkle is up to YOU.

Trust me, pulling up your big girl panties to get this done is no easy feat but with hard work and perseverance, it can most definitely be accomplished. Because it's all up to you. And from that, you come out on the other side feeling renewed, confident, happy, and peaceful again, in your own skin.

When you are happy in your own skin it's not only easier on you, believe me. In general, you will have the ability to attract friends and people effortlessly because they will see your confidence beaming, your inner light shining through. And when you have this, when you feel this way about yourself, it is easier to move on because you are living your truth.

Before we talk about moving on, let's first take a glimpse into history and science about what the female sisterhood means, as well as a rare visit from the "other woman," after the fact. It's all just a page turn away... in Chapter 10.

Chapter 10:

The Antonym of Female Rivalry is the Female Sisterhood

"I wish more women realized that helping another woman win, cheering her on, praying for her, or sharing a resource with her, does not take away from the blessing coming to them. In fact, the more you give, the more you receive. Empowering women doesn't come from selfishness but rather from selflessness."
—Selene Kinder (InspirationFeed, 2020).

Jessica's Story

"I never stripped or took money for sex or anything like that, at all. But I did work at a local chain restaurant that is known for hiring young, attractive servers who wore revealing outfits that looked like the 'All American Cheerleader, Surfer, Girl Next Door,' to put myself

through college. My day job at the clinic paid for my rent and my car. My waitressing money helped me pay for classes and everything else. I worked there a few nights a week, downtown. You would think that it'd be a hyper-competitive environment, right? With all these beautiful women and lots of guys involved? No. It was the least competitive environment I think that I've ever been in. You wouldn't have expected it in a place like that. But I actually have very fond memories of my time working there and not because of the guys.

It was because of the women I worked with. I worked with amazing women. Maybe it was just that I got lucky and I was there during a really good time, I don't know. But for that 2 to 3 years, there was a great group of girls there and it stayed that way, pretty consistently. There wasn't a lot of turnover.

We all had our differences, but it was more like a meritocracy. We had a male boss, but he didn't seem to see any differences between us, the women. He was just a nice guy. He seemed to be an 'eyes-wide-open type of guy,' he had clear communication, was all for the community, was totally transparent, etc. And if you needed any favors the person you needed to be really nice to was the hostess, because that meant you were getting seats more often and at the better tables. Yep, you can kind of size people up and I know that sounds terrible but it's the truth. But it just wasn't like any other restaurant that I've ever worked for. There was no pettiness.

All the women were very driven, extremely driven. Most of us were on our own and also had day jobs. Most of us were putting ourselves through school and did not come from money. And that is why I was driven to make money for me. To get through. It felt like...it was sad that I could go there and make more in two nights than I could at my supposedly legitimate day job. And I had the support there, versus at my day job, where there was tons of rivalry and back-stabbing.

It makes me wonder if being self-driven to that degree...that these women are always wanting to better themselves is a key quality for not getting wrapped up in female rivalry. There she is, someone who is wrapped up, not selfishly, but in doing what she's doing in terms of where she wants to go. And because of that, she has no time to worry about the other negative crap that can occur. These women were independent, and they all had plans and goals for themselves. They all had confidence in what they were doing and confidence that they were going to get there. They were on a mission and that mission had an end game goal for each of them. It was different for all of us, but inherently there was a desire to make it. And as a result, we all were very supportive of one another. We really cheered each other on."

Helping Other Women Glow

There are countless ways to support and help other women glow, without losing your own shine. Jessica's story is an example. So too, is Phoebe's. When she shared her story with me, she had a mix of negative and positive scenarios to tell. She reminisced about the very uplifting and empowering behavior she experienced from other women. That feeling stayed with her as she, later on, experienced the negative. It helped her know there were positive role models out there that wanted to help other women shine.

Phoebe. "I'm a minority. I went to college at an all-girls school on the East Coast and it was fantastic. I think it was the first time I felt that I could finally breathe. It was so very diverse, in all different ways. Those women were great role models. We were expected to move forward and just do things and no one held us back. Of course, there were some petty things, as there always are, but not like I'd experienced in high school, at all. These women were all there for each other and that was so refreshing and not what I'd experienced before."

10.1: Your Turn. Dear reader, how do you personally help other women glow? Or do you? Is this something you are conscious about doing? Or is it something that perhaps you've never taken the time to really think about? Take a moment now to write below, your thoughts and why.

_____

_____

_____

_____

The Antonym of Female Rivalry

As I've previously mentioned, female rivalry is boundless and the negative behaviors occur frequently in pretty much every single aspect of daily living, at work, home, socially, in sports, and at school. You name the place and there is no doubt that it exists. Female rivalry does not discriminate.

As women, we are not always going to see eye to eye or have all things in common with all other women, and sometimes it's a plain hard truth that we may not even like someone else. That's as it should be because if we all did the same things, liked the same things, and acted in the same manner, we'd be sheep... not humans.

It's okay that we are all different but we're also all in this life together. That means getting along and accepting those differences. It's being okay with them and not competing for something you may or may not have. This conversation makes me think of the pie analogy. Imagine,

> *a nice round, golden, freshly baked, flaky blackberry pie. You can slice it into eight specific, yet individual pieces. All pieces look the same. The triangular shape is cut the same...but no matter how hard you try to cut it those pieces are not exact. A berry will fall out; juice will run; crust will crumble. Each piece may offer you a similar experience in terms of eating the pie, they are alike, yet also different.*

We can apply this pie analogy to the following scenarios. Instead of thinking, "Well, she's a coach and I'm a coach, so obviously she's my competition because we're doing the same thing." Wrong! Think instead, "Wow, we're in the same field... I have a friend who wants to be my client. I know our working together won't be a good fit because I know her personally. I'll instead refer her to Sally who'll be a great fit."

OR, "Oh, she's getting something I also want. That sucks. I guess that prevents me from getting anything too." Wrong! Think instead, "Ok, Donna got promoted to the position I was interested in. I'm disappointed but also happy for her. Perhaps there's something else out there that may be a better fit for me. Maybe Donna can help me network because she's now in a position that offers more visibility." Let's flip that lens and work together, not against. Teamwork makes the dream work, baby.

The bottom line, however, in as much as there are certain types of personalities that judge, compete, rival, and hate, there is another side. There are also personalities that support, collaborate, respect, love, uplift, and empower. The antonym of rivalry between women, the favorable side to this negative behavior, is the *female sisterhood*. This is the positive side of relationships between women and when it works, it works so very, very well.

A friend just mentioned this quote to me the other day. I had to use it because it fits so well with what I am going to talk about in the next section, "*A rising tide lifts all boats...not just one.*" Yep. That about sums it up... perfectly.

> **Rubi.** "*I was a consultant and thrown into a project where, although I knew what I was doing and how to do it, I was quite unfamiliar with the industry of the client I was working for. I'd worked for a lot of private and public sector clients, but this client was in the financial industry and that was new to me. I worked for a few weeks by myself trying to get the lay of the land and understand all the nuances that were unique to this industry. To say the least, it was a big project with a big learning curve and adding the industry learning curve to that made it very stressful.*
>
> *Less than a month in, Sienna joined me. We had completely different personality types. She was a powerhouse, a 'get 'er done' type of person,*

who'd only ever worked in the financial industry. I am more of a 'sit back and assess the situation before I talk' type of person. I was somewhat intimidated by Sienna because of her experience and personality. On the other hand, I had a vast amount of experience that pertained to the type of work we were doing, something that was new to Sienna.

What could have been a disaster ended up being a blessing. We worked side by side for almost a year and became the dynamic duo. Because our skill sets and personalities were so different, we ended up complementing one another. There was absolutely no competition at all because we each ended up learning so much from each other. A lot of our success was based upon our open communication, our individual mindsets, and the willingness to know when to let the other one step up and take the lead. At the end of the project, we both were sad to part. We agreed that neither of us had ever worked so efficiently with another person and on top of it, had fun. To this day she is a dear friend."

Shannon. *"I started a new position with a woman named Anna. We both had the same position but worked for different people. I remember feeling very nervous when I started because she'd already been working in the job and I thought, 'What if we don't get along? What if it's negative and we end up competing with each other to see who is the best?' As it turned out, we got along great but still actually also competed with each other. We both felt like the other one was so much better at the job than how we actually viewed ourselves doing it. It was a type of positive competition as we each raised the bar for each other. It could have been a bad thing where we negatively talked down to each other because we wanted to be the 'better one' but we didn't. Instead we each thought, 'I want to be as good as her.'*

We had a mutual respect for each other. We appreciated each other and the things that we each could do. We used that to build the other one up and to figure out, 'Well if she's good at this, how can I complement it?'

It ended up being the best team ever because we would have conversations where we would help each other. It was a great positive experience. It was huge! Hands down, communication was an enormous component of that, as well as having mutual respect for each other."

10.2: Your Turn: Dear Reader, what are your thoughts regarding the sisterhood being the antonym of female rivalry? As the dependency of female relationships has evolved, where do you see yourself fitting in with your own female relationships? Is this something you are conscious of? Or is it something that perhaps you've not really taken the time to think about? Take a moment now to write below, your thoughts and why.

_____

_____

_____

_____

"Female friendships that work are relationships,
in which women help each other belong to themselves."
—Louise Bernikow (Goodreads, Inc., 2020)

The Female Sisterhood

In primitive times, women shared much more of their daily domestic living with each other than they do today. Communal lifestyles were common and, in this domain, they cooked together, participated in the care of each other's children, hunted for food, gathered for shelter and fire, all done in tandem with the support of other women.

Brené Brown tells a story about women in a remote village who all washed their clothes together by the river. When they all got washing machines, there was a sudden outbreak of depression amongst them and no one could figure out why. This "depression" was not a result of their newly acquired washing machines. No.

Rather, it stemmed from the loss of no longer having a daily sense of community with their female counterparts. Although the washing machines were much more convenient, in having them, their communal bonding time was lessened.

Because of technology, social media, and other life conveniences, we've gotten so independent that we no longer rely on each other in the manner that we used to in the "olden" days. In the present day, although women are still customarily the pillars of their family life and communities, shared living is not a commonality. Women are much more isolated from each other. They live in their own homes versus a collective setting, they have their own schedules, and their own immediate self and family needs. Occasions to get together are fewer and together-time is reduced. We do not depend on each other as we did decades earlier. Females getting together "just because" is not as much of a natural everyday support process as it once was. I'm busy, you're busy, we all understand that, and say, "we're fine." Really though, are we?

There is a female alliance void. Life is busy with work, kids, partners, etc. Many women are lonely in the sense of not belonging to a broader female circle or not having someone to confide in. We all want to trust other women and have them trust us in return to foster that sense of closeness and partnership. While it's great to get together with girlfriends, hang out and have fun, we need to acknowledge that it's not just a luxury to do so. Female friendships are essential for belonging to something socially bigger than yourself. Female friendships are essential for not feeling lonely.

In her book, *Braving the Wilderness,* Brené Brown defines belonging as,

> *"the innate human desire to be part of something larger than us. Because this yearning is so primal, we often try to acquire it by fitting in and by seeking approval, which are not only hollow substitutes for belonging, but often barriers to it. Because **true belonging** only happens when we present our authentic, imperfect selves to the world, our sense of belonging can never be greater than our level of self-acceptance" (pg. 31).*

We feel lonely when we feel like we don't belong or don't connect to others. John Cacioppa of the University of Chicago defines loneliness as, "perceived social isolation." Cacioppa further describes loneliness as,

> *"a dangerous, not just sad condition. The brains of social species have evolved to respond to the feeling of being pushed to the social perimeter, being on the outside, by going into self-preservation mode. When we feel isolated, disconnected, and lonely, we try to protect ourselves. In that mode, we want to connect, but our brain is attempting to override connection with self-protection. That means less empathy, more defensiveness, more numbing, and less sleeping" (Brown, 2019, pg. 53–54).*

Cacioppa provides insight about the biological machinery of our brains, in how it warns us when our ability to thrive and prosper is threatened.

> *"Hunger is a warning that our blood sugar is low, and we need to eat. Thirst warns us that we need to drink to avoid dehydration. Pain alerts us to potential tissue damage. And loneliness tells us that we need social connection—**something critical to our well-being as food and water**" (Brown, 2019, pg. 53–54).*

A meta-analysis study (2015) on loneliness, by researchers Holt-Lunstad, Smith & Layton highlights the fundamental necessity of needing to belong.

> *"Living with air pollution increases your odds of dying early by 5%. Living with obesity increases your odds of dying early by 20%. Excessive drinking increases your odds of dying early by 30%. And loneliness? **It increases your odds of dying early by 45%**" (Holt-Lunstad, Baker, Harris, Stephenson, & Smith, 2015).*

Do you need to read that last statistic again? I sure did, several times. Because it's utterly shocking and sad and altogether just horrible. If that won't pull at your heartstrings, I don't know what will.

I think of people being lonely in "normal" times, like when Brené's book was written. However, as I write now, during the COVID-19 Pandemic, my heart is just sad with thoughts of all of the women and men, who are lonelier now than they've ever been before, due to social distancing and the quarantine.

Fundamentally, I believe there is a deep inherent need in each of us, as women, to connect with our female friends. This connection fosters the desire for acceptance and belonging, which in turn, helps us to not feel lonely. And while it's not as much of an "essential" action as it used to be, it doesn't happen organically like it used to. "Getting together" with your girlfriends takes work, time, and energy to be a priority. We need and we must take the time to make these connections occur. It's vital for your health to do so.

If you don't have a special group of women, you can still find one. If you are currently building your special group of women, think about what you want it to look like.

If you already have this special group... think about your own female circle, your squad, your tribe, your group, your pack, your horseshoe, your sisterhood. Whatever you call it, these women have your back and share a special bond with you. They bare their souls, support, empower, encourage, and nurture you and as do you for them, in return. To circle is to, "surround, enclose, encompass." A woman's circle is a safe and sacred place for women to come together, to use their voices, to be heard and seen, to empower each other, to share wisdom... to belong.

10.3: Your Turn: Dear reader, what are your thoughts regarding female relationships and belonging? Do you agree with the concept that people are happier if they have someone they belong to, someone who supports them? Do you have a group of women that you trust and confide in, that provides an outlet of support? If not, why? If you don't, do you want one? Take a moment now to write below, your thoughts and why.

_____

_____

_____

_____

Soul Sister
"noun. a female friend not related by blood
who shares a bond that transcends
time, space and distance.
Traits include: listening and
fully understanding without judgement
or solution; knowing the right thing to say;
sharing belongings or desserts;
regularly reminding one another of their beauty."
—Unknown (The Minds Journal, 2020).

The Science Behind the Sisterhood

Not only is having a female sisterhood a wonderful outlet that helps us from feeling lonely, but there is actual science that supports the benefits of it. This is not a criticism against men. We all have males in our support system with whom we have wonderful partnerships and relationships. Women, however, just have a special bond with one another. Female friendships tend to be different than the types of relationships men traditionally have.

Oxytocin has been called "the love hormone." Research has been conducted on the power of female relationships and the hormone oxytocin. It's revealed that women, more than men, need oxytocin to maintain connections. Female to female connections increase serotonin and oxytocin. Oxytocin plays a role in social bonding and anxiety.

When men and women experience stress, they release the hormone cortisol which promotes aggression and withdrawal responses. To counter the cortisol, the body also produces oxytocin to combat stress and calm down. Furthermore, in stressful situations, men produce higher levels of testosterone and women produce higher levels of estrogen. In men, testosterone decreases the calming effects of oxytocin. In women, estrogen heightens the calming effects of oxytocin and promotes the internal yearning for social support. To sum it up, women release hormones to other women that are healthy and help to remove stress hormones.

Dr. Shelly Taylor, UCLA Scientist elaborates.

> *"Aggression and withdrawal take a physiological toll, whereas friendship brings comfort that diminishes the effects of stress. This difference in seeking social support during stressful periods is the principal way men and women differ in their response to stress, and one of the most basic differences in men's and women's behavior" (Taylor, et al, 2000).*

Mae, et al. share the results of their study on the effects of oxytocin and social sharing and which effects differ between men and women. "We now know that oxytocin increases the positive experience of sharing with a friend in females but not in males and that brain activity during sharing is differentially affected in females vs. males" (2018).

In her book, *Women's Inhumanity Against Women*, Dr. Chesler (2001) concludes,

> *"While most women envy and compete only with each other, not with men, few women can survive without bonding to at least one or two other women. Women seek female approval as much as they seek male approval. Therefore, most girls and women deny even to themselves that they envy or compete, even indirectly with those upon whom they also depend" (p. 15).*

When "solidarity behavior" works, it brings women together to contribute to their forming alliances, collaborating for a common purpose, exhibiting loyalty, and bonding. Solidarity behavior is defined as, "an awareness of shared interests, objectives, standards, and sympathies creating a psychological sense of unity of groups or classes. It refers to the ties in a society that bind people together as one" (Wikipedia, 2020).

10.4: Your Turn: Dear reader, do you agree with the scientific thoughts behind the sisterhood? If not, why? Take a moment now to write below, your thoughts and why.

_____

_____

_____

_____

"No matter how heavy the memories fall upon your heart.
No matter what has come together or what has torn us apart.
There is still a reason you made it this far.
And how, after everything that happened,
You are blooming as you are."
—Morgan Harper Nichols (Nichols, 2020).

The Flip Side of the "Other Woman"

Chances are if this type of experience has happened to you, you will never hear from the "other woman" or receive any type of closure. But what if you do? Once in a blue moon, this happens. I've mentioned numerous times throughout this book about the behavior of the "other woman," and how in circumstances often, it's a story left untold. Usually, it is. Sometimes though, albeit infrequently, it's not.

Many of the hundreds of women I've spoken with about this topic do not currently have a relationship with the "other woman," the one with whom they experienced rivalry. A few females, however, were able to add validity to the concept that they were indeed a perceived threat to the other, jealous woman, which is what these rivalrous types of behaviors stem from. Here are a few examples.

Eva's Story. Recall Eva's grade school story from Chapter 4? Eva initially had a very bleak story to share. But as our conversation progressed she continued to communicate what happened over the summer after her 5th grade school year school had ended.

Call to mind "the other girl," Clare, from Eva's narrative. Even though she and Eva were originally grade school friends from years before, remember how mean Clare was to Eva throughout the 5th grade school year. Eva recounted the following,

> *"I was so surprised that several weeks into the summer there was a sweet note in my mailbox from Clare, who'd unfriended me. I think she just got caught up in the wrath of a mean girl situation. It was sitting in our mailbox, so she must've ridden her bike to my house. I was just floored to see it there."*

Eva had kept the note and shared it with me,

> *"Hi Eva. I know it's weird for me to wright (sic) you a letter, but I just wanted to know how you are holding up? And I'm sorry that we didn't get along well this year. And I'm sorry. I would love if we could wright (sic) to each other. Stay safe and well. Your friend, Clare."*

Hazel's Story. Remember Hazel from the intro story in Chapter 3? She is now 72, and still, this experience remains with her as clear as when it happened over 50 years ago.

Hazel worked with Diane who treated her horribly, all because she was jealous of her. Hazel left that job in early July and on that same day, also had her first baby. It wasn't long after in late September that Hazel and her husband were transferred to another base in a new state.

> *"Imagine my surprise when right before we moved, I received a letter in the mail. I wish I'd have kept it. It was a letter from, of all people, Diane. I was shocked to see it. I remember clearly that it was a full-page letter, as she had a lot to say. She talked about her feelings and how bad she felt for treating me so poorly. She said she was wrong,*

she'd treated me horribly, she felt guilty about it because she shouldn't have treated me that way and was sorry for doing it. She felt that I was getting more attention than she was, and bottom line, she was jealous. She said it had nothing at all to do with me and that it stemmed from her own inadequacy."

Ilene's Story. As one of my original dissertation participants, Ilene's story has been interwoven throughout this book. She spoke about her almost decade-long experience and how it finally came to an end when the other woman retired. Although their experience of rivalry was never overtly discussed, after the two women stopped working together their relationship took on a completely different form.

"The good news is right after that she retired. And what this would mean today, well, it is a very interesting postscript to the whole thing. Two years before she retired, she got married. She got married to an acquaintance of mine whom I just absolutely adore. A really nice guy and I see her occasionally now socially and she is an absolute delight."

Katrina's Story. Go back now to Chapter 5 where Katrina painted an ugly picture about how horribly awful her co-worker was. I believe her choice name to call Darcy was "the b*tch."

"So after I'd moved, left my job, and worked with Darcy, a couple of months later I needed to call her. I was doing a similar job at my new location, but this time I was starting a brand-new practice. I had none of the basic forms that I'd used before, which I desperately needed. I called Darcy and said, 'Hey, can you do me a favor and forward all of that stuff for me? Because I didn't bring any of it with me.' She said, 'Yes, what do you need?' I pretty much needed everything which she later sent. In that same conversation, she said, 'Well, how are things going?' I said, 'They're going okay.' I said, 'How about for you?'

As the weeks went by, I called her again, several times. Each time requesting info but then we'd always chat too. I realized we'd started giving each other advice about things. It got to the point where we were saying to one another, 'I want to catch up with you, are you home later tonight?' And just like that, we found ourselves having these hour conversations. I was like, 'What IS happening???'

And before you knew it, our friendship blossomed. So now, here we are nine years later, and I would easily, hands down say, she's probably one of my closest, best friends even. I talk to her once a week. She eventually told me that she'd had an affair with the client partner. She'd always had the hots for him and never told me about it and that is why she was so upset that night in L.A. when she thought I was flirting with him. She was jealous. They were together for three years and I had no idea.

She still is very difficult and a very hard person. She really is. But somehow, we found a common ground with each other where we truly fell in love with each other. And she's so supportive. She's always behind me, you know if I'm dealing with something crazy, she's like, 'Let me help you through that.' Because I thought for sure, I'd never see her again. It's a fine line between love and hate. You know what I mean? Because when the emotions are there, it's as intense on each side. We almost laugh about how much we didn't like each other, and we've definitely talked about it multiple times.

I think the takeaway here is that we both were vulnerable at the same time. We both had some life-altering things happen to us. And that's the same reason, we ended up needing to rely on each other as human beings. It was the game-changer and we saw each other in a different light. I think it's like anything, right? When we can see something through the lens of somebody else and not only see it but physically feel it, the same pain, we can relate in a way that we never could before. And that's the secret, because it makes you closer because you have that experience to share together."

The "High School Crew" Story, Revisited

Now think back to the high school story I shared in Chapter 4, about "The Crew." How when The Crew hit the hallways, I'd felt like I'd escaped something huge and as a result, I felt relief, guilt, and sadness.

The thing is one of those Crew members was one of my best friends. We went on to be roommates in college. We've gone through a lot of things together, good and bad. We are to the present day, even amidst living on different coasts, still friends. Granted, I don't talk to her as much as I used to. But she's one of those people in my life that when the phone rings, or when I see her in person, we pick right up where we left off... no matter the time, no matter the distance.

That adolescent brain, the absence of its complete development in a high school teenager, and the lack of ability to respond to situations with good judgement is real. I lived it and witnessed exposure to the negative behavior first hand, yesterday and today. I'll go with the theory that a chunk of those girls were not in their "right mind" yet. I know I wasn't either at that age. It does not condone the behavior. It does not make it acceptable for what occurred. But I like to think, they were still growing and had not yet reached their full potential of who they were going *to be.*

I reached out to my old friend to see if she'd like to talk about this topic, knowing that it may dredge up negative memories for her. Her response was,

"To be honest, I've really tried to move past and forget those ugly times, but the memories still do linger. I was definitely a part of being unkind to my peers during those years. Thank goodness people can change. Leaving to go to college and getting out of our little town helped immensely. Then going on to become what I am today profession-wise, where my job is to bring the best out in people has been hugely pivotal as well."

These stories highlight one of the root causes of female rivalry, insecurity. When the perceived threat is gone, the vindictive, targeted behavior also goes away. Although it's extremely rare that the "other woman" and the female who is the recipient of these types of negative behaviors become friends, these stories prove that it really can happen. I like to think there are more of these positive types of stories out there.

Food for Thought: In my vast research on this topic, I've found it to be quite rare that someone who's encountered female rivalry will ever hear from the "other woman."

10.5: Your Turn: Dear reader, let's talk about the "other woman." If you've experienced this type of behavior, after it was over, have or did you have any interaction with the "other woman?" Was the rivalrous behavior directly addressed? Was an apology given? Was there blame? Was it something else entirely? If you've experienced this behavior and haven't interacted with the "other woman," would you want to? If so, why? Take a moment now to write below, your thoughts and why.

_____

_____

_____

_____

Reflection

Hindsight always offers the ability for reflection about what you would or would not do differently in a situation, and how. And while a long pause offers great insight to think, that's also not real life either because we can't just go back and wave a magic wand to have a re-do.

What we can do though, is learn. Learn from ourselves, learn from her, and hopefully, just a sliver of what is shared can be digested so that others can learn too. Perhaps, that little sliver will light a spark and that ember will become a light to spread knowledge about this important topic so that their stories did not occur in vain.

Beatrix. *"My personal experience is that that rivalry comes from insecurities on their part, which you don't really see. And it happens in really subtle and private ways. And so, it takes a while for you to realize what's going on. And sometimes you're pretty far in it before you understand what's really happening."*

Clio. *"It was a learning experience. If you'd asked me 16 years ago if I'd do it again, I would have run away with my hair on fire. Now, I can say that it helped. I mean, I've learned a lot from it."*

Dana. *"I don't want to sound like a feminist because I have had wonderful male bosses and wonderful female bosses. I think that I feel very blessed and fortunate to know a lot of people that I have professionally, that have helped me and things like that. But you just have these few eggs that you run into and I just say, 'Oh, dear God, help me through this.' And, somehow, he does. And it's hard when you go through it but you just have to…"*

Faith. *"I think women are smarter nowadays. When you have a situation or a problem, realizing the importance of getting out of it sooner rather than later would be helpful. I think I am stubborn as a person too. 'Darn it. I'm not screwing up, they are. Why should I have to leave?'"*

Hannah. *"When I came here, and this has now been about a year and a half, having learned so much about myself in these previous environments, I also have worked a lot with personality assessments. I knew that the extreme traits in your personality are the ones that can be your biggest assets and your biggest liabilities. And the two that I have, that I think were the most extreme, were—my goal orien-*

tation, which is ridiculously high, and my need to nurture is ridiculously low. So, those are ones that I have made very much an effort to really keep in check."

From Victim to Protector

Many of the women who've shared their stories with me have learned from their negative experiences. They've taken a harmful situation, applied what they learned, and flipped it into a positive. They are now women who are over cognizant of their own actions. They look out for and protect other women.

Ilene. *"I think it turned me in to even more of a feminist and I was not a feminist when I joined this organization 25 years ago. But it sure turned me into one. And so, I am hypersensitive, perhaps even to a fault, to want to look out for other women and others who just seem to be having a harder time of it. And I just have to believe, it is because of the difficult experiences that I had early on.*

This experience has stayed with me. I've moved on but it's clearly shown me that women need to stick together and support each other. This experience has made a huge impact on my profession now and my ability to empower other women, to help them find their sisterhood."

Wendy. *"Women need to tell their stories and women need to be authentic. I think we can support each other in how we do this. Our actions become part of our stories. I feel like there's so much posturing and protecting one's brand that you lose the authenticity. I really feel like it's caught my attention that men are quite as good at telling their story and women aren't as good as doing so.*

I joined a board of a non-profit charity group. It's for moms and daughters. My kids do it with me but it's also for the mother-daughter dynamic, our doing it together, and showcasing positive relationships. It's how I can contribute with other women, to make a difference."

Maggie. *"I learned early on in my career a lot of great lessons but one of the things that has stuck with me over and over again is, you don't communicate by talking. You communicate by listening. And yes, even though I may have had a lot of ideas, I now come in with my ears open. Truly listening to them... helps me better understand and support other women."*

Eleni. *"I would say in managing my own team, I really try to develop an environment of collaboration and support versus differences and competition. In my naive perception, I don't think that women thrive as much in a competitive environment as they do in a nurturing environment. Maybe that's because I feel that that's how I am. So, I try to really nurture that type of environment. I think with men, healthy competition really works, but I feel that for women it's different. When— on a good day, I do try and build bridges and find areas of mutual understanding. On a bad day, I really try, and it means that I'm more cautious in how I'm dealing with my rivalries than what I may have done back when this happened to me."*

10.6: Your Turn: Dear reader, as you've read through this book, what are your thoughts on reflection about this type of experience? If you've experienced it personally, has reflection helped you? Do you agree or disagree that something positive may have come from having experienced this type of heinous behavior? Have you personally ever taken a negative situation and applied that experience to empower other women? Take a moment now to write below, your thoughts and why.

_____

_____

_____

_____

"People will throw stones at you. Don't throw them back.
Collect them all and build an empire."
—Anonymous (Goodreads, Inc., 2020).

Moving On

In the previous chapter, I talked about the importance of forgiveness. In tandem with forgiving is the ability to move on. It's so important to acknowledge your experiences and accept the influences they've had on your life. While you can never erase negative bullying behaviors, dealing with the feelings and having knowledge of how you are impacted today will help you move forward. Grace eloquently describes her thoughts on her experience.

> **Grace.** *"There is no utopia and it's also made me realize that I can't take things like this personally because, at the end of the day, it had nothing to do with me or what I did or didn't do. It has changed me a bit and I am learning from it. It has opened my eyes in a different way, that had I not gone through this experience I may not see things the way I do now."*

As an adult, a present-day encounter from another woman or group of women may be completely innocent. But it may spark your sense of victimhood, sending you back to that little girl, that tween, that teen, or that young lady in college. Because, that little girl is always in there. Negative mean girl behaviors can bring old personas and experiences back to the surface, which means they never really go away.

When this occurs, don't get even—do better. You may not be able to change the other person's actions but letting them know they are getting to you, gives them control. Rising above and becoming engulfed in your own life, your own successes will help you leave the negativity behind. And fundamentally, that is how you win.

Bottom line, what other people think of you is absolutely none of your business! As we like to say in my house... "Nunya! It's nunya bizness!" And while that is hard to digest at times... To move on, you must have that mindset. And girl, if you don't like it, change it! You have the power to change your outcomes and that all starts from within.

Women who uplift and empower one another, *are* out there. Surround yourself with women who add value to your life, who challenge you, uplift and expand you, and who sprinkle magic into your existence just like you do in theirs. Find a tribe, a circle, a sisterhood, a pack. And ultimately know, while experiences may shape who you are, they certainly do not own you.

10.7: Your Turn: Dear reader, if you've experienced female rivalry have you been able to move on? If so, how? If not, why? What is holding you back? If you have experienced this type of behavior, have you ever reverted to the "little girl" mindset when as an adult you've been confronted with mean behavior? Do you find it easy or hard to walk away? Has it always been that way for you? How have you looked out for or uplifted other women? Take a moment now to write below, your thoughts and why.

_____

_____

_____

_____

Closing

By this point dear reader, you may be asking, "Ok, so now what? Here I am fresh off the boat of this negative experience, I've quit my job, and I've left my so-called friends, whom I now realize weren't really my true friends to begin with. What do I do now? How do I find these women who uplift, empower, support, include, and glow? Where do I find these types of women that help me shine, and find my shine too, instead of shredding my gown and ripping off my crown?"

In the past ten chapters, I've given you an overview of what female rivalry is, the various personas, what constitutes a frenemy, how to identify a vicious vixen and bolshie bully boss, the personal impacts (emotionally, physically and psychologically), how to cope, forgive and regain your shine, as well as insight to better understanding about what the female sisterhood entails. Now comes the good part... or even better part, I should say. Because I think it's all been pretty good, don't you?

The female sisterhood IS out there. Rest assured dear reader, I can promise you that! It's up to you though to uncover it, discover it, embrace it, and accredit it. You must consciously go behind frenemy lines to make a difference and truly find it. I've dedicated the last chapter of this book to tell you specifically if you are searching for answers to these questions above, how to go about finding it.

Chapter 11:

Behind Frenemy Lines: Changing the Perception

"Find Your Tribe.
You know, the ones that make you feel the most YOU.
The ones that lift you up and help you remember who you really are.
The ones that remind you that a blip in the road is just that, a blip.
They are the ones that when you walk out of a room,
they make you feel like a better person than when you walked in.
They are the ones that even if you don't see them face to face
as often as you'd like, you see them heart to heart.
You know, that kind of tribe? Who's in your tribe?"
—Jennifer Tastiloff (Zen Girl Chronicles, 2020).

Jennifer's Story

"Where I am now, we have a team of 25 that's easily two-thirds women. I have never worked with a more supportive group of women in my life. It's like lightning in a bottle! We have a group where we get together every two weeks and we listen to podcasts that support women, and we share books. Whenever somebody trips and falls instead of making a big deal about it or gossiping about it, we all swoop in and lift up.

I would say based on the age spectrum, the youngest woman on the team is 25 and the oldest is probably in her mid-fifties. In general, the culture here is really supportive. The mission statement in and of itself draws the kind of people here that are supportive because it's about inspiring the human spirit. The other main piece is, we are not micromanaged. We are all trusted, to you know, to self-select our work as long as it's for the greater good of overall development and to get out there and do our thing.

There is a younger gal in the group of women who started a podcast club. So, you know, kudos to her. She was struggling with finding her place but recognized it and acknowledged it, which is why she came to us for support and why she initially started this group. She looks to some of us as mentors and she also admits when something is not going well rather than making a stink about it.

In general, with this group of women in the year I've been here, there hasn't been one incident of gossip or rivalry. It's because of the way that we're all helping and supporting each other and sharing, you know, with the books and podcasts and all of that. It's all about support. And one woman had a pretty serious mental health issue at Christmas last year and instead of everybody gossiping about it, we all supported and asked how we could help her. It's really, it's just fantastic. I don't ever have to worry that I'm going to come into work and find out that, 'You know, so-and-so said something to so-and-so.' It's just, it's not like that here.

And, yeah. I feel like I've earned it, working here is a blessing and I've earned it."

Part I: Changing the Perception

Part I: Changing the Perception is all about the inner work. It's the thought processes that come first, such as teaching baseline behaviors and looking inward via self-reflection. It's the things you must do before you dive in and take action.

The saying, "it takes a village," rings true. I believe it takes "a village" for a lot of things we do in this life. From family support, community assistance, advocacy at work, raising children, or social strength, the list goes on. The shortened saying actually stems from a larger phrase, "It takes a village to raise a child," which is an African proverb that means,

> *"An entire community of people must interact with children for those children to experience growth and grow in a safe and healthy environment. The villagers look out for the children" (Wikipedia, 2020).*

Ultimately, it's about having support for one another, looking out for, caring for, and helping each other. While the phrase was originally intended for children, it directly applies to the phenomenon of rivalry between women and how to alter the perception that females predominantly as a whole do not get along.

Being in support of one another, wholeheartedly, is how we will change the perception of women always undermining one another. When we collectively come together with this type of open mindset, with the understanding that there are women out there who want to support one another, we have the ability to raise each other up versus tear down. That's when we begin to build a tribe, community, and sisterhood. It begins first, internally, within you. It starts with changing beliefs about yourself, and how you exhibit and project your own behaviors. It begins by stopping your inner she bully, manifesting it in your behavior, raising strong girls, and honoring current friendships.

11.1: Your Turn: Dear reader, do you agree with my analogy of "it takes a village" as being similar to female relationships and changing the perception of women not being able to support one another? Take a moment now to write below, your thoughts and why.

_____

_____

_____

_____

"So many years of education yet nobody ever taught
us how to love ourselves and why it's so important."
—Unknown (Authentic Woman, 2020).

Stop Your Inner She-Bully

Have you ever wondered why you are not attracting the right kind of people in your life? We tend to attract what we put out there. I am not saying if you've experienced female rivalry that you are the reason why it has occurred. Not at all. Nine and three quarters out of ten, you are not the reason why you've been targeted with this type of behavior. But let's look at that other very small percentage… What if your inner she-bully plays a part in how you view yourself and the vibe you are putting out to the rest of the world? A self-check is a reality check.

To shift your internal perception about yourself, you need to decolonize your mind and have accountability with your own vulnerability. You have to be critically conscious and understand the part you play in this story because you, and you alone are accountable for your actions.

Have you ever thought you were too light, too dark, not pretty, not thin, or not hip enough? Or have you compared yourself to other people on social media, thinking they were better than you? Or have you been afraid to voice your opinion for fear of what the response would be? Or have you looked in the mirror and completely critiqued your nose, hair, or eyes, all the while finding fault and negative judgement about your overall appearance?

"The average human has 60,000 thoughts per day, and 80% of them, almost 50,000 of those thoughts, are negative" (TLEX Institute, 2019). Reflect on that for a moment... some of the worst things you will ever say to or think about yourself, are remarks that you would never in a million years say to another person.

"We are what we believe we are."
—C.S. Lewis (Goodreads, Inc., 2020).

The little voice in your head. Your saboteur-inner-bully-negative-she-voice that loves to cause doubt and put you down. Consciously or not, she can be simply awful. It's true. Often. Always... we are our own worst critics.

11.2: Your Turn: Dear reader, do you have an inner-she-bully? If so, what do you say to her to curb her behavior? Is she a constant or have you found a way to manage her? If so, how? Do you agree with the thought that in order to foster positive relations with other women you first have to have a positive relationship with yourself? Take a moment now to write below, your thoughts and why.

_____

_____

_____

_____

"There is a special place in h*ll for women
who don't help other women."
—Madeleine Albright (Goodreads, Inc., 2020).

Manifest Positive Actions in Your Own Behavior

To manifest something means that whatever you focus on is what you are bringing to your reality. When it comes to your tribe, you get to choose the types of close relationships you have with other women. In order to establish these types of relationships, you need to determine what is important to you and then prioritize it.

Shelley Zalis stated that women who support other women are more successful in business (2019). To expand on that thought, Harvard Business Review research concluded,

> *That while both men and women benefit from having a network of well-connected peers across different groups, women who also have an inner circle of close female contacts are more likely to land executive positions with greater authority and higher pay, while there was no link found for the success of men in terms of gender composition of their inner circles. The reason? Women trying to rise up into leadership face cultural and systemic hurdles that make it harder for them to advance, such as unconscious bias. The study suggests that a way to overcome some of these hurdles is to form close connections with other women, who can share experiences from women who have been there, done that—from how to ask for what you're worth to bringing your unique talents to leadership (Zalis, 2019, Uzzie, 2019).*

This is motivating data to encourage women to have a strong female support system. It's important to build circles of trust, not only to share about similar barricades but to look out for, to defend, and protect each other. There is extreme power in the pack.

With these thoughts in mind, key points about ways in which to manifest positive actions in your own behavior to build better female relationships ultimately stems from the concept of Emotional Intelligence (EI). The term Emotional Intelligence first coined in 1990 by psychologists Mayer and Salovey, refers to, "one's capacity to perceive, process and regulate emotional information accurately and effectively, both within oneself and others" (Positive Psychology, 2020).

> *"Emotional intelligence forms the juncture at which cognition and emotion meet, it facilitates our capacity for resilience, motivation, empathy, reasoning, stress management, communication, and our ability to read and navigate a plethora of social situations and conflicts. EI matters and if cultivated affords one the opportunity to realize a more fulfilled and happy life" (Positive Psychology, 2020).*

Emotional Intelligence

Emotional Intelligence is a fundamental component to growing and building purposeful human relationships. Summarized by Positive Psychology of the Netherlands, the importance of EI should not go unrecognized because the first step in realizing your true potential lies in the understanding and management of your emotions. To summarize, Emotional Intelligence plays a key role, personally and professionally, in how you interact with other people. EI impacts communication skills, success at work, and in social relationships, ability to cope with stress, decision making, and motivation skills (2020). The five categories of Emotional Intelligence are:

- Self-Awareness
- Self-Regulation
- Motivation
- Empathy
- Social Skills

I first mentioned Dr. Marc Brackett, Ph.D., and Emotional Intelligence in Chapter 7. In 2020, Brené Brown interviewed Marc on her podcast, *Unlocking Us,* in the segment titled "Permission to Feel" where they eloquently verbalized the importance of EI. The basic principles of EI and the crux of their conversation very much applies to the concept I am trying to convey as it applies to female relationships:

- Finding your own voice
- Practicing bravery
- Avoiding bystander behaviors
- Manifesting positive actions in your own behaviors

Dr. Brackett developed the RULER Skills of Emotional Intelligence, an evidence-based approach to social and emotional learning that's used for educational purposes. I believe these skills can also be implemented to facilitate positive female relationships to promote collaboration over competition.

RULER is an acronym for the five skills of emotional intelligence:

1. **R**ecognizing emotions in oneself and others
2. **U**nderstanding the causes and consequences of emotions
3. **L**abeling emotions with a nuanced vocabulary
4. **E**xpressing emotions in accordance with cultural norms and social context
5. **R**egulating emotions with helpful strategies (Brackett, 2020).

I also share specific tips on awareness, communication, demonstration, empathy, and practicing the pause in the next section. Remember, it starts first within ourselves before we can appropriately and meaningfully apply it to others.

11.3: Your Turn: Dear reader, do you manifest positive actions in your own behaviors? Are you self-aware of what you do and how you do it, may have an impact on others? If so, how do you do it? Are you a proponent of Emotional Intelligence? If so, why do you think it's important? If not, why do you think it's not important? Take a moment now to write below, your thoughts and why.

_____

_____

_____

_____

"As you think about how to raise your daughter to be a confident and courageous woman, sure of herself and resilient under pressure. Begin by considering where you need to practice a little more bravery yourself. Any time you tip-toe around an awkward conversation, allow someone to treat you poorly, avoid taking a risk for fear of failure or let other people's opinions matter more than your own, you're missing an important opportunity to teach your daughter how to be brave."
—Margie Warrel (Warrel, 2016).

Raise Strong Girls

Whether you have a daughter, granddaughter, a niece, or you are a godmother to a young girl or young neighbor, you are a role model to her. What you do and how you do it influences her behavior.

When I first started my business "To Be" journey, my goal was to highlight the important topic of rivalry between women; what it means; the significance of the phenomenon; and its challenges, behaviors, coping, and recovery steps; to ultimately promote collaboration over competition. Every. Single. Time.

I've been successful in bringing attention to this serious issue. I've also had a lot of mothers reach out to ask my opinion about what they can do for their daughters, tweens, and teens who are experiencing rivalry, mean girl, and bullying types of behaviors from other girls their age. Without a doubt, a unique approach needs to be taken when sharing this topic with tweens and teens.

If you recall, in Chapter 4, I talked about how the adolescent brain is still forming. Additionally, adolescents worry less about what their parents have to say and put more focus on what others think. Add the role of the subconscious brain which controls 95% of her habits, and these factors combined will make it challenging for her to make clear decisions.

Since these young women are more susceptible to peer pressure, and because they are still discovering their voice, they may or may not have the ability to speak up on their behalf. This is a crucial stage when self-esteem is forming. As a result, the projected negative mean girl behaviors can be especially harmful because they help young women to shape incorrect beliefs about themselves.

It's pivotal that parents and other role models help guide these young girls through the negative behaviors—to help her understand who she is, what she has control of, and what she doesn't have control of. And ultimately, how to feel good about herself and not worry about what others think.

If awareness and help are not provided to adjust the bad behaviors, they will continue. As a strong woman, a mother, or someone who is a role-model to a little girl, what does your behavior say about you? Do your messages truly mirror your beliefs? Do your actions uplift and empower the young females in your life to be the best they can be?

As a strong woman, a mother, or someone who is a role-model to a young girl, you are an influencer to our future generation. It is so important to ensure our future female leaders become includers, ones that support the female sisterhood of collaboration over competition.

Do you represent positive behaviors to your daughter or are there areas where you need to practice a little more bravery? What example are you setting for your daughter to equip her to grow into a strong woman? Does what you do mirror what you say?

Dear reader, you are uniquely you, as are your daughters, sisters, nieces, and all the lovely young tweens and teens in your life. Teach them to be brave and to be strong. Be true to you. Be true to them and remember to be all that you are meant to be, to fully embrace and shine as only YOU can.

Five Tips to Teach Your Daughters How to be Brave

1. **Awareness.** When you see it, address it. Call it out. Don't be a bystander. This doesn't mean it has to be done in a rude manner. Just call it out when you see someone else doing it.

To your future fierce female say, "How do you think that comment made her feel?" Turning the situation around to where she can see the big picture and both sides of her actions. Many times words are spoken in a reactive state without clearly thinking about the ramifications they have. Don't be quiet so she can be comfortable.

2. **Communication.** As with many things in life, open, transparent communication is key.

To your little bodacious bad*ss, from an early age, have conversations with her about inclusion, being nice, and being kind. It seems quite simple, as most of us learned these traits in kindergarten. But seriously, it starts with having conversations and addressing the elephant in the room. Not just one time, but consistently. This should be an on-going conversation, with yourself and with her.

3. **Demonstrate.** What types of behavior do you exude? Think hard about that for a second. You may say one thing and then demonstrate something entirely different.

To your daring, darling diva, remember... She is always watching and that is what generates a learned behavior, more so than, *"listening to what you have to say"* ever will. The positive things and the behaviors that you emanate will show her a positive example of what being a loyal, true friend is, what being kind to others is, and what inclusion is.

4. **Empathy.** Teach and exhibit the power of empathy and compassion.

To your powerful, punky princess, if you dislike someone, dislike them alone. Don't recruit others to join your cause. Be mindful of knowing when others are expressing bad behaviors. But don't take the bad behaviors of others, or judgments of others as your own, until you experience first-hand, that it's an actual truth.

5. **Pause.** Practice the pause. Pause before judging. Pause before assuming. Pause before accusing.

To your strong, sassy spark plug, pause whenever you're about to react harshly. When emotions are high, intelligence is low. When you practice the pause, you'll avoid doing and saying things you'll regret later.

11.4: Your Turn: Do you have a young girl in your life that looks up to you? As you reflect on what she sees, does your message mirror you? What else could you be doing to make a more positive impression on her? Take a moment now to write below, your thoughts and why.

_____

_____

_____

_____

> *"Honor the friendships that allow you to pick up from*
> *where you last left off, regardless of how long it's been*
> *since you connected. The friendships that survive hiatuses,*
> *silences, and space. Those are connections that never die."*
> —Billy Chapata (Twitter, 2018).

Honor Current Friendships

Look at your current friendships, near or far. They just don't stay afloat on their own. It's natural to have an ebb and flow, especially, if distance is involved. It's not uncommon to have chunks of time in between conversations or seeing one another and then comfortably picking up right where you last saw one another, like no time has passed.

I have wonderful friendships like this. They're a gift to be cherished. One doesn't just stumble upon friendships of this kind. They take work on both sides, or else they'd just float away. Like a garden, they must be cultivated, to grow and flourish. Not all friendships will last forever. But it's important to nourish them to maintain the ones you have.

Tips to Maintain Healthy Friendships

1. **Listen!** We all have a lot going on—show interest in everything, not just the good things. Make a point of keeping up with all areas of your friend's life. Even if you have great things to share—slow down and listen to hers too.

2. **Schedule it!** When you are together, schedule your next outing before you wave good-bye. It's so easy to have several months go by and you realize you haven't seen her in a while. Put time on your calendar so you have something to look forward to.

3. **Take a Walk Down Memory Lane!** Reminisce about the good times. Shared memories can secure your bond. It's also very important to foster your bond and keep your relationship growing to continue to make new memories together.

4. **Try Something New!** Don't just eat or drink, schedule activities with her! Hike, go to an art museum, go to a winery... Shake it up a bit! This will give you more to talk about.

5. **Just Do it!** If it's been a while, don't be too proud to be the first one to reach out. For many reasons, life gets busy and time passes... if you miss her and want to see her. Let her know.

6. **Support Her!** Don't keep score. If you feel like you must keep track of what you're giving and receiving in your friendship—it's time to slow down and assess whether you have a healthy alliance. It's natural to give and take, and each of you may need extra support from time to time. That's normal. What isn't well-balanced is pointing out what you do for her, versus what she's done for you. That won't inspire, it will lead to resentment, and will ultimately push her away.

7. **Let Her Know!** If you see something that makes you think of her, share it and let her know. A quote, a joke, an old song you both like that comes on the radio... It will warm her heart to let her know she is in your thoughts.

8. **Be Reasonable!** Never expect more from her than she can realistically give. Keep your expectations reasonable. It's ok to set boundaries, as this can avoid feelings being hurt. If she just had a baby, she's probably not going to fly across the country for a girl's weekend—and that's ok! (Powerful Mind, 2019).

My Oldest Circle

I have one circle of friends I've known for over thirty years. It's my oldest circle. The great thing about this circle is we are still the same people as who we were when we were eighteen. Even though we have a few wrinkles and a grey hair or two, have moved, have our own families, have met new friends, and made new circles along the way, we still keep our bond.

What you see is what you get, meaning we truly are ourselves when we are amongst each other. I'm not saying that I am not myself around people I've met since then. But these ladies know me inside and out from the time I was a teenager. They know my goofy stories, the crazy boyfriends, and the bad sh*t. And I know theirs. To have these types of people in your life throughout distance and time is a blessing. It's a gift to be cherished.

Lucy shared thoughts about her closest circle.

> **Lucy.** *"Since high school and my college sorority days, I've always had a large group of female friends. Back then, I considered them all to be close friends but after my husband's affair, that all changed. I knew then in my heart who my real friends were. A very small group of women whom I'd confided in about what was going on stood by me during this time and they truly helped me to get through it. I don't know what I would have done without them. I mean, it was unconditional love. I realized then that my inner circle was a lot smaller, but I didn't care. I still don't. It's who you can trust...and trust with your biggest, heaviest ugliest secret that counts. That's when you truly know that she has your back and is there for you."*

11.5: Your Turn: Dear reader, look at your current female friendships. How do you honor them? Are they a priority for you or are they something that is "just there"? What are some special things you do, to let her know a friend is special to you? Take a moment now to write below, your thoughts and why.

_____

_____

_____

_____

Part II: Behind Frenemy Lines

Part II: Behind Frenemy Lines, is all about the action you take, versus part 1, which is the internal work. This is how you dive in and do it. Let's go!

Rivalry between women deprives women of female colleagues and companionship. It prevents women from relying on our natural allies, *each other*. We must raise each other up and reverse the stereotype that women do not support each other. Collaboration versus competition is the ticket to do so.

As an individual woman, you have power. Collectively, when you are a part of a group of women, you have an even greater impact than you do by yourself. Just think about that for a second and let it sink in… Now look at your circle. They are the constant, the ones who uplift, expand, and empower you. They are the ones that are there for you, no matter what, through thick and thin. They build up and do not tear down. This. Is. A. True. Friend.

If you don't have a circle, a squad, a pack, a horseshoe, a tribe… you need to find one. And hopefully, this book is showing you how to do that.

"Alone, we can do so little; together, we can do so much."
—Helen Keller (Goodreads, Inc., 2020).

Find or Maintain Your Sisterhood

To keep your tiara sparkling to its finest luster you must make a plan, create a strategy to dive in, and go behind frenemy lines. They don't have to be followed in any particular order. They are here to guide you along the path to finding your true sisterhood. You are in charge of your friendship-destiny. It is in this way you will win the frenemy-war and be victorious. If you already have a sisterhood to call your own, hallelujah! Rejoice in that and hold on tight because they are precious beings in your life.

If you don't have a sisterhood but want one, crave one, know you will be a better person if you have one... rest easy, my fair lady, it can happen to you too. It takes work, but it's well worth it to have these types of women surround you, as a part of your sisterhood, and as part of your circle.

Trust Your Gut

The first person, networking place, women's group, or thing that you try out may not be a good fit. It may sound crazy, but interview them! It doesn't have to be formal. When you interview someone, you are doing your due diligence to ensure it's a good fit on both sides. You don't want to waste your time, or theirs. To find a good fit for a group, consider looking at trial memberships. And remember, just because you go once, meet someone once, or check something out one time, you are not always guaranteed a perfect fit. And that is completely ok!

I've been in my local area for 10+ years now and I am still finding out about new groups and new things to do. It may seem like the process crawls at a snails' pace but if you put your effort into finding a group—it will eventually happen.

When that whisper speaks, it's important to listen to it. When your brain makes decisions, it uses a combination of emotion and logic. This emotion, this *intuition* is hard-wired in our brains. The butterfly feeling in our stomachs is our nerve cells talking to us. This *gut feeling* is our ability to feel, know, and understand things without deliberately thinking about them. Our past experiences, the understanding we obtained from them, and our existing awareness guides our intuition.

Intuition guides you. Whether always conscious or not, throughout my life I've relied on my gut instinct. Big or small, professional or personal, it has helped me make decisions and find my path.

Intuition is different from fear. Intuition is the ability to understand something immediately without the need for conscious reasoning. It is about the present, not the future or past. Fear is an unpleasant emotion, a heaviness, or feeling of anxiety, caused by the outcome of something or the safety and well-being of someone. Fear often focuses on the past or future.

11.6: Your Turn: Dear reader, do you listen to your inner whisper? How has it directed you, in your life? Is it a constant? Do you think it guides you? Take a moment now to write below, your thoughts and why.

_____

_____

_____

_____

Get Your "Date" on!

Approach finding your people, friendships, social interactions, or group-networking like "dating." For example, did your significant other just magically fall out of the sky? Nope, I doubt it! Neither do BFFs or spaces for women, nor networking groups. When you were dating your significant other, even prior to dating your significant other... you had a type. This includes interests you wanted to share such as a similar foundation or background, ethical, religious beliefs, etc. There are specific deal breakers to a "yay" or "nay" for progressing forward. The same goes for finding girlfriends or women's groups.

I, not-really-on-purpose, "dated" one of my now good girlfriends. We were at a local restaurant and had passed each other in the hallway. Almost simultaneously we both said, "I really like your haircut!" We laughed and then chatted for a few minutes. It turned out we'd both moved to the area about the same time and were finding it difficult to meet new girlfriends. We set up a lunch date. On the way to meet her for lunch, I had some apprehension. "What am I doing?" I thought. Turns out, as we discussed later, we both had similar feelings on our way to lunch, we both likened it to going on a first date! Giving in to a bit of nervousness worked in my favor because she's been a dear friend now, for almost a decade.

I also had a not so great "women's group" dating experience. We'd just moved from D.C. to Richmond. We were renting a house with no young families near us. I stayed at home with my 9-month old daughter and at the same time was focused on writing my dissertation. I didn't have many opportunities to meet new people, or so I told myself. To say I was craving adult female friendships was an understatement! I found a local women's group online. From what I'd gathered via research, it seemed right up my alley. Plus it was at a local wine bar near my house... "Absolutely perfect!" I thought. I was excited to attend the meeting and come out with a new bestie!

Based on what I read online, I was ready for an encounter with similar like-minded women. I could not have been more wrong. Thankfully, the wine was good. The evening loomed... In hindsight, I should have just gotten up and left. There was no depth to the conversation. The women talked about clipping coupons and the types of clothes their kids were wearing. I'd thought the whole point of this particular social outing was to get out of the house, bond as adults, and get to know one another personally, not a mommy and me meet-up. There is absolutely nothing wrong with this type of meet-up, it simply was not what I was looking for at that point in time. My husband, who'd encouraged me to attend and had been excited about the potential, asked how it was when I got home to which I immediately burst into tears and said, "It was awful." Needless to say, I didn't go back. In reading the online description, it sounded like a good match but this group simply was not the right fit for me.

I had another pretty fabulous "women's networking and business coach" dating experience. While I was in the midst of launching my "To Be" business, I realized that I needed to hire a business coach. I wanted someone who'd also helped other female-owned businesses like mine get on the right track. I did some research, found a coach online, and immediately hired her. And at the same time, I also signed up to go on a European work-on-your-business-and-relax-at-the-same-time retreat with her and six other women. I completely dove into the experience, feet first! I think this was a bit shocking to her and in hindsight, me too. But in that moment, it just felt right.

I met a great group of diverse women, several of whom I later worked with to further my business. All of whom, I now consider to be friends. In fact, this special group of women was my segue to an entirely different group of new women in my home city who are complete bad*sses. They uplift; they empower; they support; and they include. When I am with any of them, I feel completely at home. Had I not trusted my initial instinct, I would not have met these lovely ladies. I am so glad that I did!

11.7: Your Turn: Dear reader, have you ever likened finding new female friends as "dating?" Have you ever done this before? If so, what was it like? How did it make you feel? How else do you go about finding new female friends? Take a moment now to write below, your thoughts and why.

_____

_____

_____

_____

Finding a Sisterhood at Work

I typically don't seek out the working environment to find my new BFF. Can it happen? Of course it can! I've almost always approached work with the mindset of:

- I'm there to do a job.
- I'm happy keeping my professional and personal life separate. (Especially if I am in a position where I've managed or led people).

However, I've almost always taken a friendship or two with me when I've left any type of job. In all honesty, with as much time as you spend with people and if you click with them, it's kind of hard not to.

Because I've talked so much about female rivalry at work, it's important to highlight ways in which to proactively avoid negative rivalrous types of behavior in an organizational setting. At least, as best as what you have the power or control to do. Hopefully, by providing the following points you will have better insight as to how to potentially avoid a negative experience at work.

It's important to realize that company cultures can differ greatly amongst organizations. If you are coming out of a previous negative experience or simply want to embark on your new journey eyes wide open, there are a couple of things you can do to be aware of what is going on culturally:

1. Vet the culture prior to being hired.
2. Establish communication with other women, after you are hired.

Vet the Culture

Investigate. Put the feelers out. There are several ways to research organizational culture. Ask around:

- **Search Out the Company's Social Media Presence.** You can go through a company's tweets, videos, and social media posts to gain insight into what is important to them/the team.
- **Use Your Social Media Network.** See if anyone you know, or anyone you know that they may know, can provide information on a paticular company, team, group, etc. Don't just settle for talking to associates. If you can, speak with partners, customers, suppliers, etc.
- **Know What You Want.** Consider what you've liked or disliked in previous jobs pertaining to colleagues, managers, and senior leadership. Think about what type of office you thrive in, what types of people you work best with, and what your core values and principles are. Have these points in mind when you conduct your search.
- **Ask Different People the Same Questions.** Have a list of specific questions to ask the various people you meet when you conduct your search. This will provide insight for consistency.

Establish Communication With Other Women

It's important to establish and implement transparent communication with other women after you are hired. Take the reins, you strong and fearless female! By commanding control, you will encounter direct communication instead of passively experiencing it.

Gain insight about what is going on with other women within the organization to better understand what is occurring in different divisions, departments, teams, etc. Having a group to collaborate with, at and across all levels, provides a dedicated space to share challenges and successes. It also reduces the feeling of competition for an imaginary allocation at the top (McNulty, 2018).

> *"Because women seeking positions of executive leadership often face cultural and political hurdles that men typically do not, they benefit from an inner circle of close female contacts that can share private information about things like an organization's attitudes toward female leaders, which helps strengthen women's job search, interviewing, and negotiation strategies" (Uzzi, 2019).*

Open communication in an office will help everyone understand unique challenges all females may each be going through on their own. You may not know, if others as a group, are collectively experiencing the same things until you discuss them. Open communication can improve the flow of information and relieve tension and anxiety. Some ways to do this are as follows:

- Host women-only coffee chats, lunches, or happy hours.
- Create open channels of communication, in person, or in a private social channel, members only group.
- Reach out to women new to the organization to share advice and personal experiences. Find commonality topics that may help you bond.
- Have an open-door policy.
- Openly be a champion for other women.
- Sponsor other women. This involves connecting a protégé with opportunities and contacts and advocating on their behalf, as opposed to the more advice-focused role of mentorship (McNulty, 2018).

To make this work and be inclusive, your actions don't have to be huge, nor does it have to be run from the top down. Just start by reaching out and making connections. You'll be surprised to see it grow from there, as other women will also want and benefit from this type of interaction and support (McNulty, 2018).

11.8: Your Turn: Dear reader, have you taken a job only to realize that it wasn't a good fit culturally? If so, what did you do? Have you ever vetted a company prior to accepting a job? If so, how did you do this? Did you find you were given truthful answers that helped you make the right decision for you? Have you ever been a part of a women's only network within a company you worked for? If so, did you find that it offered valuable, truthful insight and a true support system? Take a moment now to write below, your thoughts and why.

_____

_____

_____

_____

Have a Sounding Board

Find someone to bounce those ideas off of! Having a group of supportive women on your side, so you can get the "skinny" on things, can help you step outside of yourself to gain additional insight and perspective. And really, it doesn't have to be made up of just women, it can be a male figure in your life, a family member, a mentor, a friend, a colleague, a neighbor, or a coach, etc.... Having a sounding board can help you to reflect about some of the news steps you are taking.

On a personal level,

> *"a sounding board may be an individual you can go to with anything that will hear you out and listen. Sometimes they offer advice but the benefit they give is essentially in the listening. It's a person you trust so much that you can say anything that pops into your head and they'll hear you out without judgement"* (Hedrick, 2015).

A sounding board is helpful because:

• It makes space for you to think things through.

- By explaining your ideas and issues to someone else, it can clarify your own thinking.
- Having your thinking challenged in a safe environment gives you the chance to develop your ideas further, and if necessary, change direction completely with no adverse consequences (Business Matters, 2008).

11.9: Your Turn: Dear reader, do you have a sounding board, someone you can go to, to bounce ideas off of? Male or female? How is that relationship reciprocated? Take a moment now to write below, your thoughts and why.

_____

_____

_____

_____

Be Inclusive

I've been burned before as I'm sure you've been burned before too. What has happened to you may help shape your path, but it does not have to define your future. Chalk it up to a learning experience and move on. If you let being burned control you, you lessen the opportunity for new beginnings and new chances to cross your path. It's important to focus on being an includer versus an excluder.

If someone new moves into your neighborhood, the PTA, your church, athletic club, etc., welcome her. You may not know where she is coming from, likewise, you also may never know if you are looking at your new BFF! The point is, don't assume. You just never know who is placed on your path at exactly the right moment in time.

I've read about the concept of the "horseshoe" versus a "circle" as it pertains to female groups. This concept focuses on breaking open your circle to become a horseshoe. Think in terms of a U-shape versus an O-shape. It's noticing who is on the outside and inviting them in. It's making room for more.

In her book, *Untamed,* Glennon Doyle talks about circles and horseshoes, "I hate how people stand in circles. I wish we'd all agree to stand around in horseshoes, with room available for awkward outsiders to join" (2020, p. 107). She further elaborates the horseshoe concept in a Twitter post, "Horseshoes are better than circles. Leave space. Always leave space. Horseshoes of friends > that circles of friends. Life can be lonely. Stand in horseshoes" (2018).

I've heard some women say they don't like the concept of "the circle" as they find it barring, "A tight wall that no one else can get into. The new girl or the person that doesn't have their own circle can't get in. You are either a part of the circle or outside of the circle" (Blinn, 2020). I get that.

I also get, and yes, I'm aware this may cause some type of controversy, that while you can be inviting, kind, and friendly, you are simply not going to be friends with everyone. I'm calling it as I see it. You can always be inclusive but that doesn't mean that everyone in your horseshoe will always be in your inner circle.

Does that mean excluding someone? Absolutely not! You should always be nice. You should always include and invite in. It just means you may not have that much in common with her, have the time, interests, and vice versa, on the level it takes to be connected with her closer.

Glennon Doyle sums up the concept of inclusion nicely in a Twitter post.

> *"If you are standing with other women in a circle and there is a woman standing along in your circle's vicinity—the thing to do is notice her, smile at her, over a bit and say, 'Hi, come join us!' Even if she decides to not join your circle—even if she looks at you like you are crazy—inviting her in is STILL THE THING TO DO. This advice is meant for both literal and figurative circles. WIDEN YOUR CIRCLE. ALL THE TIME" (2014).*

It's also okay too, for your circle to reduce in size. Your circles will evolve as you evolve. Sometimes you don't have the time to maintain contact with a lot of people. Sometimes you realize you no longer have things in common.

And sometimes, situations change and you just naturally drift apart due to age, stages, and phases you are in.

Food for Thought: It's okay to make your circle smaller with true friends you trust versus having a bigger circle of women of whom you don't trust.

Raising Includers

My husband and I are raising our daughter, both of our children, to be includers. It includes being mindful, modeling kindness, and accepting others as they are. It enables their generation to have respect for themselves *and* others, so they grow strong with wild hearts, yet are also fierce with compassion. It means demonstrating values of:

- Collaboration over competition
- Progress over perfection
- Benevolent over b*tchy
- Belonging over bullying
- Respect over rivalry
- Support over smear
- Grace over gossip
- Harmony over hate
- Empowerment over envy
- Avoiding the fear of failure
- Extending gratitude and forgiveness
- Being grounded in authenticity

Being an includer however, does not mean letting people walk all over you... Quite the opposite. It's knowing who you are as a person, being firm in your beliefs but also being able to recognize when a friend, phase, stage, relationship, or job has ended and is no longer healthy for you. It's liberating to say, "this isn't serving me" and walk away.

11.10: Your Turn: Dear reader, are you inclusive? Is this a behavior you are conscious of doing? Or is it something you haven't really given much thought to? If you have children in your life, are you teaching them too, to be inclusive? If so, how are you doing this? What do you think of the concept of the horseshoe versus a circle? Is there a difference to you, about them? Take a moment now to write below, your thoughts and why.

_____

_____

_____

_____

Queens Supporting Queens

I don't usually watch the Grammy Awards but my daughter is a huge Ariana Grande fan, so in 2020 we watched some of it on TV. I was so touched by the behaviors that two female artists exhibited.

At the January 2020 Grammy Awards,

> *Billie Eilish, who'd already won five trophies, and Lizzo, who had 3 trophies, were rooting for other women. Both wanted other women to win their Grammys. Billie made history as the second artist ever and youngest on top of that to scoop up the Grammy's four biggest awards. She was very humble and thankful in her first three acceptances. It was her fourth win for Album of the Year that caught people's and the cameras' attention. Because while they were announcing the winner, Billie could be seen repeating, 'Please don't be me, please don't be me.' When she got onstage to accept her award, she began her speech by saying, 'Can I just say that I think Ariana Grande deserves this? 'Thank U Next' got me through some sh*t, and I think it deserves this win, more than anything in the world.' The camera cut to Ariana in the audience, who blew Billie a kiss and shouted, 'Take your moment, girl!' These two women showcased a true female-sisterhood-bond-*

ing...and the importance of artists and people in general, supporting each other's achievements.

Lizzo also took a moment from her spotlight to shine the light on another artist during the Grammy show. She showed Beyoncé some love. The category was stacked, with Lizzo, Billie, Ariana Grande, and Taylor Swift nominated...before the award was announced, Lizzo could be seen chanting the name of only one of her competitors, Beyoncé. This action highlights a true sisterhood act, Lizzo showing support for her competitor rather than cross her fingers and pray for herself to win. This speaks volumes about her character (Bate, 2020).

This gets right to the heart of what my messages highlight about the female sisterhood. It also sets such a kick-ass, public example of what I am trying to teach my daughter, of what we all should be teaching our girls: Queens supporting Queens. Girls supporting girls. Women supporting women.

11.11: Your Turn: Dear reader do you compete or empower, as it pertains to other women? Is this something you consciously think about? Why or why not? Are other female relationships important to you? Has this book helped you to gain perspective of how to find a sisterhood and authentic female relationships? Take a moment now to write below, your thoughts and why.

_____

_____

_____

_____

Closing

It is up to each of us individually to work in conjunction with one another to change the negative perception... and shift to a "mindset of abundance." Let's show the world that womanhood has evolved. We should be able to support and coexist with one another without drama, competition, gossip, or bullying types of behaviors. We should be able to uplift, empower, and advocate collaboration over competition. The ticket in doing so, is in doing it together.

Last Word

"and perhaps what made her beautiful, was not her appearance, or what she achieved. but in her love and in her courage and in her audacity to believe; no matter the darkness around her. light ran wild within her, and that was the way she came alive, and it showed up in everything."
—Morgan Harper Nichols (Goodreads, Inc. 2020).

When I first began to investigate this phenomenon of rivalry between women, I was very surprised about the enthusiasm this topic revealed and the earnestness of women wanting to share their stories. These women also knew of other women in this type of situation, in their personal lives, socially, and within the working environment, had been affected. These brave, brave women shared with me some of the most vulnerable moments of their lives. Yet in doing so, it made them stronger. It gave them the ability to fight their inner demons and release the heaviness of these awful behaviors. In turn, it is also helping other women to find their voice too.

I became aware of how common this phenomenon really is. A reality began to unfold. It painted a picture of what women who experienced these behaviors are all about. It's not a pretty picture, but it's one that reveals truth, honesty, and ultimately for many of these women, the act of forgiveness.

Although it was very painful when the situation occurred, all the women who shared their stories were motivated to talk about their experiences, often with undisguised emotion and insight as to how vulnerable they truly were in this situation. The insight of these women is emotionally powerful, even while their narratives were frequently disturbing.

The purpose of my diving into this research was to better understand the lived experience of rivalry between women. According to professors Evelyn Fox Keller & Helene Moglen (1987), "competition denied in principle, but unavoidable in practice, surfaces in forms that may be far more wounding, and perhaps even fiercer and more destructive" (p. 34).

My role in this endeavor is to tell "her" story. I want to showcase the occurrence of rivalry in everyday living. And, I want to highlight the fact that rivalry between women does not discriminate. The unveiling of these stories supports the notion that negative rivalrous behaviors create obstacles in every-day life, regardless of where it occurs.

Their stories speak of a silent epidemic that is occurring daily. It can take place in any environment, an organizational setting, your neighborhood, social events, clubs, or sports. Their stories are ones that, with more insight and awareness, need not occur.

The individual descriptions and experiences portrayed by each woman interviewed are unique and cannot be simplified into a generic meaning. Their shared experiences are individual and personal. However, once the individual experience was revealed in conjunction with the other experiences, the mean-ing went beyond each individual woman and was contemplated for deeper meaning as a collective whole.

This collective whole highlights the enormity of this phenomenon. This issue... until we address it head-on, it will not go away. It's time to talk about the elephant in the room. The one we're afraid to address because we'll be called *over-sensitive*... we'll be the b*tch. They'll say we're *not tough enough* to "play the game," or we don't have what it takes to be in power. Let's prove them wrong. We can do this, together.

"Be Brave.
Your bravery wins a thousand battles you can't see, because your
bravery strengthens a thousand others to win their battles too."
—Ann Voskamp (Ann Voskamp, 2020).

It's Time.

It's time to focus on bonding together as women, to get to know each other as real people instead of labels.

It's time to focus on doing what we absolutely can to lift each other up instead of counting how many track meets she missed or if she is buying instead of making cupcakes for the school party. A strong woman stands up for herself. A stronger woman stands up for everyone else.

It's time to focus on the beauty and strength of having a solid support system. One that comes with the understanding, knowledge, and trust, that your sister is there for you unconditionally—no matter what and how you do it.

It's time to halt judgment, stop the guilt, and put an end to projecting assumptions on each other about what is right and wrong. The rivalry is there and clearly exists on both sides. Let's change that perception and the reality...

It's time we stood up to it. When we unite and work together to support, uplift, and empower one another, we can do great things. No matter what camp you reside in, she is not better than you, nor you better than her. No one is more perfect than another.

It's time to build your own table. If you are not getting a seat at the table, build your own. Build your own circle, seek your own sisterhood, find a new tribe.

It's time ladies. It's time to make a change. Choose to be a woman who lifts others up instead of someone who puts others down.

Because I am so very passionate about this topic, I will end as I began. My sincere hope is that the stories I share with you will help you to understand the truth about what rivalry between women truly means. You should know, especially if you have ever or are currently experiencing it... That you can say, "*It's not just me,*" and know you are not alone.

Let's be the ones who change the game and the world.

It's time.

—Amber

You Already Are. It's Time To Be.

About the Author

Amber Tichenor has a Ph.D. in Industrial/ Organizational (I/O) Psychology and is the founder of To Be, Coaching + Consulting®. A thought leader on the topic of women's rivalry, Amber has 20+ years' experience as an Organizational Change Strategy and Leadership consultant where she helped guide businesses through transformational change.

Amber is deeply passionate about addressing the phenomenon of rivalry between women, and wrote her PhD thesis about this issue. She consults with organizations, offers speaking engagements, and workshops on this important topic—what it means, the importance of the phenomenon, the challenges and behaviors it presents, along with coping, and recovery steps.

Amber's goal is to promote collaboration over competition, to empower women to find their voice, leave the rivalry behind, and team up with a community of like-minded women who support each other, to be unstoppable together.

Visit her website: https://www.tobecoachingandconsulting.com

Resources

I've included some resources that I've found to be helpful for finding a sisterhood or various types of female networking groups. Some I've personally been involved in and others I've heard about from other women.

There are so many resources available that provide support. These are just a few that I personally know of, have been shared with me, or I've stumbled upon in my research that I know are beneficial to this topic.

R.1: Your Turn: Dear reader, are there resources that you utilize for support, as it pertains to what I've discussed in this book? If so, how did you find them?

If you know of others that I've missed, that you would recommend, please let me know as I'll add it to my list!

Books.
Agrawal, Radha. (2018). Belong. Find Your People, Create Community & Live a More Connected Life. New York, NY. Workman Publishing Co.

Brackett, Marc. (2019). Permission to Feel. The Power of Emotional Intelligence to Achieve Well-Being and Success. New York, NY. Celadon Books.

Brown, B. (2019). Braving the Wilderness: The Quest for True Belonging. New York. Random House Trade Paperbacks.

Devereux-Mills, Anne. (2019) The Parlay Effect: How Female Connections Can Change the World. San Francisco, CA. Parlay House Books.

Doyle, Glennon (2020). Untamed. New York, NY. Dial Press a Division of Random House.

Goldin, Kara. (2020). Undaunted: Overcoming Doubts and Doubters. New York, NY: Harper Collins.

Harder, Lori. (2018). A Tribe Called Bliss. Break Through Superficial Friendships, Create Real Connections, Reach Your Highest Potential. New York, NY. Gallery Books.

Janna, Tiffany. (2020). Subtle Acts of Inclusion. Oakland, CA: Berrett-Koehler Publishers.

Kelleher, Seo. (2020). Don't Be a B*tch, Be an Alpha: How to Unlock Your Magic, Play Big, and Change the World. Richmond, VA. Alpha Sisters Publishing.

Leyba, Cara, A. (2015). Girl Code. Unlocking the Secrets to Success, Sanity + Happiness for the Female Entrepreneur. New York, NY. Penguin Publishing, a Division of Random House.

Sandberg, Sheryl. (2013). Lean In. Women, Work and the Will to Lead. New York, NY. Knopf, Borzoi Books, a Division of Random House.

Shapiro-Barash, S. (2006). Tripping the Prom Queen: The Truth About Women and Rivalry. New York, NY: St. Martin's.

Shipman, Claire & Kay, Katty. (2018). The Confidence Code For Girls. New York, NY: Harper Collins.

Sincero, Jen. (2018). You Are A Badass Every Day: How to Keep Your Motivation Strong, Your Vibe High, and Your Quest For Transformation Unstoppable. New York, NY: Viking.

Wintsch, Katherine. (2019). Slay Like A Mother: How To Destroy What's Holding You Back So You Can Live The Life You Want. Naperville, IL: Sourcebooks.

Wiseman, Rosalind. (2016). Queen Bees and Wannabees. New York, NY: Harmony Books.

National + International Groups.

Anne Devereux-Mills Parlay House Network: https://parlayhouse.com

Parlay House is an inclusive series of gatherings for women that foster intimate conversations that don't happen in other parts of your life. They don't network: they ignite meaningful bonds between strangers. Started in San Francisco, recurring Parlay House events now happen in SF, New York, London, Paris, Oakland, Denver, Washington D.C., Seattle, and Atlanta—with more to come!!

Lean In: https://leanin.org/circles

The Lean In Circles community is a vibrant network of women in almost every country. Since 2013, they've been connecting over shared experiences, building each other up, and cheering each other on.

Sallie Krawchek's Ellevate Network: https://www.ellevatenetwork.com

A professional network of women supporting each other across companies to change the culture of business at large. (It began as "85 Broads," a network of Goldman alumni that drew its name from the old GS headquarters address before Krawcheck, a Merrill alumna, bought and expanded it).

Richmond, Virginia, USA Groups.

Alpha Female Sisterhood: https://www.facebook.com/groups/alphafemale-sisterhood

Alpha Female Sisterhood is a Facebook group where strong women lift one another up and grow together. It's a place where empowered women can embrace their alpha female energy, empower themselves to play big to live their purpose, and encourage and support other women to do the same. Have to ask permission to join.

Boss Babes RVA: https://www.facebook.com/groups/bossbabesrva/about

Founded in 2014. Boss Babes RVA was founded as an outlet for female entrepreneurs to hang out, uplift each other, learn from one another, and surround themselves with motivated, passionate, and creative individuals.

The Boss Babes RVA Facebook group is a place to discuss the topics of:

- education
- networking
- mentorship
- collaboration

as it relates to business and career growth. 'Boss' can mean owning your own business or merely owning your own path in your career development. We've reserved the term 'Babes' for anyone who is female-identifying.

FABWOMEN: https://fabwomen.me

FABWOMEN is a diverse community of women committed to personal and professional development through creation of lasting connections. FABWOMEN seeks to purposefully empower, encourage, motivate, and celebrate the diversity of womanhood by creating a safe space for dialogue, by building strong personal networks and by providing opportunities for growth and education for the purpose of self-discovery and acceptance of one's authentic self.

On Purpose Woman Global Community, Private Facebook Group: https://www.facebook.com/groups/onpurposenetworkingforwomen/about

The mission of this group is "to connect women around the world to their gifts, their purpose and each other." It's an exciting big vision based on the concept and belief that we crave connection and community and it's important to know we're not alone. Group co-leaders: Ginny Robertson and Kathryn Yarborough.

On Purpose Woman Magazine: http://onpurposewomancommunity.com/about-magazine/

Originally founded by Ginny Robertson, the "On Purpose Woman Magazine" is headquartered in the Baltimore-Washington area. In 2018, Ginny teamed up with entrepreneur Kathryn Yarborough to bring On Purpose Woman Magazine back in digital format. The "On Purpose Magazine," is a *force for good* and is now read by women across the United States and around the globe and is a place for women's voices to be heard.

Rebelle: https://www.rebellecon.com

Rebelle's Mission is to amplify the voices of women who are doing it differently, and learn alongside one another. It's a trusted group of like-minded women to confide in, a group that is eager to listen without judgment. A virtual community.

Rev Up Society: https://www.maryfoley.com

A community for women entrepreneurs committed to success. Rev Up is a community that inspires you to achieve your most ambitious business goals, encouraging you to take bold action. The Rev Up Society is a group of clear-minded women entrepreneurs who are inspired by their work and committed to success. Together, members of the Rev Up Society provide a strong and supportive community where you can confide your challenges, mastermind new strategies, and celebrate your wins.

Glossary of Terms

Aggression is defined as, "hostile or violent behavior or attitudes toward another; readiness to attack or confront. The action or an act of attacking without provocation. Forceful and sometimes overly assertive pursuit of one's aims and interests" (New Oxford Dictionary, 2019). Wikipedia further defines the term as,

> *overt or covert, often harmful, social interaction with the intention of inflicting damage or other unpleasantness upon another individual. It may occur either reactively or without provocation. In humans, aggression can be caused by various triggers, from frustration to feeling disrespected (2020).*

> *Aggression is defined as, "behavior whose intent is to harm another" (Chapter 2, pg. 3). (Duncan et al, 2004).*

Control is defined as, "the power to influence or direct people's behavior or the course of events. The power to restrain something. The means of limiting or regulating something" (New Oxford Dictionary, 2019).

Covert Aggression is defined as, "a personality employing a potent one-two punch: the covert-aggressive conceals aggressive intent to ensure you never really see what's coming; and he or she exploits your normal sensitivities, conscientiousness, and other vulnerabilities to manipulate you into succumbing" (Bellows 2015).

Demeaning is defined as, "causing someone to lose their dignity and the respect of others. To demean is to do something that is beneath one's dignity; to conduct oneself in a particular way" (New Oxford Dictionary, 2019).

Direct Aggression as defined by the APA Dictionary of Psychology is, "aggressive behavior directed toward the source of frustration or anger" (2018).

Humiliation is defined as, "the action of humiliating someone of the state of being humiliated. To humiliate someone is to make (someone) feel ashamed and foolish by injuring their dignity and self-respect, especially publicly" (New Oxford Dictionary, 2019).

Indirect Aggression is defined as, "any behavior aimed at the goal of harming another living being that is delivered circuitously through another person or object, even if it must nevertheless be intended to harm someone" (Richardson & Green, 2003). "It's the use of the non-physical act of meanness, cruelty, or offense. It's also known as social aggression or relational aggression since it's used to harm a person's relationships or social standing" (Wikipedia, 2020). Dr. Bjorkqvist references indirect aggression, "when social skills develop, even more sophisticated strategies of aggression are made possible, with the aggressor being able to harm a target person without even being identified" (1994, p. 179).

Intangible is defined as, "unable to be touched or grasped; not having a physical presence. Difficult or impossible to define or understand; vague and abstract. Not precisely measurable" (New Oxford Dictionary, 2019).

Public Humiliation or public shaming is defined by Wikipedia as, "a form of punishment whose main feature is dishonoring or disgracing a person, usually an offender or a prisoner, especially in a public place" (2020).

Rivalry as A Banner for Broader Behaviors. As may be gleaned from the research insight descriptions, rivalry is often a "banner" for other broader behaviors that a woman experiences, or a result of other broader circumstances she is dealing with.

Social Intelligence is defined as, "the ability to understand and manage men and women and boys and girls, to act wisely in human relations." (Chapter 2) (1920 by Edward Thorndike). Psychologist Nicholas Humphrey of Cambridge, MA (1986) believes that it is social intelligence that defines who we are as humans.

Tangible is defined as, "perceptible by touch. Clear and definite; real" (New Oxford Dictionary, 2019).

References

First Word

Native Partnership. (2020). *Native American Proverb Quote*. Retrieved August 6, 2020 from, http://www.nativepartnership.org/site/Page-Server?pagename=ThousandVoices_home

Vocabulary.Com. (2020). *Rivalry*. Retrieved August 5, 2020 from, https://www.vocabulary.com/dictionary/rivalry

Part One

Quotesphilia, Inc. (2020). *Matshona Dhliwayo Quote*. Retrieved October from, https://quotesphilia.com/author/matshona-dhliwayo-quotes/qpn-7867171/

Chapter 1

Adichie, Chimamanda, Ngozi. (2014). *We Should All Be Feminists*. Random House. New York, NY.

American Psychological Association (APA). (2018). *Direct Aggression*. Retrieved January 10, from, https://dictionary.apa.org/direct-aggression

Bellows, A. (2015). Are You the Target of Covert Aggression? *Psych Central*. The Mixing Bowl. Retrieved January 10, 2020 from, https://blogs.psychcentral.com/mixing-bowl/2015/12/are-you-the-target-of-covert-aggression/

Briles, J. (1989). *Woman to Woman: From Sabotage to Support*. Far Hills, NJ: New Horizon.

Bjorkqvist, K. (1994). Sex Differences in Physical, Verbal and Indirect Aggression: A Review of Recent Research. *Sex Roles*, 30 (3/4), 177–188.

Chesler, P. (2001). *Woman's Inhumanity to Woman*. NY: Thunders' Mouth/Nation.

Duncan, L. & Owen-Smith, A. (2006). Powerlessness and the Use of Indirect Aggression in Friendships. *Sex Roles*, 55, 493–502.

Fey, Tina. (2004). *The Weekend Warrior by Chris Kattan*. Retrieved April 22, 2020 from, https://archive.is/20120710074402/http://jam.canoe.ca/Television/TV_Shows/S/Saturday_Night_Live/2004/04/28/pf-733201.html

Kattan, Chris. (2004). Weekend Warrior. Jam.canoe.ca. April 28, 2004. Archived from the original on July 10, 2012. Retrieved August 5, 2020 from, https://archive.is/20120710074402/http:/jam.canoe.ca/Television/TV_Shows/S/Saturday_Night_Live/2004/04/28/pf-733201.html

Loya, B.N., Cowan, G., Walters, C. (2006). The role of Social Comparison and Body Consciousness in Women's Hostility Toward Women. *Sex Roles*, 54, 575–583.

Lugones, M., Spelman, E. (1987). Competition, Compassion, & Community: Models for a Feminist Ethos. In Miner & Longino (Ed.), *Competition a feminist taboo?*, (pp 234–247). New York, NY: The Feminist.

Matsumoto, D. (1987). One Young Woman in Publishing. In Miner & Longino (Ed.), *competition a feminist taboo?*, (pp 81–91). New York, NY: The Feminist.

Miner, , V., Longino, H.E. (1987). *Competition: A feminist taboo?* New York, NY: The Feminist.

Goodreads, inc. (2020). *Adrienne Rich quote*. Retrieved August 5, 2020 from, https://www.goodreads.com/author/quotes/29947.Adrienne_Rich

Reddit. (2020). *Cherokee Proverb*. Retrieved August 5, 2020 from, https://www.reddit.com/r/quotes/comments/sve4i/an_old_cherokee_told_his_grandson/

Richardson, D.S., Green, L.R. (2006). Direct and indirect aggression: Relationships as Social Context. *Journal of Applied Social Psychology*, 36(10), 2492–2508.

Richardson, D.S., Green, L.R. (2003). Defining Direct and Indirect Aggression: The Richardson Conflict Response Questionnaire. RIPA/ IRSP, 16(2), 11–30. Presses Universitaires de Grenoble. Retrieved March 10, 2020 from, https://www.researchgate.net/publication/285080399_Defining_direct_and_indirect_aggression_The_Richardson_Conflict_Response_Questionnaire

Rojahn, K., Fischer, A.H., Willemsen, T.M. (1997). The social identities of female leaders in different cultural contexts. *Feminism & Psychology*, 7(2), 183–207.

Shapiro-Barash, S. (2006). Tripping the Prom Queen: The Truth About Women and Rivalry. New York, NY: St. Martin's.

Soukhanov, A.H. (2001). *Microsoft encarta college library*. New York, NY: St. Martin's

Thompson, William. R. (2001). Identifying Rivals and Rivalries in World Politics. *International Studies Quarterly*. 45 (4): 557–586.

Urban Dictionary (2020). *Keyboard courage*. Retrieved April 14, 2020 from, https://www.urbandictionary.com/define.php?term=keyboard%20courage

Wikipedia. (2020). *Competition*. Retrieved April 10, 2020 from, https://en.wikipedia.org/wiki/Competition

Wikipedia. (2020). *Public Humiliation*. Retrieved January 10, 2020, from, https://en.wikipedia.org/wiki/Public_humiliation

Wiseman, Rosalind. (2016). Queen Bees and Wannabes, 3rd Edition. Helping Your Daughter Survive Cliques, Gossip, Boys, and the New Realities of Girl World. Crown Publishing Group, a division of Penguin Random House LLC., New York, NY

Chapter 2

Painter, N.E. (1987). Foreword. In Minder & Longino (Ed.), *Competition a feminist taboo?*, (pp 21–37). New York, NY: The Feminist.

Bandura, A. (1980). The social learning theory of aggression. In R.A. Falk & S.S. Kim (Ed.), *The War System: An interdisciplinary approach*. Boulder, CO: Westview.

Bjorkqvist, K. (1994). Sex differences in physical, verbal and indirect aggression: A review of recent research. *Sex Roles*, 30 (3/4), 177–188.

Bjorkqvist, K., Osterman, K., Lagerspetz, M.J., (1992). Direct and Indirect Aggression Scales (DIAS). Retrieved from, http://www.vasa.abo.fi/svf/up/dias.htm

Brehm, S., S., Kassin, Saul, Fein, S. (2005). *Social Psychology (6th ed)*. Boston, MA: Houghton Mifflin.

Buss, A. H. (1961). *The Psychology of Aggression*. NY: John Wiley & Sons, Inc.

Campbell, A. (1993). *Men, women and aggression*. NY: Basic Books.

Chesler, P. (2001). *Woman's inhumanity to woman*. NY: Thunders' Mouth/Nation.

Dollard, J., Doob, L.W., Miller, N. E., Mowrer, O.H., & Sears, R. R. (1939). *Frustration and aggression*. New Haven, CT: Yale University.

Douglas, Susan J. (1994). Where the girls *are: growing up female with the mass media* ([Nachdr.] ed.). New York: Times Books. p. 221.

Douglas, Susan J.; Michaels, Meredith W. (2004). *The mommy myth. The idealization of motherhood and how it has undermined women.* (Advance uncorrected proof. ed.). New York: Free Press. p. 235.

Dowd, Maureen (2005). *Are men necessary? When sexes collide.* New York, N.Y.: G.P. Putnam's Sons. ISBN 0399153322.

Duncan, L. & Owen-Smith, A. (2006). Powerlessness and the use of indirect aggression in friendships. *Sex Roles*, 55, 493–502.

Ganaie, M.Y., Mudasir, Hafiz. (2015). A Study of Social Intelligence & Academic Achievement of College Students of District Srinagar, J&K, India. *Journal of American Science* 2015;11(3). Retrieved April 8, 2020 from, http://www.jofamericanscience.org/journals/amsci/am110315/004_2810 7am110315_23_27.pdf

Heim, Pat; Susan A. Murphy; Golant, Susan K. (2003). *In the company of women: indirect aggression among women: why we hurt each other and how to stop.* (1st pbk. ed.). New York: Jeremy P. Tarcher/Putnam.

Herbst, Philip H. (2001). Wimmin, wimps & wallflowers: an encyclopaedic dictionary of gender and sexual orientation bias in the United States. Yarmouth, Me: Intercultural Press [u.,a.] p. 46.

Humphrey, Nicholas (1986). *The Inner Eye: Social Intelligence in Evolution,* Faber & Faber, 1986; Oxford University Press 2002,

James, Caryn. (2016). Why We Just Love a Good Catfight. *The Wall Street Journal* (pages A11–A12) https://www.wsj.com/articles/why-we-love-a-good-catfight-1488386736

Pozner, Jennifer L. (2010). *Reality bites back: the troubling truth about guilty pleasure TV.* Berkeley, CA: Seal Press. pp. 99–100. ISBN 978-1580052658.

Richardson, D.S., Green, L.R. (2006). Direct and indirect aggression: Relationships as social context. *Journal of Applied Social Psychology*, 36(10), 2492–2508.

Riggio, Ronald. E. (2014). What is social intelligence? Why does it matter? *Psychology Today.* Retrieved December 26, 2019 from, https://www.psychologytoday.com/us/blog/cutting-edge-leadership/201407/what-is-social-intelligence-why-does-it-matter

Shapiro Barash, S. (2006). *Tripping the Prom Queen.* St. Martin's Press. New York, NY.

Sweeney, Kathleen (2007). Maiden USA: Girl icons come of age. New York: Peter Lang. p. 122.

Thorndike, E.L. (1920). Intelligence and its use. *Harper's Magazine*, 140, 227–235., Social Intelligence.

Wikipedia. (2020). *Catfight.* Retrieved April 10, 2020 from, https://en.wikipedia.org/wiki/Catfight

Wikipedia. (2020). *Stranger Danger.* Retrieved August 5, 2020 from, https://en.wikipedia.org/wiki/Stranger_danger

Chapter 3

Admin. (2011). Femme Magazine. Guy's Girl. Retrieved January 22, 2020 from, https://femmagazine.com/the-guys-girl/.

Boyes, Alice. (2013). The 3 Types of Frenemies. *Psychology Today*. Retrieved January 20, 2020, from, https://www.psychologytoday.com/us/blog/in-practice/201304/the-3-types-frenemies

Cardwell, Mike (1999). *Dictionary of Psychology*. Chicago Fitzroy Dearborn.

Chesler, P. (2001). *Woman's Inhumanity to Woman*. NY: Thunders' Mouth/ Nation.

Clarke, Katrina (April 8, 2017). Five Types of Frenemies and the Signs that You have One. *CBC News*. Retrieved January 20, 2020.

Edwards, Vanessa Van (April 7, 2017). The Science of Frenemies. *Medium*. Retrieved January 20, 2020.

Federal Glass Ceiling Commission. (1995). Solid Investments: Making full use of the Nation's Human Capital. Archived. 2014-11-08 at the *Wayback Machine*. Washington, D.C.: U.S. Department of Labor, November 1995, p. 13–15.

Goodreads, Inc. (2020). *Maya Angelou Quote*. Retrieved August 5, 2020 from, https://www.goodreads.com/author/quotes/3503.Maya_Angelou

Haufrect, Sarah. (2018). Behind frenemy lines. *Psychology Today*. Retrieved January 20, 2020, from, https://www.psychologytoday.com/us/blog/the-bonds-we-make/201802/behind-frenemy-lines

Jap, Sandy (2017). Are you partners or frenemies? *AMA.org*. Archived from, *The Original*, on February 9, 2019.

Jones, Ernest. (1964) *The Life and Work of Sigmund Freud* (1964) p. 37.

Jung, Carl Gustav. (August 1, 1971). *Psychological Types*. Collected Works of C.G. Jung. 6. Princeton University Press.

Kanter, R.M. (1977). *Men and Women of the Corporation*. New York, NY: Basic Books.

Kelly, J. (2012, March 8). 10 Types of Teens: A field guide to teenagers. *TLC Family*. Retrieved October 31, 2012 from, https://lifestyle.howstuff-works.com/family/parenting/tweens-teens/10-types-of-teens.htm

Labrum, Chris. (nd). Cliques: poverty & prejudice: Gangs of all colors. *EDGE*. Retrieved 10 February 2016 from, https://web.stanford.edu/class/e297c/poverty_prejudice/gangcolor/cliques.htm

Leary, Mark, R. (October 19, 2011). "Personality and persona: personality processes in self presentation". *Journal of Personality*. 79 (6): 1191–1218.

Maddock, S. (1999) *Challenging Women*. Sage, London.

Mavin, S. (2006). Venus Envy. Problematizing Solidarity Behavior and Queen Bees. Women in Management Review.

McNulty, Anne Welsh. (2018). Don't underestimate the power of women supporting each other at work. *Harvard Business Review*. Retrieved June 20, 2020, from, https://hbr.org/2018/09/dont-underestimate-the-power-of-women-supporting-each-other-at-work

Medela. (2020). 10 Ways You Might be Mom-shaming. *Medela USA*. Retrieved July 28, 2020 from, https://www.medela.us/breastfeeding/articles/10-ways-you-might-be-mom-shaming

Merriam Webster Dictionary. (2019). *Bully*. Retrieved XX from, https://www.merriam-webster.com/dictionary/bully?utm_campaign=sd&utm_medium=serp&utm_source=jsonld

Mitford, Jessica. (2010). *Poison Penmanship: the gentle are of muckraking*. New York Review Books. P. 218.

Oxford English Dictionary. (2020). *Abuser*. Retrieved January 20, 2020 from, https://www.oxfordlearnersdictionaries.com/us/definition/english/abuser?q=abuser

Oxford English Dictionary. (2020). *Brown-nose*. Retrieved January 20, 2020 from https://www.oxfordlearnersdictionaries.com/us/definition/english/brown-nose?q=brown-nose

Oxford English Dictionary. (2020). *Bully*. Retrieved October 7, 2019, from, https://www.oxfordlearnersdictionaries.com/us/definition/english/bully_1?q=bully

Oxford English Dictionary. (2020). *Friend*. Retrieved October 7, 2019, from, https://www.oxfordlearnersdictionaries.com/us/definition/english/friend_1?q=friend

Oxford Dictionary. (2019). *Frenemy*. Retrieved October 7, 2019, from, https://www.oxfordlearnersdictionaries.com/us/definition/english/frene-my?q=frenemy

Oxford English Dictionary. (2019). Mean. Retrieved January 20, 2020 from, https://www.oxfordlearnersdictionaries.com/us/definition/english/mean_1?q=mean

Oxford English Dictionary. (2019). Persona. Retrieved January 20, 2020 from, https://www.oxfordlearnersdictionaries.com/us/definition/english/persona?q=persona

Ringrose, Jessica; Walkerdine, Valerie (2008). What Does it Mean to Be a Girl in the Twenty-First Century?. In Reid-Walsh, Jacqueline (ed.). *Girl Culture: Studying girl culture : a readers' guide.* ABC-CLIO.

Ryan, Liz. (2017). Frenemies at Work. *Business Week.* Retrieved August 6, 2020 from, https://www.bloomberg.com/news/articles/2007-06-14/frenemics-at-workbusinessweek-business-news-stock-market-and-financial-advice

Salkind, Neil (2008). Cliques. *Encyclopedia of Educational Psychology.* Sage Publications.

Simply Psychology. (2011). Stereotypes. Archived from, *The Original*, on 11 February 2011. Retrieved 25 March 2018 from, www.simplypsychology.org

Staines, G., Travis, C., Jayaratne, T.E. (1973). The queen bee syndrome. *Psychology Today*, 7(8), 55-60.

Steiner, Leslie Morgan (2007). *The Mommy Wars.* New York. Random House.

Stern, Sussana. (2001). Sexual Selves on the World Wide Web: Adolescent Girls' Home Pages as Sites for Sexual Self-Expression; Sexual Teens, Sexual Media, Lawrence Erlbaum Associates.

Tracy, K. (2003) The Girl's Got Bite: The Original Unauthorized Guide to Buffy's World. Macmillan. p 37.

Urban Dictionary. 2020. *Backstabber*. Retrieved January, 20, 2020 from, https://www.urbandictionary.com/define.php?term=backstabber

Urban Dictionary. 2020. Brown-Noser. Retrieved January 20, 2020 from, https://www.urbandictionary.com/define.php?term=brown-noser

Urban Dictionary. 2020. Guys Girl. Retrieved January 20, 2020 from, https://www.urbandictionary.com/define.php?term=guy%27s%20girl

Wacjman, J. (1998). *Managing Like a Man, Blackwell,* Oxford.

Werner, Carly. (2019). What's 'self-gaslighting' and how do I unlearn it? Retrieved March 7, 2020 from, https://www.healthline.com/health/mental-health/unlearning-self-gaslighting

Wikipedia. (2020). *Gaslighting.* Retrieved, March 7, 2020 from, https://en.wikipedia.org/wiki/Gaslighting

Wikipedia. (2020). *Microaggression.* Retrieved, March 7, 2020 from, https://en.wikipedia.org/wiki/Microaggression

Wiley, John (2012). The Blackwell Encyclopedia of Gender and Sexuality Studies. Vol. 5. John Wiley and Sons.

Williams, K. D., Forgas, J. P., & von Hippel, W. (Eds.). (2005). The social Outcast: Ostracism, social Exclusion, Rejection, and Bullying. New York: *Psychology Press.* Retrieved March 7, 2020 from, http://psychology.iresearchnet.com/social-psychology/interpersonal-relationships/social-exclusion/

Wiseman, Rosalind. (2011). Girls' cliques: What role does your daughter play? *iVillage.* Retrieved December 2019 from, https://www.today.com/parents

York Morris, Susan. (2017). *How To Recognize Gaslighting and get help.* Retrieved March 7, 2020 from, https://www.healthline.com/health/gaslighting

YourDictionary.Com, 2020. *Backstabber.* Retrieved January 20, 2020 from https://www.yourdictionary.com/backstabber

Part Two

Star Wars, Inc. (2020) Obi-Wan Kenobi Quote. The Lawless, Season 5, Episode 16. Retrieved October from, https://www.starwars.com/news/20-star-wars-the-clone-wars-quotes

Chapter 4

Goodreads, Inc. (2020). *Germaine Greer Quote.* Retrieved August from, https://www.goodreads.com/author/quotes/56667.Germaine_Greer?page=4

Marra, Gail. (2018). *The Adolescent Brain*. Retrieved June 20, 2020 from, https://www.gailmarrahypnotherapy.com/9-things-you-may-not-have-known-about-your-subconscious-mind/

Massachusetts Institute of Technology (MIT). (2020). *Bystander.* Retrieved, March 3, 2020 from, http://web.mit.edu/bystanders/definition/index.html

Merriam Webster Dictionary. (2020). *Vicious*. Retrieved August 5, 2020 from, https://www.merriam-webster.com/dictionary/vicious

Merriam Webster Dictionary. (2020). *Vixen*. Retrieved August 5, 2020 from, https://www.merriam-webster.com/dictionary/vixen

Chapter 5

Brainy Quote. (2020). *Muhammad Ali Junnah quote*. Retrieved August 5, 2020 from, https://www.brainyquote.com/quotes/muhammad_ali_jinnah_372004

Bariso, Jason. (2020). After years of research, Google discovered the secret weapon to building a great team. It's a lesson in emotional intelligence. *EQ Applied*. Retrieved July 31, 2020 from, https://www.inc.com/justin-bariso/after-years-of-research-google-discovered-secret-weapon-to-building-a-great-team-its-a-lesson-in-emotional-intelligence.html

Business Dictionary (2020). *Organizational Culture* Retrieved February 5, 2020 from, http://www.businessdictionary.com/definition/organizational-culture.html

Ely. R.J. (1994). The effects of organizational demographics on social identity on relationships among professional women. *Administrative Science Quarterly*, 39, 203-238.

Gotham Culture (2020). *Organizational Culture*. Retrieved February 5, 2020 from, https://gothamculture.com/what-is-organizational-culture-definition/

Greer, G. (2000). *The Whole Woman*. Anchor, London.

Houlis, Annamarie. (2018). *70% of Female Executives Feel Bullied By Women—Here's How to Stop it*. Retrieved May 15, 2019 from, https://www.theladders.com/career-advice/author/annamariehoulis

Kanter, R.M. (1977). *Men and Women of the Corporation*. New York, NY: Basic Books.

Mavin, S. (2006). Venus envy: problematizing solidarity behavior and Queen Bees. *Women in Management Review*. Newcastle University.

Leading With Honor. (2020). *Perry Belcher quote*. Retrieved August 5, 2020 from, https://www.leadingwithhonor.com/leading-with-honor-wisdom-for-today-january-24-2020/

Mavin, S. (2006a). Venus Envy: Problematizing Solidarity Behavior and Queen Bees. *Women in Management Review*, 21(4), 264–276.

Merriam Webster Dictionary. (2020). *Bolshie*. Retrieved August 5, 2020 from, https://www.merriam-webster.com/dictionary/bolshie

Merriam Webster Dictionary. (2020). *Bully*. Retrieved August 5, 2020 from, https://www.merriam-webster.com/dictionary/bully

Rozovsky, Julia. (2015). *The five keys to a successful Google team*. Retrieved July 31, 2020 from, https://www.michigan.gov/documents/mdhhs/Google-and-Psychological-Safety_684425_7.pdf

Urban Dictionary. (2020). *Venus*. Retrieved August 5, 2020 from, https://www.urbandictionary.com/define.php?term=Venus

Chapter 6

Cannon, Walter, B. (1915). Bodily Changes in Pain, Hunger, Fear and Rage: An Account of Recent Researches into the Function of Emotional Excitement. *Appleton-Century-Crofts*. P. 211.

Cannon, Walter. (1932). *Wisdom of the Body*. United States: W.W. Norton & Company. ISBN 978-0393002058.

Dr. Chesler (2001) Chesler, P. (2001). *Woman's Inhumanity to Woman*. NY: Thunders' Mouth/ Nation.

Goodreads, Inc. (2020). *N.K. Jemison Quote*. Retrieved August 5, 2020 from, https://www.goodreads.com/quotes/tag/bullies

Harvard. (2011). Understanding the stress response. *Harvard Health Publishing*. Retrieved August 5, 2020 from, https://www.health.harvard.edu/staying-healthy/understanding-the-stress-response

Houlis, Annamarie. (2018). *70% of Female Executives Feel Bullied By Women—Here's How to Stop it*. Retrieved May 15, 2019 from, https://www.theladders.com/career-advice/author/annamariehoulis

Jansen, A; Nguyen, X; Karpitsky, V; Mettenleiter, M (27 October 1995). Central Command Neurons of the Sympathetic Nervous System: Basis of the Fight-or-Flight Response. *Science Magazine*. 5236 (270).

Klein, Sarah. (2013). Adrenaline, cortisol, norepinephrine: The three major stress hormones explained. *Huffington Post*. Retrieved 16 August 2019 from, https://www.huffpost.com/entry/adrenaline-cortisol-stress-hormones_n_3112800

Philpot, Richard; Liebst, Lasse Suonperä; Levine, Mark; Bernasco, Wim; Lindegaard, Marie Rosenkrantz (2019). "Would I be helped? Cross-national CCTV footage shows that intervention is the norm in public conflicts". *American Psychologist*. doi:10.1037/amp0000469. hdl:10871/37604. ISSN 1935–990X. PMID 31157529.

Reach Out. (2020). *What does being a bystander mean?* Retrieved February 11, 2020 from, https://au.reachout.com/articles/what-does-being-a-bystander-mean

Urban Dictionary. (2020). *Fight or Flight*. Retrieved February 11, 2020 from, https://www.urbandictionary.com/define.php?term=fight+or+flight

Wikipedia. (2020). *Victim Blaming*. Retrieved, March 7, 2020 from, https://en.wikipedia.org/wiki/Victim_blaming

Victim Blaming (PDF). Canadian Resource Centre for Victims of Crime. Retrieved February 11, 2020 from, https://crcvc.ca/docs/victim_blaming.pdf

Manitoba Trauma Information + Education Centre. (2013). Fight, Flight, Freeze Responses. Retrieved August 6, from, https://trauma-recovery.ca/impact-effects-of-trauma/fight-flight-freeze-responses/

Part Three

Goodreads, inc. (2020). *Akshay Vasu quote*. Retrieved October 7, 2020 from, https://www.goodreads.com/quotes/8072397-tell-me-about-the-light-that-you-are-trying-to

Chapter 7

APA Dictionary. (2007). *Emotion*. Retrieved August 5, 2020 from, https://dictionary.apa.org/emotion

Brackett, Marc. (2020). *Yale Center for Emotional Intelligence*. Retrieved August 5, from, 2020, https://www.marcbrackett.com/about/yale-center-for-emotional-intelligence/

Goodreads, Inc. (2020). *Miguel Ruiz quote*. Retrieved August 5, 2020 from, https://www.goodreads.com/author/quotes/4402.Miguel_Ruiz

New Oxford American Dictionary. (2005). *Encumbrance*. Retrieved August 6, 2020 from, https://www.oxfordlearnersdictionaries.com/us/definition/english/encumbrance?q=encumbrance

Landy, F. J., & Conte, J. M. (2007). Work in the 21st century: An introduction to Industrial and Organizational Psychology (2nd ed). Malden, MA: Blackwell.

Lazarus, R. S. (1993). From psychological stress to the emotions: A history of changing outlooks. *Annual Review of Psychology*, 44: 1-21.

Stern, Robin. (2009). Are You Being Gaslighted? The Process of Gaslighting Happens In Stages. *Psychology Today*. Retrieved, March 7, 2020 from, https://www.psychologytoday.com/us/blog/power-in-relationships/200905/are-you-being-gaslighted

Warter, Carlos. (2019). *Carlos Warter quote*. Forgiveness exercise: Forgiving your enemies...and your loved ones. *InnerSelf.* Retrieved August 5, 2020 from, https://innerself.com/content/personal/attitudes-transformed/forgiveness/5633-forgiving-your-enemies.html

York Morris, Susan. (2017). *How To Recognize Gaslighting and get help*. Retrieved March 7, 2020 from, https://www.healthline.com/health/gaslighting

Chapter 8

American Psychological Association (APA). (2018). *Reactive coping*. Retrieved, February 18, 2020 from, https://dictionary.apa.org/reactive-coping

Lazarus, R. S. (1993). From psychological stress to the emotions: A history of changing outlooks. *Annual Review of Psychology*, 44: 1–21.

Goodreads, Inc. (2020). *Alice Walker quote*. Retrieved August 5, 2020 from, https://www.goodreads.com/quotes/856195-some-periods-of-our-growth-are-so-confusing-that-we

Merriam Webster Dictionary. (2020). *Self-Awareness*. Retrieved, February 18, 2020 from, https://www.merriam-webster.com/dictionary/self-awareness

Wikipedia. (2020). *Self-Awareness*. Retrieved, February 18, 2020 from, https://en.wikipedia.org/wiki/Self-awareness

Wikipedia. (2020). *Coping*. Retrieved, February 18, 2020 from, https://en.wikipedia.org/wiki/Coping

Chapter 9

American Psychological Association (APA). (2018). *Proactive coping*. Retrieved, February 18, 2020 from, https://dictionary.apa.org/proactive-coping

American Psychological Association (APA). (2018). *Mindfulness*. Retrieved, February 18, 2020 from, https://dictionary.apa.org/mindfulness

Barker, Eric. (2012). What's Worse: Physical Pain or Social Pain. *The Business Insider*. Retrieved, October 1, 2019 from, https://www.businessinsider.com/whats-worse-physical-pain-or-social-pain-2012-8

Daily Inspiration Quotes. (2020). *Erin Van Vurin quote*. Retrieved August 5, 2020 from, https://www.dailyinspirationalquotes.in/2016/12/theres-going-painful-moments-life-will-change-entire-world-matter-minutes-moments-will-change-let-make-stronger-smarter-kinder/

Daily Inspiration Quotes. (2020). *Unknown quote*. Retrieved August 5, 2020 from, https://www.dailyinspirationalquotes.in/2016/01/i-forgive-people-but-that-doesnt-mean-i-accept-their-behavior-or-trust-them-i-forgive-them-for-me-so-i-can-let-go-and-move-on-with-my-life-unknown/

Firestone, Lisa. (2018). Dealing With Unresolved Trauma. *Psychology Today*. Retrieved October 1, 2019 from, https://www.psychologytoday.com/us/blog/compassion-matters/201803/dealing-unresolved-trauma

Goodreads, Inc. (2020). *Jack Rose quote*. Retrieved August 5, 2020 from, https://www.goodreads.com/quotes/181824-opposition-can-be-your-friend-opposition-can-be-the-fire

Goodreads, Inc. (2021). Nelson Mandela quote. Retrieved January 12, 2021 from, https://www.goodreads.com/quotes/tag/fear

Houlis, Annamarie. (2018). *70% of Female Executives Feel Bullied By Women—Here's How to Stop It.* Retrieved May 15, 2019 from, https://www.theladders.com/career-advice/author/annamariehoulis

Kim, S. H., Vincent, L. C., & Goncalo, J. A. (2013). Outside advantage: Can social rejection fuel creative thought? *Journal of Experimental Psychology*: General, 142(3), 605–611.conn

Luskin, F. (2010). *This Emotional Life, PBS Special.* Palo Alto, CA: Stanford University. Retrieved May 30, 2011 from www.LearningtoForgive.com

Mind Journal. (2020). *Tanya Markul quote.* Retrieved August 5, 2020 from, https://themindsjournal.com/healing-messy-alienation/

Psychological Science. (2008). "When hurt will not heal: exploring the capacity to relive social and physical pain." Aug;19(8):789–95.

Rock, David. (2011). Your Brain at Work: Strategies for Overcoming Distraction, Regaining Focus, and Working Smarter All Day Long.

Stone, M. (2002). Forgiveness in the workplace. *Industrial and Commercial Training.* 34:(6/7).

University of Michigan. sapac.umich.edu. (2018). Bystander Intervention. A proactive bystander is an individual who accepts personal responsibility for a situation and intervenes to ensure the well-being and/or safety of others. Retrieved, February 18, 2020 from, https://sapac.umich.edu/article/bystander-intervention

Chapter 10

Barcella, L. (2017). *Healthline. According to Science, Your Girl Squad Can Help You Release More Oxytocin.* Retrieved February 29, 2020 from, https://www.healthline.com/health/womens-health/benefits-of-a-girlsquad-and-female-friendships#1

Brown, B. (2019). *Braving the Wilderness: The Quest for True Belonging.* New York. Random House Trade Paperbacks.

Cacioppo, John, T. and Patrick, W.(2008). *Loneliness: Human Nature and the Need for Social Connection.* New York. Norton.

Chesler, P. (2001). *Woman's Inhumanity to Woman*. NY: Thunders' Mouth/ Nation.

Holt-Lunstad, J., Baker, M. Harris, T., Stephenson, D. Smith, T.B. (2015). "Loneliness and Social Isolation as Risk Factors for Mortality: A Meta-Analytic Review," *Perspectives on Psychological Science*, 10(2), 227–37.

InspirationFeed. (2020). *Selene Kinder quote*. Retrieved August 5, 2020 from, https://inspirationfeed.com/women-quotes/

Goldman, B. (2013). Stanford Medicine News Center. "'*Love Hormone' May Play Wider Role In Social Interaction Than Previously Thought.*" Retrieved, February 29, 2020 from, https://med.stanford.edu/news/all-news/2013/09/love-hormone-may-play-wider-role-in-social-interaction-than-previously-thought-scientists-say.html

Goodreads, Inc. (2020). *Anonymous quote*. Retrieved August 5, 2020 from, https://www.goodreads.com/quotes/9659588-when-people-throw-stones-at-you-don-t-throw-them-back

Goodreads, Inc. (2020). *Louise Bernikow quote*. Retrieved August from, https://www.goodreads.com/quotes/148947-female-friendships-that-work-are-relationships-in-which-women-help

Mae, et al. (2018). Sex- and context dependent effects of oxytocin on social sharing. *NeuroImage*. Vol. 183. Pp 62–72. Retrieved February 29, 2020 from, https://www.sciencedirect.com/science/article/abs/pii/S1053811918306918

Minds Journal. (2020). *Soul Sister Quote*. Retrieved August from, https://the-mindsjournal.com/soul-sister/

Mom.com. (2020). Women in isolation story, per Brene Brown. Retrieved August 5, 2020 from, https://mom.com/momlife/loneliness-mother-hood-isolation-friendships

Nichols, Morgan. (2020). *Morgan Harper Nichols quote*. Retrieved August 5, 2020 from, https://morganharpernichols.com

Taylor, Shelley E.; Klein, Laura Cousino; Lewis, Brian P.; Gruenewald, Tara L.; Gurung, Regan A. R.; Updegraff, John A. (2000). "Biobehavioral responses to stress in females: Tend-and-befriend, not fight-or-flight".

Psychological Review. **107** (3): 411–29. CiteSeerX 10.1.1.386.912. doi:10.1037/0033-295X.107.3.411. PMID 1094127

Wikipedia. (2020). *Solidarity*. Retrieved August 5, 2020 from, https://en.wikipedia.org/wiki/Solidarity

Chapter 11

Authentic Woman. (2020). Unknown quote. Retrieved August 5, 2020 from, https://authenticwoman.co/so-many-years-of-education-yet-nobody-ever-taught-us-how-to-love-ourselves-and-why-its-so-important/

Bate, Ellie (2020). Billie Eilish and Lizzo both wanted other women to win their grammys and people are loving the sisterhood. BuzzFeed. News. Retrieved, January 27, 2020, from, https://www.buzzfeed.com/eleanorbate/billie-eilish-lizzo-ariana-grande-beyonce-grammys?utm_source=dynamic&utm_campaign=bffbbuzzfeedvideo&ref=bffbbuzzfeed-video&fbclid=IwAR0jnzb5Wlm8Oa4pTb6Zziu-Hu772TDBqZIqJPZxP-mjaX7Ewp5FbRFfLxs8

Blinn. (2020). Friendships: why horseshoes are better than circles. Crystal Cattle the life of a farmgirl and everything with it. Retrieved August 5, 2020 https://www.crystalblin.com/2020/02/friendships-why-horseshoes-are-better.html

Brackett, Marc. (2020). What is RULER? The Ruler Approach. Retrieved August 5, 2020 from, https://www.rulerapproach.org/about/what-is-ruler/

Business Matters/ (2008). The value of a sounding board. Business Matters. Retrieved August 5, 2020 from, https://www.bmmagazine.co.uk/in-business/advice/the-value-of-a-sounding-board/

Chapata, Billy. (2018). Billy Chapata quote. Retrieved August 5, 2020 from, https://twitter.com/iambrillyant/status/1008408948502859778?lang=en

Doyle, Glennon (2020). Untamed. New York, NY. Dial Press a Division of Random House.

Doyle, Glennon. (2018). Twitter quote. Retrieved, January 11, 2021 from, https://twitter.com/glennondoyle/status/1004003626656915457?lang=en

Doyle, Glennon. (2014). Twitter quote. Retrieved, August 5, 2020 from, https://twitter.com/GlennonDoyle/status/1004003626656915457/photo/1

https://greatbendpost.com/posts/5e3c7e787d7daa72b30ecaaf

Goodreads, Inc. (2020). C. S. Lewis quote. Retrieved August 5, 2020 from, https://www.goodreads.com/quotes/155077-we-are-what-we-believe-we-are

Goodreads, Inc. (2020). Helen Keller quote. Retrieved August 5, 2020 from, https://www.goodreads.com/quotes/9411-alone-we-can-do-so-little-together-we-can-do

Goodreads, Inc. (2020). Madeleine Albright quote. Retrieved August 5, 2020 from, https://www.goodreads.com/quotes/14328-there-is-a-special-place-in-h*ll-for-women-who

McNulty, Anne Welsh. (2018). Don't underestimate the power of women supporting each other at work. Harvard Business Review. Retrieved June 20, 2020, from, https://hbr.org/2018/09/dont-underestimate-the-power-of-women-supporting-each-other-at-work

Hedrick. (2015). Why It's important to have a sounding board. Psych Central. Retrieved August 5, 2020 from, https://blogs.psychcentral.com/two-minds/2015/05/why-its-important-to-have-a-sounding-board/

Positive Psychology. (2020). The importance of emotional intelligence. Positive Psychology. Retrieved July 18, 2020, from, https://positivepsychology.com/importance-of-emotional-intelligence/

Powerful Mind. (2019). 8 ways to keep your friendships strong. Powerful Mind. Retrieved April 4, 2020 from, http://powerfulmind.co/keep-your-friendships-strong/

TLEX Institute (2019). How to effortlessly have more positive thoughts. TLEX Institute. Retrieved December 3, 2019 from, https://tlexinstitute.com/how-to-effortlessly-have-more-positive-thoughts/

Uzzi, Brian. (2019) Research: Men and women need different kinds of networks to succeed. Harvard Business Review. Retrieved June 20, 2020 from, https://hbr.org/2019/02/research-men-and-women-need-different-kinds-of-networks-to-succeed

Warrell, Margie. (2016). How to raise brave girls. Margie Warrell, Live Bravely. Retrieved August 5, 2020 from, https://margiewarrell.com/how-to-raise-brave-girls/

Wikipedia (2020). It takes a village, African proverb. Retrieved August 5, 2020 from, https://en.wikipedia.org/wiki/It_takes_a_village

Your Dictionary. (2020). Sounding board. Retrieved August 5, 2020 from, https://www.yourdictionary.com/sounding-board

Zalis, Shelley. (2019). Power of the Pack: Women who support women are more successful. Forbes. Retrieved June 20, 2020, from, https://www.forbes.com/sites/shelleyzalis/2019/03/06/power-of-the-pack-women-who-support-women-are-more-successful/#5cf189771771

Zen Girl Chronicles. (2020). Jennifer Tastiloff quote. Retrieved August 6, from, http://www.zengirlchronicles.com/2013/05/find-your-tribe.html

Last Word

Goodreads, inc. (2020). *Morgan Harper Nichols quote*. Retrieved August 6, 2020 from, https://www.goodreads.com/author/quotes/14780318.Morgan_Harper_Nichols

Keller, Evelyn, Fox., & Moglen, Helene. (1987). Competition and feminism: Conflicts for academic women. *Signs*. Vol. 12. (3)., pp. 493511.

Show Up Now. (2020). *Ann Voskamp quote*. Retrieved August 6, 2020 from, https://annvoskamp.com/2020/04/this-is-a-war-where-are-the-prayer-warriors-to-win-this-battle-pandemicprayers/

A free ebook edition
is available with the
purchase of this book.

To claim your free ebook edition:

1. Visit MorganJamesBOGO.com
2. Sign your name CLEARLY in the space
3. Complete the form and submit a photo of the entire copyright page
4. You or your friend can download the ebook to your preferred device

Morgan James BOGO™

A **FREE** ebook edition is available for you
or a friend with the purchase of this print book.

CLEARLY SIGN YOUR NAME ABOVE

Instructions to claim your free ebook edition:
1. Visit MorganJamesBOGO.com
2. Sign your name CLEARLY in the space above
3. Complete the form and submit a photo of this entire page
4. You or your friend can download the ebook to your preferred device

Print & Digital Together Forever.

Snap a photo

Free ebook

Read anywhere

9 781631 955419